*READINGS IN AMERICAN HISTORY*

# AMERICA FIRSTHAND

Volume I *FROM SETTLEMENT TO RECONSTRUCTION*

*Third Edition*

*ROBERT D. MARCUS*
State University of New York College at Brockport

*and*

*DAVID BURNER*
State University of New York at Stony Brook

*ST. MARTIN'S PRESS*
New York

Acquisitions editor: Louise H. Waller
Manager, publishing services: Emily Berleth
Editor, publishing services: Doug Bell
Project management: Publication Services
Production supervisor: Alan Fischer
Art director: Sheree Goodman
Cover design: Rod Hernandez
Cover art: Francis Guy, *Winter Scene in Brooklyn*, c. 1817–1820. The Brooklyn Museum 97.13. Gift of The Brooklyn Institute of Arts and Sciences.

Library of Congress Catalog Card Number: 94-65215



Manufactured in the United States of America.
98765
fedcba

For information, write:
St. Martin's Press, Inc.
175 Fifth Avenue
New York, NY 10010

ISBN: 0-312-10162-7

Acknowledgments
Acknowledgments and copyrights are continued at the back of the book on pages 291–292, which constitute an extension of the copyright page.

# *Preface*

The third edition of *America Firsthand* responds to the increasing difficulty of teaching and learning American history. In the three years since the publication of the second edition, the challenges of studying American history have continued to grow, as both historians and students have become more conscious of the voices that either have been silent or have remained outside the canon of the American past as it is studied in the present.

We believe that students need to find exemplars of themselves in the past. *America Firsthand* was written to help them discover how the diversities of past experience and recent scholarship can respond to that need. The focus is on people who speak directly of their own experiences. In this edition we continue to pay attention to the voices of women, African Americans, native Americans, and others whose lives until recently have been lost in mainstream history. Insofar as is possible, individuals are presented in their own words and in selections long enough to be memorable, personal, and immediate. The accounts of indentured servants, runaway slaves, cowboys, factory workers, civil rights activists, homeless people, and many others offer students opportunities to identify with a wide range of human experience.

We have retained enough political and military documents to maintain the traditional markers of United States history; these continue to provide a useful narrative framework. In this third edition, however, we continue to emphasize social history in the belief that personal remembrances create a sense of identification with the past. New readings include George R. T. Hewes telling of his own role in the Boston Tea Party, Captain John Ross's experience of the "trail of tears," an eyewitness description of the storming of the Alamo, Timothy Shay Arthur's depiction of a tavern, a memoir of frustrating attempts to establish industry in the antebellum South, and Sarah Jane Foster's account of working to educate ex-slaves after the Civil War. Volume II contains such new documents as letters from African-American soldiers during World War II, accounts of the Chinese-American town in California, a nurse's experience in the Vietnam War, the memoirs of an agrarian radical woman editor, and the letters of a German-American immigrant farmer.

Visual sources have been added to both volumes. Readers can view the American Revolution through the eyes of English cartoonists, see the toys with which nineteenth-century American children played, view the Hampton Institute through the work of a pioneer woman photographer, and see how everyday Americans survived the Great Depression.

While the readings convey the experiences and forces of specific personalities, they include observations on the American Revolution and the Civil War, on Reconstruction, the Great Depression, and the war in Vietnam.

All teachers and students must struggle with the problem of connecting traditional chronology with the new materials of social history, and no formula for doing that is without its problems. We have offered a set of connections that, in combination with a good United States history textbook, will be workable for many courses. Careful headnotes and questions at the end of each section help make the essential links from the personalities to the times in which those personalities lived.

*America Firsthand,* third edition, explores in even greater concreteness than the preceding edition the many ways of being American and the multitudinous minds and characters that make up a diverse history and nation. We see the American experience through the perspective of many cultures and diverse people who have in common that, in some form, they have left behind a vivid record of the world they inhabited and the times they experienced. We hope these recollections serve as fertile ground in which students can begin to root their own interest in history, and their own perception of the times in which they live.

## *Acknowledgments*

The authors wish to thank the following individuals who reviewed the third edition of *America Firsthand* for St. Martin's Press: Donald S. Castro, California State Polytechnic University, Pomona; Truman R. Clark, Tomball College; Joseph R. Fischer, Pennsylvania State University; Patrick J. Furlong, Indiana University, South Bend; Dee Garceau, University of Montana; Kalman Goldstein, Fairleigh Dickinson University; Gael Graham, Western Carolina University; Barbara Handy-Marchello, University of North Dakota; Stephen E. Jess, Southwestern Michigan College; Judith N. Kerr, Towson State University; Mary M. Stolberg; and Mary Miley Theobald, Virginia Commonwealth University.

## *Contents*

# PART I | DISCOVERY AND EARLY SETTLEMENT

*The Age of Exploration combined the ambitions of science and humanism emerging from the Renaissance with older hopes of discovering the lost tribes of Israel and of reaching the trade of the Orient by sailing west. Accounts of the New World, such as the one found in Colón's life of Columbus, flooded Europe with reports that were as much a product of the confused dreams of the age as they were of the realities of America.*

*The people in this new land were named Indians by explorers who mistook the Americas for the East Indies or the Orient. These native Americans had their own complex culture, which rapidly came into conflict with that of the white explorers and settlers. Bartolomé de Las Casas's report of the Spanish conquest captures the full horrors of that first encounter. Chief Johnson's account of the Mohawk chief Hiawatha presents a native American legend of the building of the Iroquois Confederacy in upstate New York. And Father Le Jeune's account of his experience in Canada suggests how little understanding existed even between friendly whites and receptive native Americans.*

*The New World's wilderness imposed reality upon the Old World's visions in strange and surprising ways. Men lusted for El Dorado but found their gold in Virginia tobacco fields or on the Grand Banks of Newfoundland. Many even found new freedoms for themselves—although black slavery and race warfare also developed at this time. Religion flourished in the colonies, as it did throughout the seventeenth-century world, but the new American environment altered society so that the churches found themselves in a losing competition with the more mundane requirements for adapting to the harshness of the colonial frontier and its economic life.*

*In both Virginia and New England the tremendous difficulties of making a settlement required that the new settlers have a firm belief in their mission. Some of the brutal realities of life in the colonies are recounted by John White and by the son of William Pond. Religious motives played a role in both settlements but were far stronger in New England. While John Smith was largely concerned with selling his Virginia to prospective investors and settlers, Puritans like Samuel Willard and Cotton Mather worried about the state of both their own and their children's souls.*

*Children could freely be sold, sent away, or punished by their parents almost without restriction. Along with society's concern for the rearing and educating of children came a hypersensitivity about their behavior, as in the overreaction of otherwise sensible adults to the ill-mannered or sometimes merely inconvenient actions of children. As if to exempt themselves from having any part in creating a society in which not everyone had achieved perfection, the adults gave great credence to supernatural explanations of the causes of children's unhappiness or recalcitrance. A misbehaving child was easily seen as a victim or perpetrator of witchcraft. In some cases, the young person became the body through which the Devil operated in the material world, or at least so thought the Puritan divine Cotton Mather.*

FERNANDO COLÓN

# 1 The Life of the Admiral Christopher Columbus

*The idea of sailing west to reach the riches of the East Indies and the Asian mainland was much in vogue with literate Europeans during the late fifteenth century. Learned people agreed that the earth was round; their only questions were how long and how dangerous would be a trip to reach the Orient.*

*Christopher Columbus, the son of an obscure Genoan weaver, and himself a weaver of ambitious dreams, made his historic voyage to the New World in 1492. Sailing with a tiny fleet of three ships and a crew of ninety sailors, he found the thirty-three-day crossing easier than was his nearly decade-long effort to find royal patrons willing to support it. The trip drew not only on his own skills as an expert ship's captain, but also on his ability to plan such an expedition, obtain governmental approval and financing, and finally, demonstrate (or advertise) its success so that such explorations could continue. (Columbus himself was to make a total of four voyages to the New World.)*

*The explorations that followed Columbus—those of Cabot, Verrazano, Cartier, and many others—benefited from a new maritime technology borrowed from Arab sailors and from a variety of new vessels such as the light-weight caravels employed by Columbus. Mariners also perfected sails and various types of riggings that gave ships added stability and greater maneuverability on the open seas. And when leaving sight of the coast, new navigational aids—charts, compasses, and astrolabes—permitted them to determine their position with some, though not perfect, accuracy.*

*One of the basic documents from which we know the life of Columbus, Colón's biography of the admiral, was written by a loyal son who accompanied his father on the last of his voyages to the New World. The son literally lived on his father's legacy, for the Crown awarded Colón income from the labors of 400 Indian slaves.*

## HOW THE ADMIRAL SAILED FROM THE GRAND CANARY AND CONTINUED HIS VOYAGE OF DISCOVERY, AND WHAT HAPPENED TO HIM ON THE OCEAN

On the afternoon of Friday, September 1st, the ships having been made ready in all respects, the Admiral hoisted sails and set out from the

Grand Canary. Next day they reached Gomera, where they passed four more days in taking on meat, wood, and water. And on the morning of the Thursday following, September 6, 1492, which day may be taken to mark the beginning of the enterprise and the ocean crossing, the Admiral sailed westward from Gomera; but he made little headway on account of feeble and variable winds.

At daybreak on Sunday, he found he was nine leagues west of the island of Ferro. This day they completely lost sight of land, and many sighed and wept for fear they would not see it again for a long time. The Admiral comforted them with great promises of lands and riches. To sustain their hope and dispel their fears of a long voyage he decided to reckon less leagues than they actually made, telling them they had covered only fifteen leagues that day, though they had actually gone eighteen. He did this that they might not think themselves so great a distance from Spain as they really were, but for himself he kept a secret accurate reckoning.

Continuing their voyage, at sundown of Tuesday, September 11th, about one hundred and fifty leagues west of the island of Ferro, the Admiral saw a large fragment of mast that may have belonged to a ship of 120 tons and that seemed to have been in the water for a long time. In this region and farther west the currents set strongly to the northeast. At midnight of September 13th, after the fleet had run another fifty leagues westwards, the needles were found to vary half a point to the northwest, and in the morning a little more than half a point to the northeast. From this the Admiral knew that the needle did not point to the polestar, but to some other fixed and invisible point. No one had ever noticed this variation before, so he had good reason to be surprised at it. Three days later, almost one hundred leagues west of that area, he was even more surprised to find that at midnight the needles varied a whole point to the northwest, while in the morning they again pointed directly to the polestar.

Saturday night, September 15th, as they were almost three hundred leagues west of Ferro, a prodigious flame fell from the sky into the sea, some four or five leagues from the ships, toward the southwest, although the weather was as balmy as in April, with a mild wind blowing from the northeast to the southeast and the currents setting to the northeast. The *Niña's* people told the Admiral that the previous Friday they had seen a *garjao* and another bird called *rabo de junco*; they were much surprised by these birds, the first they had seen on the voyage.

They were even more surprised the next day, Sunday, to see the surface of the water covered with a great mass of yellowish green weed, which seemed to have been torn away from some island or reef. The next day they saw much more of this weed; many therefore affirmed they must certainly be near land, especially since they saw a live crab amid these mats of weed; the weed resembled star grass, save that it had long stalks and shoots, and was loaded with fruit like the mastic tree. They also observed that the sea water was less salty by half than before. That night they were followed by many tunny fish that swam about the ships, coming so near that the *Niña's* people killed one with a harpoon.

About three hundred and seventy leagues from Ferro they saw another *rabo de junco*; this bird is so called because its tail forms a long plume [and in Spanish the word *rabo* means "tail"].

The Tuesday following, September 18th, Martin Alonso Pinzón, who had gone ahead in the *Pinta*, a very fast sailer, lay to for the Admiral to come up and informed him he had seen a great flight of birds moving westward, a sign that made Pinzón hopeful of finding land that night; and at sundown he thought he actually saw land some fifteen leagues to the north, covered by darkness and clouds. All the ship's people wanted the Admiral to search in that direction, but he would not waste his time upon it, because it was not the place where his calculations made him expect to find land. That night, after sailing for eleven days under full sail and running ever before the wind, they took in their topsails because the wind had freshened.

## *HOW ALL THE SHIP'S PEOPLE, BEING EAGER TO REACH LAND, WERE VERY ATTENTIVE TO THE THINGS THEY SAW IN THE SEA*

As this was the first voyage of that kind for all the men in the fleet, they grew frightened at finding themselves so far from land without prospect of aid, and did not cease to grumble among themselves. Seeing nothing but water and sky all about, they paid the closest attention to all they observed, as was natural for men who had gone a greater distance from land than any had ever done before. So I shall mention all the things to which they assigned any importance (but only in telling of the first voyage), though I will not take note of those minor signs that are commonly and frequently observed at sea.

On the morning of September 19th a pelican flew over the Admiral's ship, followed by others in the afternoon. This gave him some hope of soon sighting land, for he reflected that these birds would not have flown far from land. Accordingly, when it grew calm, the ship's people sounded with two hundred fathoms of line; they found no bottom, but noted that now the currents set to the southwest. Again, on Thursday, the 20th of the month, two hours before noon, two pelicans flew over the ship and a while later came another; the sailors also caught a bird like a heron, save that it was black, with a white tuft on its head and feet like a duck's, as is common with water birds. They also caught a little fish and saw much weed of the kind mentioned before. At daybreak three little birds flew singing over the ship; they flew away when the sun came out, but left the comforting thought that unlike the other large water birds, which might have come a great distance, these little birds could not have come from afar. Three hours later they saw another bird that came from the west-northwest, and next day, in the afternoon, they saw another *rabo de junco* and a pelican; they also saw more seaweed than ever before, stretching northward as far as they could see. This also comforted them, since they concluded it must come from some nearby land; but at times it caused them great fright, because in places the weed was so thickly matted that it held back the ships. And since fear conjures up imaginary terrors, they even feared lest the weed grow so thick that there might happen to them what is supposed to have happened to St. Amador in the frozen sea that is said to hold ships fast. That is why they kept as clear as possible of those mats of weed.

The next day they sighted a whale, and the Saturday following, September 22d, some *pardelas* were seen. During those three days the wind blew from the southwest, more westerly at some times than at others; and though this wind was contrary to his design, the Admiral wrote that he found it very helpful. For one of the bogeys his people had been scaring themselves with was the idea that since the wind was always at their backs, they would never have a wind in those waters for returning to Spain. Then, when they got such a wind, they would complain that it was inconstant, and that since there was no heavy sea, that proved it would never blow hard enough to return them the great distance they had come from Spain. To this the Admiral would reply that must be because they were near land, which kept the sea smooth, and he sought to convince them as well as he could. But [in his journal] he wrote that he stood in need of God's aid, such as Moses had when he was leading the Jews out of Egypt and they dared not lay violent hands upon him on account of the miracles that God wrought by his own means. So, says the Admiral, it happened with him on this voyage. For soon after, on Sunday, September 23d, there arose a wind from the west-northwest, with a rough sea such as the people wanted; also, three hours before noon, a turtledove flew over the ship, and in the afternoon they saw a pelican, a small river bird, some white birds, and some crabs among the weed. Next day they saw another pelican, and many *pardelas* flying out of the west, and some little fish, some of which the sailors caught with harpoons, because they would not bite at hooks.

## *HOW THE MEN GRUMBLED BECAUSE OF THEIR DESIRE TO RETURN, AND HOW CERTAIN SIGNS AND TOKENS OF LAND MADE THEM CONTINUE GLADLY ON THEIR COURSE*

As these signs proved fruitless, the men grew ever more restless and fearful. They met together in the holds of the ships, saying that the

Admiral in his mad fantasy proposed to make himself a lord at the cost of their lives or die in the attempt; that they had already tempted fortune as much as their duty required and had sailed farther from land than any others had done. Why, then, should they work their own ruin by continuing that voyage, since they were already running short of provisions and the ships had so many leaks and faults that even now they were hardly fit to retrace the great distance they had traveled? Certainly (said they), none would blame them for deciding to return but rather would hold them for very brave men for having enlisted on such a voyage and having sailed so far. And since the Admiral was a foreigner without favor at Court and one whose views had been rejected and criticized by many wise and learned men, none would speak in his defense and all would believe what they said, attributing to ignorance and ineptitude whatever he might say to justify himself. Others said they had heard enough gab. If the Admiral would not turn back, they should heave him overboard and report in Spain that he had fallen in accidentally while observing the stars; and none would question their story. That, said they, was the best means of assuring their safe return.

The grumbling, lamenting, and plotting went on day after day; and at last the Admiral himself became aware of their faithlessness and wicked designs against him. Therefore at times he addressed them with fair words; again, very passionately, as if fearless of death, he threatened punishment to any who hindered his voyage. By these different means he managed somewhat to calm their fears and check their machinations. To bolster their hopes he reminded them of the signs and tokens mentioned above, assuring them they would soon sight land. After that they looked most diligently for those signs and thought each hour a year until land was reached.

Finally, at sunset of Tuesday, September 25th, while the Admiral was talking with Pinzón, whose ship had come close alongside, Pinzón suddenly cried out, "Land, land, sir! I claim the reward!" And he pointed to a bulk that clearly resembled an island and lay about twenty-five leagues distant. At this the people felt such joy and relief that they offered thanks to God. The Admiral himself gave some credit to that claim until nightfall, and wishing to please them that they might not oppose continuing the voyage, he gratified their wishes and steered in that direction a good part of the night. But next morning they knew that what they had supposed to be land was nothing more than squall clouds, which often resemble land.

So, to the grief and vexation of most of his people, they again sailed westward, as they had done since leaving Spin, save when the winds were contrary. Ever vigilant for signs, they sighted a pelican and a *rabo de junco* and other birds of that kind. The morning of Thursday, September 27th, they saw another pelican flying west to east; they also saw many fish with gilded backs, and caught one of these fish with a harpoon. A *rabo de junco* flew close by; and they noted that for the last few days the currents had not been as constant and regular as before but changed with the tides; the quantity of seaweed also diminished.

Next day all the ships caught fish with gilded backs, and on Saturday they saw a frigate bird. This is a sea bird, but never does it rest upon the water, for it flies through the air pursuing pelicans until from fright they drop their excrement, which it catches in the air for its food; by such tricky hunting does the frigate bird sustain itself in those seas. It is said to be most commonly found near the Cape Verdes. A little later they saw two more pelicans and many flying fish, which are a span long and have two little wings like a bat; these fish sometimes fly about the height of a lance above the water, rising in the air like a harquebus shot, and occasionally they fall into the ships. After dinner the Admiral's people also saw much weed lying in the north-south direction, something they had often seen before, and three more pelicans and a frigate bird, which followed them.

Sunday morning four *rabos de junco* flew over the ship, and the fact that they came together made the people believe that land must be near, especially since a little while later four more pelicans passed by; they also saw many emperor fish, which resemble the fish called *chopos* in that they have a very hard skin and are not good to eat.

Although very attentive to these signs, the Admiral did not neglect the portents of the heavens or the courses of the stars. He was much surprised to observe that in this region the Guards appeared at night directly to the west, while at daybreak they were directly northeast. From this he concluded that during one night the ships traveled only three lines or nine [astronomical] hours, and by observation he found this to be true every night. He also noted that in the evening the needles varied a whole point, while at dawn they pointed directly to the polestar. This fact greatly disquieted and confused the pilots, until he told them its cause was the circle described by the polestar about the pole. This explanation partly allayed their fears, for these variations on a voyage into such strange and distant regions made them very apprehensive.

## *HOW THEY CONTINUED TO SEE THE ABOVE-MENTIONED SIGNS AND TOKENS AND OTHERS THAT WERE EVEN MORE HOPEFUL, WHICH GAVE THEM SOME COMFORT*

At sunrise on Monday, October 1st, a pelican flew over the ship, and two hours before noon came two more; the direction of the weed was now east to west. In the morning of that day the pilot of the Admiral's flagship said they were 578 leagues west of Ferro, and the Admiral put the figure at 584; but from his secret reckoning he knew they had traveled 707 leagues, a difference of 129 between his count and the pilot's. The reckonings of the other two ships varied even more widely; in the afternoon of the Wednesday following, the *Niña's* pilot claimed they had sailed 540 leagues, while the *Pinta's* set the figure at 634. Allowing for the distance they had covered the past three days, their reckonings still fell far short of the true and reasonable total, for they had always sailed with a stiff wind at their backs. But the Admiral dissembled this error that his people might not grow even more frightened, finding themselves so far from home.

Next day, October 2d, they saw many fish and caught a small tunny. They also saw a white bird like a sea gull and many *pardelas.* The seaweed was now withered and almost reduced to powder.

Next day, seeing no birds save some *pardelas,* the men feared they unknowingly had passed between some islands; for they thought the great multitude of birds they had seen were birds of passage bound from one island to another. The Admiral's people wished to turn off in one or another direction to look for those lands, but he refused because he feared to lose the fair wind that was carrying him due west along what he believed to be the best and most certain route to the Indies. Besides, he reflected that he would lose respect and credit for his voyage if he beat aimlessly about from place to place looking for lands whose position he had claimed to know most accurately. Because of this refusal, the men were on the point of mutiny, grumbling and plotting against him. But God was pleased to assist him with new signs, for on Thursday, October 4th, they saw a flight of more than forty *pardelas* and two pelicans which came so near the ships that a grummet hit one with a stone. They had previously seen another bird like a *rabo de junco* and one resembling a sea gull, and many flying fish fell into the ships. Next day another *rabo de junco* flew over the ship, and a pelican came from the west; many *pardelas* were seen.

At daybreak of the Sunday following, October 7th, they saw what appeared to be land lying westward; but since it was indistinct, none wished to claim having made the discovery, not for fear of being shamed if proved wrong but for fear of losing the 10,000 maravedís promised by the Catholic Sovereigns to the first person sighting land. In order to prevent men from crying "land, land!" at every moment and causing unjustified feelings of joy, the Admiral had ordered that one who claimed to have seen land and did not make good his claim in the space of three days would lose the reward even if afterwards he should actually see it. Being warned of this, none of the people on the Admiral's ship dared cry out "land, land!" but the *Niña,* which was a better sailer and so ranged ahead, fired a gun and broke out flags as a sign that she had sighted land.

But the farther they sailed the more their spirits fell, until at last that illusion of land faded clean away. God, however, was pleased to offer them some small comfort; for they saw many large flocks of birds, more varied in kind than those they had seen before, and others of small land birds which were flying from the west to the southwest in search of food. Being now a great distance from Spain, and convinced that such small birds would not fly far from land, the Admiral changed course from west to southwest, noting [in his journal] that he was making a slight deviation from his main course in imitation of the Portuguese, who made most of their discoveries by attending to the flights of birds. He did this especially because the birds they saw were flying in almost the very same direction where he always expected land to be found. He reminded the men that he had often told them they must not expect to strike land until they had sailed seven hundred and fifty leagues west of the Canaries; he had also said that the island of Española, then called Cipango, would be found in that area. He would doubtless have found it, too, had he not accepted the truth of the report that that island extended from north to south, and so did not run far enough south to hit it; as a result, Española and the other Caribbean islands now lay on his left, to the south, whither those birds were flying.

Being, then, so near land, they saw a great abundance and variety of birds. On Monday, October 8th, there came to the ship twelve vari-colored birds of the kind that sing in the fields; after flying for a while about the ship they continued on their way. The other ships also sighted many birds flying to the southwest; and that night they saw many large birds and flocks of small birds that came from the north and flew after the rest. They also saw many tunny fish, and in the morning they saw a *garjao,* a pelican, ducks, and little birds that flew in the same direction as the others; they noted that the air was as fresh and fragrant as in April in Seville.

But by this time the men's anxiety and desire to sight land had reached such a pitch that no sign of any kind would satisfy them. And though on Wednesday, October 10th, they saw birds passing overhead both night and day, they did not cease to complain nor the Admiral to reprove them for their small spirit, telling them that for better or worse they must go through with the enterprise of the Indies on which the Catholic Sovereigns had sent them.

## *HOW THE ADMIRAL SIGHTED THE FIRST LAND, THIS BEING AN ISLAND IN THE ARCHIPELAGO CALLED THE BAHAMAS*

Our Lord, perceiving how difficult was the Admiral's situation because of his many opponents, was pleased on the afternoon of Thursday, October 11th, to give them clear indications that they were near land, which cheered the men greatly. First the flagship's people saw a green branch pass near the ship, and later, a large green fish of the kind that is found near reefs. Then the *Pinta's* people saw a cane and a stick; and they fished up another stick skillfully carved, a small board, and an abundance of weeds of the kind that grow on the shore. The *Niña's* crew saw other signs of the same kind, as well as a thorn branch loaded with red berries that seemed to be freshly cut.

These signs, and his own reasoning, convinced the Admiral that land must be near. That night, therefore, after they had sung the Hail Mary as seamen are accustomed to do at nightfall, he spoke to the men of the favor that Our Lord had shown them by conducting them so safely and prosperously with fair winds and a clear course, and by comforting them with signs that daily grew more abundant. And he prayed them to be very watchful that night, reminding them that in the first article of the instructions issued to each ship at the Canaries he had given orders to do no night-sailing after reaching a point seven hundred leagues from those islands, but that the great desire of all to see land had decided him to sail on that night. They must make amends for this temerity by keeping a sharp lookout, for he was most confident that land was near; and to him who first sighted it he would give a velvet doublet in addition to the annuity for life of 10,000 maravedís that their Highnesses had promised.

That same night, about two hours before midnight, as the Admiral stood on the sterncastle, he saw a light, but he says it was so uncertain a thing that he dared not announce it was land. He called Pedro Gutiérrez, butler to the King, and asked him if he saw that light. He replied that he did, so they called Rodrigo Sánchez of Segovia to have a look, but he was too slow in coming to the place from which the light could be seen. After that they saw it only once or twice. This made them think it might be a light or torch belonging to fishermen or travelers who alternately raised and lowered it, or perhaps were going from house to house; for the light appeared and disappeared so quickly that few believed it to be a sign of land.

Being now very watchful, they held on their course until about two hours after midnight, when the *Pinta,* a speedy sailer that ranged far ahead, fired the signal for land. A sailor named Rodrigo de Triana first sighted it while they were still two leagues away. It was not he who received the grant of 10,000 maravedís from the Catholic Sovereigns, however, but the Admiral, who had first seen the light amid the darkness, signifying the spiritual light with which he was to illuminate those parts.

Land being now very near, all the ship's people impatiently awaited the coming of day, thinking the time endless till they could enjoy what they had so long desired.

## *HOW THE ADMIRAL WENT ASHORE AND TOOK POSSESSION OF THE LAND IN THE NAME OF THE CATHOLIC SOVEREIGNS*

At daybreak they saw an island about fifteen leagues in length, very level, full of green trees and abounding in springs, with a large lake in the middle, and inhabited by a multitude of people who hastened to the shore, astounded and marveling at the sight of the ships, which they took for animals. These people could hardly wait to see what sort of things the ships were. The Christians were no less eager to know what manner of people they had to do with. Their wishes were soon satisfied, for as soon as they had cast anchor the Admiral went ashore with an armed boat, displaying the royal standard. The captains of the other two ships did the same in their boats with the banner of the expedition, on which was depicted a green cross with an F on one side, and crowns in honor of Ferdinand and Isabella on the other.

After all had rendered thanks to Our Lord, kneeling on the ground and kissing it with tears of joy for His great favor to them, the Admiral arose and gave this island the name San Salvador. Then, in the presence of the many natives assembled there, he took possession of it in the name of the Catholic Sovereigns with appropriate ceremony and words. The Christians forthwith accepted him as admiral and viceroy and swore obedience to him as the representative of their Highnesses, with such show of pleasure and joy as so great a victory deserved; and they begged his pardon for the injuries that through fear and little faith they had done him.

Many Indians assembled to watch this celebration and rejoicing, and the Admiral, perceiving they were a gentle, peaceful, and very simple people, gave them little red caps and glass beads which they hung about their necks, together with other trifles that they cherished as if they were precious stones of great price.

## *OF THE CONDITION AND CUSTOMS OF THOSE PEOPLE, AND WHAT THE ADMIRAL SAW ON THAT ISLAND*

The Admiral having returned to his boats, the Indians followed him thither and even to the ships, some swimming and others paddling in their canoes; they brought parrots, skeins of woven cotton, darts, and other things, which they exchanged for glass beads, hawk's bells, and other trifles. Being a people of primitive simplicity, they all went about as naked as their mothers bore them; and a woman who was there wore no more clothes than the men. They were all young, not above thirty years of age, and of good stature. Their hair was straight, thick, very black, and short —that is, cut above the ears—though some let it grow down to their shoulders and tied it about their heads with a stout cord so that it looked like a woman's tress. They had handsome features, spoiled somewhat by their unpleasantly broad foreheads. They were of middle stature, well formed and sturdy, with olive-colored skins that gave them the appearance of Canary Islanders or sunburned peasants. Some were painted black, others white, and still others red; some painted only the face, others the whole body, and others only the eyes or nose.

They had no arms like ours, nor knew thereof; for when the Christians showed them a naked sword, they foolishly grasped it by the blade and cut themselves. Nor have they anything of iron, for their darts are sticks with sharpened points that they harden in the fire, arming the end with a fish's tooth instead of an iron point. Some Indians had scars left by wounds on their bodies; asked by signs what had caused them, they replied, also by signs, that the natives of other islands came on raids to capture them and they had received their wounds in defending themselves. They appeared fluent in speech and intelligent, easily repeating words that they had once heard. The only animals of any kind on the island were parrots, which they brought with the things mentioned above for barter. This traffic continued till nightfall.

Next morning, October 13th, many of these people came to the beach and paddled to the ships in their little boats, called canoes; these are made from the bole of a tree hollowed out like a trough, all in one piece. The larger ones hold forty to forty-five persons; the smaller ones are of all sizes, down to one holding but a single man. The Indians row with paddles like baker's peels or those used in dressing hemp. But their paddles are not attached to the sides of the boat as ours are; they dip them in the water and pull back with a strong stroke. So light and skillfully made are these canoes that if one overturns, the Indian rowers immediately begin to swim and right it and shake the canoe from side to side like a weaver's shuttle until it is more than half empty, bailing out the rest of the water with gourds that they carry for this purpose.

That day they brought the same things to barter as the previous day, giving all they had, in exchange for some trifle. They had no jewels or metal objects except some gold pendants which they wear hanging from a hole made through the nostrils. Asked whence came that gold, they replied by signs, from the south, where lived a king who had many tiles and vessels of gold. They added that to the south and southwest there were many other islands and large countries. Being very eager to obtain our things, and having nothing more to give in exchange, they picked up anything they could lay their hands on as soon as they came aboard, were it only a piece of broken crockery or part of a glazed bowl, then jumped into the sea and swam ashore with it. . . .

*BARTOLOMÉ DE LAS CASAS*

# 2 The Destruction of the Indies

*Bartolomé de Las Casas (1474–1566) spent most of his long life attempting to protect the native Americans against the massacres, tortures, slavery, tribute, and forced labor imposed on them by their Spanish conquerors. His powerful writings created the image of Spanish conquest often called the "Black Legend," a vision of destruction and cruelty once thought unparalleled. Modern scholars generally accept the accuracy of Las Casas's shocking portraits of devastation, many of which he personally witnessed. Today, however, many view these horrors not as the outcome of some peculiar Spanish cruelty but as characteristic of the bloody "Columbian encounter" between Europeans and other cultures in the age of exploration and conquest.*

## *SHORT REPORT OF THE DESTRUCTION OF THE WEST INDIES*

The Indies were discovered in the year fourteen hundred and ninety-two. The year following, Spanish Christians went to inhabit them, so that it is since forty-nine years that numbers of Spaniards have gone there: and the first land, that they invaded to inhabit, was the large and most delightful Isle of Hispaniola [present-day Dominican Republic and Haiti], which has a circumference of six hundred leagues.

2. There are numberless other islands, and very large ones, all around on every side, that were all—and we have seen it—as inhabited and full of their native Indian peoples as any country in the world.

3. Of the continent, the nearest part of which is more than two hundred and fifty leagues distant from this Island, more than ten thousand leagues of maritime coast have been discovered, and more is discovered every day; all that has been discovered up to the year forty-nine is full of people, like a hive of bees, so that it seems as though God had placed all, or the greater part of the entire human race in these countries.

4. God has created all these numberless people to be quite the simplest, without malice or duplicity, most obedient, most faithful to their natural Lords, and to the Christians, whom they serve; the most humble, most patient, most peaceful, and calm, without strife nor tumults; not wrangling, nor querulous, as free from uproar, hate and desire of revenge, as any in the world.

5. They are likewise the most delicate people, weak and of feeble constitution, and less than any other can they bear fatigue, and they very easily die of whatsoever infirmity; so much so, that not even the sons of our Princes and of nobles, brought up in royal and gentle life, are more delicate than they; although there are among them such as are of the peasant class. They are also a very poor people, who of worldly goods possess little, nor wish to possess: and they are therefore neither proud, nor ambitious, nor avaricious.

6. Their food is so poor, that it would seem that of the Holy Fathers in the desert was not scantier nor less pleasing. Their way of dressing is usually to go naked, covering the private parts; and at most they cover themselves with a cotton cover, which would be about equal to one and a half or two ells square of cloth. Their beds are of matting, and they mostly sleep in certain things like hanging nets, called in the language of Hispaniola *hamacas*.

7. They are likewise of a clean, unspoiled, and vivacious intellect, very capable, and receptive to every good doctrine; most prompt to accept our Holy Catholic Faith, to be endowed with virtuous customs; and they have as little difficulty with such things as any people created by God in the world.

8. Once they have begun to learn of matters pertaining to faith, they are so importunate to know them, and in frequenting the sacraments and divine service of the Church, that to tell the truth, the clergy have need to be endowed of God with the gift of pre-eminent patience to bear with them: and finally, I have heard many lay Spaniards frequently say many years ago, (unable to deny the goodness of those they saw) certainly these people were the most blessed of the earth, had they only knowledge of God.

9. Among these gentle sheep, gifted by their Maker with the above qualities, the Spaniards entered as soon as they knew them, like wolves, tigers, and lions which had been starving for many days, and since forty years they have done nothing else; nor do they otherwise at the present day, than outrage, slay, afflict, torment, and destroy them with strange and new, and divers kinds of cruelty, never before seen, nor heard of, nor read of, of which some few will be told below: to such extremes has this gone that, whereas there were more than three million souls, whom we saw in Hispaniola, there are to-day, not two hundred of the native population left.

10. The island of Cuba is almost as long as the distance from Valladolid to Rome; it is now almost entirely deserted. The islands of San Juan [Porto Rico], and Jamaica, very large and happy and pleasing islands, are both desolate. The Lucaya Isles lie near Hispaniola and Cuba to the north and number more than sixty, including those that are called the Giants, and other large and small Islands; the poorest of these, which is more fertile, and pleasing than the King's garden in Seville, is the healthiest country in the world, and contained more than

five hundred thousand souls, but to-day there remains not even a single creature. All were killed in transporting them, to Hispaniola, because it was seen that the native population there was disappearing.

11. A ship went three years later to look for the people that had been left after the gathering in, because a good Christian was moved by compassion to convert and win those that were found to Christ; only eleven persons, whom I saw, were found.

12. More than thirty other islands, about the Isle of San Juan, are destroyed and depopulated, for the same reason. All these islands cover more than two thousand leagues of land, entirely depopulated and deserted.

13. We are assured that our Spaniards, with their cruelty and execrable works, have depopulated and made desolate the great continent, and that more than ten Kingdoms, larger than all Spain, counting Aragon and Portugal, and twice as much territory as from Seville to Jerusalem (which is more than two thousand leagues), although formerly full of people, are now deserted.

14. We give as a real and true reckoning, that in the said forty years, more than twelve million persons, men, and women, and children, have perished unjustly and through tyranny, by the infernal deeds and tyranny of the Christians; and I truly believe, nor think I am deceived, that it is more than fifteen.

15. Two ordinary and principal methods have the self-styled Christians, who have gone there, employed in extirpating these miserable nations and removing them from the face of the earth. The one, by unjust, cruel and tyrannous wars. The other, by slaying all those, who might aspire to, or sigh for, or think of liberty, or to escape from the torments that they suffer, such as all the native Lords, and adult men; for generally, they leave none alive in the wars, except the young men and the women, whom they oppress with the hardest, most horrible, and roughest servitude, to which either man or beast, can ever be put. To these two ways of infernal tyranny, all the many and divers other ways, which are numberless, of exterminating these people, are reduced, resolved, or sub-ordered according to kind.

16. The reason why the Christians have killed and destroyed such infinite numbers of souls, is solely because they have made gold their ultimate aim, seeking to load themselves with riches in the shortest time and to mount by high steps, disproportioned to their condition: namely by their insatiable avarice and ambition, the greatest, that could be on the earth. These lands, being so happy and so rich, and the people so humble, so patient, and so easily subjugated, they have had no more respect, nor consideration nor have they taken more account of them (I speak with truth of what I have seen during all the aforementioned time) than,—I will not say of animals, for would to God they had considered and treated them as animals,—but as even less than the dung in the streets.

17. In this way have they cared for their lives—and for their souls: and therefore, all the millions above mentioned have died without faith, and without sacraments. And it is a publicly known truth, admitted, and confessed by all, even by the tyrants and homicides themselves, that the Indians throughout the Indies never did any harm to the Christians: they even esteemed them as coming from heaven, until they and their neighbours had suffered the same many evils, thefts, deaths, violence and visitations at their hands.

## *OF HISPANIOLA*

In the island of Hispaniola—which was the first, as we have said, to be invaded by the Christians—the immense massacres and destruction of these people began. It was the first to be destroyed and made into a desert. The Christians began by taking the women and children, to use and to abuse them, and to eat of the substance of their toil and labour, instead of contenting themselves with what the Indians gave them spontaneously, according to the means of each. Such stores are always small; because they keep no more than they ordinarily need, which they acquire with little labour; but what is enough for three households, of ten persons each, for a month, a Christian eats and destroys in one day. From their using force, violence and other kinds of vexations, the Indians began to perceive that these men could not have come from heaven.

2. Some hid their provisions, others, their wives and children: others fled to the mountains to escape from people of such harsh and terrible intercourse. The Christians gave them blows in the face, beatings and cudgellings, even laying hands on the lords of the land. They reached such recklessness and effrontery, that a Christian captain violated the lawful wife of the chief king and lord of all the island.

3. After this deed, the Indians consulted to devise means of driving the Christians from their country. They took up their weapons, which are poor enough and little fitted for attack, being of little force and not even good for defence. For this reason, all their wars are little more than games with sticks, such as children play in our countries.

4. The Christians, with their horses and swords and lances, began to slaughter and practise strange cruelty among them. They penetrated into the country and spared neither children nor the aged, nor pregnant women, nor those in child labour, all of whom they ran through the body and lacerated, as though they were assaulting so many lambs herded in their sheepfold.

5. They made bets as to who would slit a man in two, or cut off his head at one blow: or they opened up his bowels. They tore the babes from their mothers' breast by the feet, and dashed their heads against the rocks. Others they seized by the shoulders and threw into

the rivers, laughing and joking, and when they fell into the water they exclaimed: "boil body of so and so!" They spitted the bodies of other babes, together with their mothers and all who were before them, on their swords.

6. They made a gallows just high enough for the feet to nearly touch the ground, and by thirteens, in honour and reverence of our Redeemer and the twelve Apostles, they put wood underneath and, with fire, they burned the Indians alive.

7. They wrapped the bodies of others entirely in dry straw, binding them in it and setting fire to it; and so they burned them. They cut off the hands of all they wished to take alive, made them carry them fastened on to them, and said: "Go and carry letters": that is; take the news to those who have fled to the mountains.

8. They generally killed the lords and nobles in the following way. They made wooden gridirons of stakes, bound them upon them, and made a slow fire beneath: thus the victims gave up the spirit by degrees, emitting cries of despair in their torture.

9. I once saw that they had four or five of the chief lords stretched on the gridirons to burn them, and I think also there were two or three pairs of gridirons, where they were burning others; and because they cried aloud and annoyed the captain or prevented him sleeping, he commanded that they should strangle them: the officer who was burning them was worse than a hangman and did not wish to suffocate them, but with his own hands he gagged them, so that they should not make themselves heard, and he stirred up the fire, until they roasted slowly, according to his pleasure. I know his name, and knew also his relations in Seville. I saw all the above things and numberless others.

10. And because all the people who could flee, hid among the mountains and climbed the crags to escape from men so deprived of humanity, so wicked, such wild beasts, exterminators and capital enemies of all the human race, the Spaniards taught and trained the fiercest boar-hounds to tear an Indian to pieces as soon as they saw him, so that they more willingly attacked and ate one, than if he had been a boar. These hounds made great havoc and slaughter.

11. And because sometimes, though rarely, the Indians killed a few Christians for just cause, they made a law among themselves, that for one Christian whom the Indians killed, the Christians should kill a hundred Indians.

CHIEF ELIAS JOHNSON

# 3 On the Founding of the Indian Nations

*When the first European settlers reached North America, they encountered people who themselves had complex values and traditions. For over two hundred years after its organization in about 1570, the Iroquois Confederacy, also known as the Five Indian Nations (later the Tuscarora joined as the sixth nation), dominated upstate New York and blocked the way west for British settlers in New England and the Hudson Valley. Richly embroidered native American legend attributed the founding of the Confederacy to Hiawatha, a leader of the Mohawks—one of the five nations—whom native American lore eventually transformed into a wise and powerful god. Hiawatha, according to the legend, saw common ground among the five nations that enabled them to create an effective confederacy without sacrificing their autonomy. The American republic would wrestle with a similar problem, as Benjamin Franklin foresaw. Franklin, in fact, was so impressed with the structure of the Iroquois Confederacy that he recommended its government to the colonies as a model for joining separate sovereign states into a powerful nation.*

*We learn of Hiawatha from Chief Elias Johnson, whose nation, the Tuscarora, had migrated from North Carolina in the early eighteenth century to join the Iroquois Confederacy in New York. He collected the oral traditions of the Iroquois people, many of which had passed from generation to generation for centuries. His book,* Legends, Traditions, and Laws of the Iroquois, or Six Nations, and History of the Tuscarora Indians, *published in 1881, is a standard reference on the history of the Iroquois.*

When another day had expired, the council again met. Hiawatha entered the assembly with even more than ordinary attention, and every eye was fixed upon him, when he began to address the council in the following words:

"Friends and Brothers:—You being members of many tribes, you have come from a great distance; the voice of war has aroused you up; you are afraid of your homes, your wives and your children; you trembled for your safety. Believe me, I am with you. My heart beats with your hearts. We are one. We have one common object. We come to promote our common interest, and to determine how this can be best done.

"To oppose those hordes of northern tribes, singly and alone, would prove certain destruction. We can make no progress in that way.

We must unite ourselves into one common band of brothers. We must have but one voice. Many voices makes confusion. We must have one fire, one pipe and one war club. This will give us strength. If our warriors are united they can defeat the enemy and drive them from our land; if we do this, we are safe.

"Onondaga, you are the people sitting under the shadow of the *Great Tree,* whose branches spread far and wide, and whose roots sink deep into the earth. You shall be the first nation, because you are warlike and mighty.

"Oneida, and you, the people who recline your bodies against the *Everlasting Stone,* that cannot be moved, shall be the second nation, because you always give good counsel.

"Seneca, and you, the people who have your habitation at the foot of the *Great Mountain,* and are overshadowed by its crags, shall be the third nation, because you are all greatly gifted in speech.

"Cayuga, you, whose dwelling is in the *Dark Forest,* and whose home is everywhere, shall be the fourth nation, because of your superior cunning in hunting.

"Mohawk, and you, the people who live in the open country, and possess much wisdom, shall be the fifth nation, because you understand better the art of raising corn and beans and making cabins.

"You five great and powerful nations, with your tribes, must unite and have one common interest, and no foe shall disturb or subdue you.

"And you of the different nations of the south, and you of the west, may place yourselves under our protection, and we will protect you. We earnestly desire the alliance and friendship of you all. . . .

"If we unite in one band the Great Spirit will smile upon us, and we shall be free, prosperous and happy; but if we shall remain as we are we shall incur his displeasure. We shall be enslaved, and perhaps annihilated forever.

"Brothers, these are the words of Hiawatha. Let them sink deep into your hearts. I have done."

A deep and impressive silence followed the delivery of this speech. On the following day the council again assembled to act on it. High wisdom recommended this deliberation.

The union of the tribes into one confederacy was discussed and unanimously adopted. To denote the character and intimacy of the union they employed the figure of a single council-house, or lodge, whose boundaries be co-extensive with their territories. Hence the name of Ako-no-shu-ne, who were called the Iroquois. . . .

Hiawatha, the guardian and founder of the league, having now accomplished the will of the Great Spirit, immediately prepared to make his final departure. Before the great council, which had adopted his advice just before dispersing, he arose, with a dignified air, and addressed them in the following manner:

"Friends and Brothers:—I have now fulfilled my mission here below; I have furnished you seeds and grains for your gardens; I have removed obstructions from your waters, and made the forest habitable by teaching you how to expel its monsters; I have given you fishing places and hunting grounds; I have instructed you in the making and using of war implements; I have taught you how to cultivate corn, and many other arts and gifts. I have been allowed by the Great Spirit to communicate to you. Last of all, I have aided you to form a league of friendship and union. If you preserve this, and admit no foreign element of power by the admission of other nations, you will always be free, numerous and happy. If other tribes and nations are admitted to your councils, they will sow the seed of jealousy and discord, and you will become few, feeble and enslaved.

"Friends and brothers, these are the last words you will hear from the lips of Hiawatha. The Great Creator of our bodies calls me to go; I have patiently awaited his summons; I am ready to go. Farewell."

As the voice of the wise man ceased, sweet strains of music from the air burst on the ears of the multitude. The whole sky appeared to be filled with melody; and while all eyes were directed to catch glimpses of the sights, and enjoy strains of the celestial music that filled the sky, Hiawatha was seen, seated in his snow-white canoe, amid the air, *rising, rising* with every choral chant that burst out. As he rose the sound of the music became more soft and faint, until he vanished amid the summer clouds, and the melody ceased. . . .

JOHN WHITE

# 4 The Lost Colony of Roanoke

*For all his celebrated bravery and dash, Sir Walter Raleigh, who financed and directed the first English settlement in the New World, was a careful planner. He first tried to unlock the royal treasury; then when Queen Elizabeth I said no, he used his own capital and enterprise to proceed. He sent two exploratory expeditions in 1584 and 1585 before launching a full-scale settlement in 1587 at Roanoke Island, in what is now North Carolina but was then called Virginia. Under the command of Governor John White—an artist, a trusted leader, and a skillful writer—117 colonists, including 17 women and 9 children, sailed in three ships to the new land. White then returned to England in order to resupply the colony. What he found on his return in 1590 forms one of the first and most interesting of American historical mysteries. The English did not attempt the settlement of Virginia again until the founding of the Jamestown colony in 1607.*

In the year of our Lord 1587 Sir Walter Raleigh intending to persevere in the planting of his country of Virginia, prepared a new colony of one hundred and fifty men to be sent thither, under the charge of John White, whom he appointed Governor, and also appointed unto him twelve Assistants, unto whom he gave a charter, and incorporated them by the name of Governor and Assistants of the City of Raleigh in Virginia.

/ / /

The two and twentieth of July we arrived safe at Hatorask, where our ship and pinnace anchored. The Governor went aboard the pinnace, accompanied with forty of his best men, intending to pass up to Roanoke forthwith, hoping there to find those fifteen Englishmen, which Sir Richard Grenville had left there the year before, with whom he meant to have conference, concerning the state of the country and savages, meaning after he had so done, to return again to the fleet, and pass along the coast, to the Bay of Chesapeake, where we intended to make our seat and fort, according to the charge given us among other directions in writing, under the hand of Sir Walter Raleigh. But as soon as we were put with our pinnace from the ship, a Gentleman by the means of Ferdinando, who was appointed to return for England, called to the sailors in the pinnace, charging them not to bring any of the planters back again, but to leave them in the Island, except the Governor, & two or three such as he approved, saying that the summer was fair spent, wherefore he would land all the planters in no other place. Unto this were all the sailors, both in the pinnace and ship, persuaded by the Master, wherefore it booted not the Governor to contend with them, but passed to Roanoke, and the same night at sunset went aland on the Island, in the place where our fifteen men were left. But we found none of them, nor any sign that they had been there, saving only we found the bones of one of those fifteen, which the savages had slain long before.

The three and twentieth of July the Governor with divers of his company, walked to the North end of the island, where Master Ralph Lane had his fort, with sundry necessary and decent dwelling houses, made by his men about it the year before, where we hoped to find some signs or certain knowledge of our fifteen men. When we came there, we found the fort razed down, but all the houses standing unhurt, saving that the nether rooms of them, and also the fort were overgrown with melons of diverse sorts, and deer within them, feeding on those melons. So we returned to our company, without hope of ever seeing any of the fifteen men living.

The same day order was given that every man should be employed for the repairing of those houses, which we found standing, and also to make other new cottages for such as should be needed.

The 25th of July our flyboat and the rest of our planters arrived all safe at Hatoraske, to the great joy and comfort of the whole company.

/ / /

On the twenty-eighth, George Howe, one of our twelve assistants was slain by diverse savages, which were come over to Roanoke, either for purposes to spy on our company, and what a number we were, or else to hunt deer, which were many on the island. These savages, being secretly hidden among high reeds, often times killing deer when the deer were asleep, spied our man wading in the water alone, almost naked, without any weapons except a small forked stick, catching crabs and also being strayed two miles from his company, and shot him in the water, where they gave him sixteen wounds with their arrows. And after they had slain him with their wooden swords, they beat his head in pieces, and fled over the water to the main land.

On the thirtieth of July Master Stafford and twenty of our men passed by water to the island of Croatoan, with Manteo, who had his mother, and many of his kindred dwelling in that island, of whom we hoped to understand some news of our fifteen men, but especially to learn the disposition of the people of the country towards us, and to renew our old friendship with them. At our first landing they seemed as though they would fight with us: but perceiving us begin to march with our shot towards them, they turned their backs, and fled. Then Manteo their country man called to them in their own language, whom, as soon as they heard, they returned, and threw away their bows and arrows, and some of them came unto us embracing and entertaining us friendly, desiring us not to gather or spill any of their corn, for that they had little. We answered them, that neither their corn, nor any of us, and things of theirs, should be diminished by any of us, and that our coming was only to renew the old love, that was between us and them at the first, and to live with them as brethren and friends: which answer seemed to please them well, wherefore they requested us to walk up to their town, who there feasted us after their manner, and desired us earnestly, that there might be some token or badge given them of us, whereby we might know them to be our friends, when we met them anywhere out of the town or island. They told us further, that for want of some such badge, divers of them were hurt the year before, being found out of the island by master Lane his company, whereof they showed us one, which at that very instant lay lame, and had lain of that hurt ever since: but they said they knew our men mistook them, and hurt them instead of Winginos men, wherefore they held us excused.

August

The next day we had conference further with them, concerning the people of Secotan, Aquascogoc, and, Pomeiok, willing them of Croatoan to certify the people of those towns, that if they would accept our friendship, we would willingly receive them again, and that all unfriendly dealings past on both parts, should be utterly forgiven and forgotten. To this the chief men of Croatoan answered, that they would gladly do the best they could, and within seven days, bring the Werowances and chief governors of those towns with them, to our governor at Roanoke, or their answer. We also understood of the men of Croatoan, that our man master Howe was slain by the remnant of Winginos men dwelling then at Dasamonguepeuk, with whom Wanchese kept company: and also we understood by them of Croatoan, how that the 15 Englishmen left at Roanoke the year before, by Sir Richard Grenville, were suddenly set upon, by 30 of the men of Secotan, Aquascogoc, and Dasamonguepeuk, in manner following. They conveyed themselves secretly behind the trees, near the houses where our men carelessly lived. And having perceived that of those fifteen they could see but eleven only, two of those savages appeared to the eleven Englishmen, calling to them by friendly signs, that but two of their chiefest men should come unarmed to speak with those two savages, who seemed also to be unarmed. Wherefore two of the chiefest of our Englishmen went gladly to them: but whilst one of those savages traitorously embraced one of our men, the other with his sword of wood, which he had secretly hidden under his mantel, stroke him on the head and slew him, and presently the other eight and twenty savages showed themselves. The other Englishman perceiving this, fled to his company, whom the savages pursued with their bows and arrows so fast, that the Englishmen were forced to take to the house wherein all their victuals and weapons were. But the savages forthwith set the same on fire by means whereof our men were forced to take up such weapons as come first to hand, and without order to run forth among the savages, with whom they skirmished above an hour. In this skirmish another of our men was shot into the mouth with an arrow, whereof he died. And also one of the Savages was shot into the side by one of our men, with a wild fire arrow, whereof he died presently.

The place where they fought was of great advantage to the Savages, by means of the thick trees, behind which the Savages through their nimbleness, defended themselves, and so offended our men with their arrows, that our men being some of them hurt, retired fighting to the water side, where their boat lay, with which they fled towards Hatorask. By that time they had rowed but a quarter of a mile, they spied their four fellows coming from a creek thereby, where they had been to fetch Oysters: these four they received into their boat, leaving Roanoke, and landed on a little Island on the right hand of our entrance into the harbour of Hatorask, where they remained a while, but afterward departed, whither as yet we know not.

Having now sufficiently dispatched our business at Croatoan, the same day we departed friendly, taking our leave, and came aboard the fleet at Hatorask.

The eighth of August, the Governor having long expected the coming of the Werwoances of Pomeiok, Aquascogoc, Secotan, and Dasamonguepeuk, seeing that the seven days were past, within which they promised to come in, or to send their answers by the men of Croatoan, and no tidings of them heard, being certainly also informed by those men of Croatoan, that the remnant of Wingina his men, which were left alive, who dwelt at Dasamonquepeuk, were they which had slain George Howe, and were also at the driving of our eleven Englishmen from Roanoke, he thought to defer the revenge thereof no longer. Wherefore the same night about midnight, he passed over the water, accompanied with Captain Stafford, and 24 men, whereof Manteo was one, whom we took with us to be our guide to the place where those Savages dwelt, where he behaved himself toward us as a most faithful Englishman.

The next day, being the 9th of August, in the morning so early that it was yet dark, we landed near the dwelling place of our enemies, & very secretly conveyed our selves through the woods, to that side, where we had their houses between us and the water. And having spied their fire, and some sitting about it, we presently set on them. The miserable souls herewith amazed, fled into a place of thick reeds, growing fast by, where our men perceiving them, shot one of them through the body with a bullet, and therewith we entered the reeds, among which we hoped to acquit their evil doing towards us, but we were deceived, for those Savages were our friends, and were come from Croatoan to gather the corn & fruit of that place, because they understood our enemies were fled immediately after they had slain George Howe, and for haste had left all their corn, tobacco, and pompions standing in such sort, that all had been devoured of the birds and deer, if it had not been gathered in time. But they had like to have paid dearly for it: for it was so dark, that they being naked, and their men and women apparelled all so like others, we knew not but that they were all men. And if that one of them which was a Werowance's wife had not had a child at her back, she had been slain in stead of a man, and as happen was, another Savage knew master Stafford, and ran to him, calling him by his name, whereby he was saved. Finding our selves thus disappointed of our purpose, we gathered all the corn, peas, pompions, and tobacco that we found ripe, leaving the rest unspoiled, and took Menatoan his wife, with the young child, and the other Savages with us over the water to Roanoke. Although the mistaking of these Savages somewhat grieved Manteo, yet he imputed their harm to their own folly, saying to them, that if their Wiroances had kept their promise in coming to the Governor at the day appointed, they had not known that mischance.

The 13th of August our Savage Manteo, by the commandment of Sir Walter Raleigh, was christened in Roanoke, and called Lord thereof, and of Dasamonguepeuk, in reward of his faithful service.

The 18th of August Eleanor, daughter of the Governor, and wife to Ananias Dare one of the Assistants, was delivered of a daughter in Roanoke, and the same was christened there the Sunday following, and because this child was the first Christian born in Virginia, she was named Virginia. By this time our ships had unladen the goods and victuals of the planters, and began to take in wood and fresh water, and to new caulk and trim them for England. The planters also prepared their letters and tokens to send back into England.

/ / /

At this time some controversies arose between the Governor and Assistants, about choosing two out of the twelve Assistants, which should go back as factors for the company into England: for every one of them refused, save only one, which all other thought not sufficient. But at length by much persuading of the Governor, Christopher Cooper only agreed to go for England. But the next day, through the persuasion of divers of his familiar friends, he changed his mind so that now the matter stood as at the first.

The next day, the 22nd of August, the whole company both of the Assistants and planters came to the Governor, and with one voice requested him to return himself into England, for the better and sooner obtaining of supplies, and other necessaries for them: but he refused it, and alleged many sufficient causes, why he would not: the one was, that he could not so suddenly return back again without his great discredit, leaving the action, and so many whom he partly had procured through his persuasions, to leave their native country, and undertake that voyage, and that some enemies to him and the action at his return into England would not spare to slander falsely both him and the action, by saying, he went to Virginia, but politically, and to no other end but to lead so many into a country, in which he never meant to stay himself, and there to leave them behind him. Also he alleged, that seeing they intended to remove 40 miles further up into the main presently, he being then absent, his stuff and goods might be both spoiled and most of them pilfered away in the carriage, so that at his return he should be either forced to provide himself of all such things again, or else at his coming again to Virginia find himself utterly unfurnished, whereof already he had found some proof, being but once from them but three days. Wherefore he concluded that he would not go himself.

The next day, not only the Assistants but divers others, as well women as men, began to renew their requests to the Governor again, to take upon him to return into England for the supply, and dispatch of all such things as there were to be done, promising to make him their bond under all their hands and seals for the safe preserving of all his goods for him at his return to Virginia, so that if any part thereof were spoiled or lost, they would see it restored to him, or his Assigns, whensoever the same should be missed and demanded: which bond, with a testimony under their hands and seals, they forthwith made, and delivered into his hands.

/ / /

Return—1590

[Because of the War of the Spanish Armada, White could not return until 1590. He recounts what he found.]

The next morning being the 17th of August, our boats and company were prepared again to go up to Roanoke. . . . The admiral's boat was halfway toward the shore, when Captain Spicer put off from his ship. The Admiral's boat first passed the breach, but not without some danger of sinking, for we had a sea break into our boat which filled us half full of water, but by the will of God and careful steerage of Captain Cooke we came safe ashore, saving only that our furniture, victuals, match and powder were much wet and spoiled. For at this time the wind blew at Northeast and direct into the harbour so great a gale, that the Sea broke extremely on the bar, and the tide went very forcibly at the entrance. By that time our admiral's boat was hauled ashore, and most of our things taken out to dry, Captain Spicer came to the entrance of the breach with his mast standing up, and was half passed over, but by the rash and indiscreet steerage of Ralph Skinner his Master's mate, a very dangerous Sea broke into their boat and overset them quite.... They were eleven in all, and seven of the chiefest were drowned.... This mischance did so much discomfort the sailors, that they were all of one mind not to go any further to seek the planters. But in the end by the commandment and persuasion of me and Captain Cooke, they prepared the boats. And seeing the Captain and me so resolute, they seemed much more willing.

Our boats and all things fitted again, we put off from Hatorask, being the number of nineteen persons in both boats: but before we could get to the place, where our planters were left, it was so exceedingly dark, that we overshot the place a quarter of a mile. There we spied towards the North end of the island the light of a great fire through the woods, to the which we presently rowed. When we came right over against it, we let fall our grapnel near the shore, and sounded with a trumpet a call, and afterwards many familiar English tunes of songs, and called to them friendly; but we had no answer. We therefore landed at daybreak, and coming to the fire, we found the grass and sundry rotten trees burning about the place. From hence we went through the woods to that part of the island directly over against Dasamongwepeuk, and from thence we returned by the water side, round about the North point of the island, until we came to the place where I left our Colony in the year 1587.

In all this way we saw in the sand the print of the savages' feet of two or three sort trodden the night, and as we entered up the sandy bank upon a tree, in the very brow thereof were curiously carved these fair Roman letters C R O: which letters presently we knew to signify the place, where I should find the planters seated, according to a secret token agreed upon between them and me at my last departure from them, which was, that in any ways they should not fail to write or carve on the trees or posts of the doors the name of the place where they should be seated; for at my coming away they were prepared to remove from Roanoke 50 miles into the main. Therefore at my departure from them in A.D. 1587 I willed them, that if they should happen to be distressed in any of those places, that then they should carve over the letters or name, a Cross ✠ in this form, but we found no such sign of distress.

And having well considered of this, we passed toward the place where they were left in sundry houses, but we found the houses taken down, and the place very strongly enclosed with a high palisade of great trees, with continues and flankers very Fort-like, and one of the chief trees or posts at the right side of the entrance had the bark taken off, and 5 foot from the ground in fair Capital letters was graven CROATOAN without any cross or sign of distress. This done, we entered into the palisade, where we found many bars of iron, two pigs of lead, four iron fowlers, iron sacker-shot, and such like heavy things, thrown here and there, almost overgrown with grass and weeds. From thence we went along by the water side, towards the point of the Creek to see if we could find any of their boats or pinnace, but we could perceive no sign of them, nor any of the last falkons and small ordinance which were left with them, at my departure from them.

At our return from the Creek, some of our sailors meeting us, told us that they had found where divers chests had been hidden, and long since dug up again and broken up, and much of the goods in them spoiled and scattered about, but nothing left, of such things as the Savages knew any use of, undefaced. Presently Captain Cooke and I went to the place, which was in the end of an old trench, made two years past by Captain Amadas: where we found five chests, that had been carefully hidden of the Planters, and of the same chests three were my own, and about the place many of my things spoiled and broken, and my books torn from the covers, the frames of some of my pictures and maps rotten and spoiled with rain, and my armor almost eaten through with rust. This could be no other but the deed of the Savages our enemies at Dasamongwepeuk, who had watched the departure of our men to Croatoan; and as soon as they were departed, dug up every place where they suspected any thing to be buried. But although it much grieved me to see such spoil of my goods, yet on the other side I greatly joyed that I had safely found a certain token of their safe being at Croatoan, which is the place where Manteo was born, and the savages of the island our friends.

When we had seen in this place so much as we could, we returned to our boats, and departed from the shore towards our ship, with as much speed as we could: for the weather began to overcast, and very likely that a foul and stormy night would ensue. Therefore the same evening with much danger and labor, we got ourselves aboard, by which time the wind and seas were so greatly risen, that we doubted our cables and anchors would scarcely hold until morning. Wherefore the Captain caused the boat to be manned with five lusty men, who could swim all well, and sent them to the little island on the right hand of the harbor, to bring aboard six of our men, who had filled our cask with fresh water. The boat the same night returned aboard with our men, but all our cask ready filled they left behind, impossible to be had aboard with out danger of casting away both men and boats: for this night proved very stormy and foul.

The next morning it was agreed by the Captain and myself, with the Master and others, to weigh anchor, and go for the place at Croatoan, where our planters were: for that then the wind was good for that place, and also to leave that cask with fresh water on shore in the island until our return. So then they brought the cable to the Captain, but when the anchor was almost apeck, the cable broke, by means whereof we lost another anchor, wherewith we drove so fast into the shore that we were forced to let fall a third anchor: which came so fast home that the ship was almost aground by Kenricks mounts: so that we were forced to let slip the cable end for end. And if it had not chanced that we had fallen into a channel of deeper water, closer by the shore than we accompted of, we could never have gone clear of the point that lies to the Southwards of Kenricks mounts. Being thus clear of some dangers, and gotten into deeper waters, but not without some loss: for we had but one cable and anchor left us of four, and the weather grew to be fouler and fouler, our victuals scarce, and our cask and fresh water lost: it was therefore determined that we should go for Saint John or some other island to the Southward for fresh water. And it was further proposed, that if we could any way supply our wants of victuals and other necessaries, either at Hispaniola, Saint John, or Trinidad, that then we should continue in the Indies all the winter following, with hope to make two rich voyages of one, and at our return to visit our countrymen at Virginia. The captain and the whole company in the Admiral (with my earnest petitions) thereunto agreed, so that it rested only to know what the Master of the Moonlight our consort would do herein. But when we demanded them if they would accompany us in that new determination, they alleged that their weak and leaky ship was not able to continue it; wherefore the same night we parted, leaving the Moonlight to go directly for England, and the Admiral set his course for Trinidad, which course we kept two days.

*FATHER PAUL LE JEUNE*

# 5 *Encounter with the Indians*

*The Society of Jesus of the Roman Catholic Church, known usually as the Jesuits, in the sixteenth and seventeenth century energetically proselytized in virtually every Portuguese, Spanish, and French colony. Coming from a world and culture apart from their new clientele, the first Jesuit missionaries arrived in French Canada in 1632 determined to bring Christianity to the native Americans by living with them, learning their languages, educating their children, and demonstrating (sometimes at the cost of their lives) that they were as brave as the native American warriors. The Jesuits played a major role in cementing French alliances with many native American nations across Canada and into the Ohio Valley. This gave France a strategic position in the New World, hemming the colonies of British North America against the eastern seaboard until French power was destroyed in the mid-eighteenth century. The Jesuits in Canada reported regularly on their ministry. These reports form an important account of native American life and greatly influenced the European perception of the New World.*

*Father Paul Le Jeune, born in France in 1591, became a Jesuit in 1613. He had been a professor of rhetoric as well as Superior of the Jesuit House at Dieppe before he radically changed his activities by going to French North America in 1632. Le Jeune worked with the native Americans until 1649. He died in Paris in 1664.*

*Le Jeune found much to admire in the native Americans, as well as much that he could neither understand nor accept. The reports below, written from Quebec in August 1634, indicate how little whites and native Americans could understand one another, even when they shared common hardships.*

## *CHAPTER IV. ON THE BELIEF, SUPERSTITIONS, AND ERRORS OF THE MONTAGNAIS SAVAGES.*

I have already reported that the Savages believe that a certain one named Atahocam had created the world, and that one named Messou had restored it. I have questioned upon this subject the famous Sorcerer and the old man with whom I passed the Winter; they answered that they did not know who was the first Author of the world,—that it was perhaps Atahocam, but that was not certain; that they only spoke of Atahocam as one speaks of a thing so far distant that nothing sure can be known about it; . . .

As to the Messou, they hold that he restored the world, which was destroyed in the flood; whence it appears that they have some tradition of that great universal deluge which happened in the time of Noë. . . .

They also say that all animals, of every species, have an elder brother, who is, as it were, the source and origin of all individuals, and this elder brother is wonderfully great and powerful. . . . Now these elders of all the animals are the juniors of the Messou. Behold him well related, this worthy restorer of the Universe, he is elder brother to all beasts. If any one, when asleep, sees the elder or progenitor of some animals, he will have a fortunate chase; if he sees the elder of the Beavers, he will take Beavers; if he sees the elder of the Elks, he will take Elks, possessing the juniors through the favor of their senior whom he has seen in the dream. . . .

Their Religion, or rather their superstition, consists besides in praying; but O, my God, what prayers they make! In the morning, when the little children come out from their Cabins, they shout, *Cacouakhi, Pakhais Amiscouakhi, Pakhais Mousouakhi, Pakhais,* "Come Porcupines; come, Beavers; come, Elk;" and this is all of their prayers.

When the Savages sneeze, and sometimes even at other times, during the Winter, they cry out in a loud voice, *Etouctaian miraouinam an Mirouscamikhi,* "I shall be very glad to see the Spring."

At other times, I have heard them pray for the Spring, or for deliverance from evils and other similar things; and they express all these things in the form of desires, crying out as loudly as they can, "I would be very glad if this day would continue, if the wind would change," etc. I could not say to whom these wishes are addressed, for they themselves do not know, at least those whom I have asked have not been able to enlighten me. . . .

These are some of their superstitions. How much dust there is in their eyes, and how much trouble there will be to remove it that they may see the beautiful light of truth! I believe, nevertheless, that any one who knew their language perfectly, in order to give them good reasons promptly, would soon make them laugh at their own stupidity; for sometimes I have made them ashamed and confused, although I speak almost entirely by my hands, I mean by signs. . . .

## *CHAPTER V. ON THE GOOD THINGS WHICH ARE FOUND AMONG THE SAVAGES.*

If we begin with physical advantages, I will say that they possess these in abundance. They are tall, erect, strong, well proportioned, agile; and there is nothing effeminate in their appearance. Those little Fops that are seen elsewhere are only caricatures of men, compared with our Savages. I almost believed, heretofore, that the Pictures of the Roman Emperors represented the ideal of the painters rather than men who had ever existed, so strong and powerful are their heads; but I see here upon the shoulders of these people the heads of Julius Caesar, of Pompey, of Augustus, of Otho, and of others, that I have seen in France, drawn upon paper, or in relief on medallions.

As to the mind of the Savage, it is of good quality. I believe that souls are all made from the same stock, and that they do not materially differ; hence, these barbarians having well formed bodies, and organs well regulated and well arranged, their minds ought to work with ease. Education and instruction alone are lacking. Their soul is a soil which is naturally good, but loaded down with all the evils that a land abandoned since the birth of the world can produce. I naturally compare our Savages with certain villagers, because both are usually without education, though our Peasants are superior in this regard; and yet I have not seen any one thus far, of those who have come to this country, who does not confess and frankly admit that the Savages are more intelligent than our ordinary peasants.

Moreover, if it is a great blessing to be free from a great evil, our Savages are happy; for the two tyrants who provide hell and torture for many of our Europeans, do not reign in their great forests,—I mean ambition and avarice. As they have neither political organization, nor offices, nor dignities, nor any authority, for they only obey their Chief through good will toward him, therefore they never kill each other to acquire these honors. Also, as they are contented with a mere living, not one of them gives himself to the Devil to acquire wealth.

They make a pretence of never getting angry, not because of the beauty of this virtue, for which they have not even a name, but for their own contentment and happiness, I mean, to avoid the bitterness caused by anger. The Sorcerer said to me one day, speaking of one of our Frenchmen, "He has no sense, he gets angry; as for me, nothing can disturb me; let hunger oppress me, let my nearest relation pass to the other life, let the Hiroquois, our enemies, massacre our people, I never get angry." What he says is not an article of faith; for, as he is more haughty than any other Savage, so I have seen him oftener out of humor than any of them; it is true also that he often restrains and governs himself by force, especially when I expose his foolishness. I have only heard one Savage pronounce this word, *Ninichcatihin,* "I am angry," and he only said it once. But I noticed that they kept their eyes on him, for when these Barbarians are angry, they are dangerous and unrestrained.

Whoever professes not to get angry, ought also to make a profession of patience; the Savages surpass us to such an extent, in this respect, that we ought to be ashamed. I saw them, in their hardships and in their labors, suffer with cheerfulness. My host, wondering at the great number of people who I told him were in France, asked me if the men were good, if they did not become angry, if they were patient. I have never seen such patience as is shown by a sick Savage. You may yell, storm, jump, dance, and he will scarcely ever complain. I found myself, with them, threatened with great suffering; they said to me, "We shall be sometimes two days, sometimes three, without eating, for lack of food; take courage, *Chihiné*, let thy soul be strong to endure suffering and hardship; keep thyself from being sad, otherwise thou wilt be sick; see how we do not cease to laugh, although we have little to eat." One thing alone casts them down,—it is when they see death, for they fear this beyond measure; take away this apprehension from the Savages, and they will endure all kinds of degradation and discomfort, and all kinds of trials and suffering very patiently. . . .

They are very much attached to each other, and agree admirably. You do not see any disputes, quarrels, enmities, or reproaches among them. Men leave the arrangement of the household to the women, without interfering with them; they cut, and decide, and give away as they please, without making the husband angry. . . .

## *CHAPTER VI. ON THEIR VICES AND THEIR IMPERFECTIONS.*

The Savages, being filled with errors, are also haughty and proud. Humility is born of truth, vanity of error and falsehood. They are void of the knowledge of truth, and are in consequence, mainly occupied with thought of themselves. They imagine that they ought by right of birth, to enjoy the liberty of Wild ass colts, rendering no homage to any one whomsoever, except when they like. They have reproached me a hundred times because we fear our Captains, while they laugh at and make sport of theirs. All the authority of their chief is in his tongue's end; for he is powerful in so far as he is eloquent; and, even if he kills himself talking and haranguing, he will not be obeyed unless he pleases the Savages. . . .

I have shown in my former letters how vindictive the Savages are toward their enemies, with what fury and cruelty they treat them, eating them after they have made them suffer all that an incarnate fiend could invent. This fury is common to the women as well as to the men, and they even surpass the latter in this respect. I have said that they eat the lice they find upon themselves, not that they like the taste of them, but because they want to bite those that bite them.

These people are very little moved by compassion. When any one is sick in their Cabins, they ordinarily do not cease to cry and storm, and make as much noise as if everybody were in good health. They do not know what it is to take care of a poor invalid, and to give him the food which is good for him; if he asks for something to drink, it is given to him, if he asks for something to eat, it is given to him, but otherwise he is neglected; to coax him with love and gentleness, is a language which they do not understand. As long as a patient can eat, they will carry or drag him with them; if he stops eating, they believe that it is all over with him and kill him, as much to free him from the sufferings that he is enduring, as to relieve themselves of the trouble of taking him with them when they go to some other place. I have both admired and pitied the patience of the invalids whom I have seen among them.

The Savages are slanderous beyond all belief; I say, also among themselves, for they do not even spare their nearest relations, and with it all they are deceitful. For, if one speaks ill of another, they all jeer with loud laughter; if the other appears upon the scene, the first one will show him as much affection and treat him with as much love, as if he had elevated him to the third heaven by his praise. The reason of this is, it seems to me, that their slanders and derision do not come from malicious hearts or from infected mouths, but from a mind which says what it thinks in order to give itself free scope, and which seeks gratification from everything, even from slander and mockery. Hence they are not troubled even if they are told that others are making sport of them, or have injured their reputation. All they usually answer to such talk is, *mama irinisiou,* "He has no sense, he does not know what he is talking about;" and at the first opportunity they will pay their slanderer in the same coin, returning him the like.

Lying is as natural to Savages as talking, not among themselves, but to strangers. Hence it can be said that fear and hope, in one word, interest, is the measure of their fidelity. I would not be willing to trust them, except as they would fear to be punished if they had failed in their duty, or hoped to be rewarded if they were faithful to it. They do not know what it is to keep a secret, to keep their word, and to love with constancy,—especially those who are not of their nation, for they are harmonious among themselves, and their slanders and raillery do not disturb their peace and friendly intercourse. . . .

## *CHAPTER XII. WHAT ONE MUST SUFFER IN WINTERING WITH THE SAVAGES.*

In order to have some conception of the beauty of this edifice, its construction must be described. I shall speak from knowledge, for I have often helped to build it. Now, when we arrived at the place where we were to camp, the women, armed with axes, went here and there in the great forests, cutting the framework of the hostelry where we were to lodge; meantime the men, having drawn the plan thereof, cleared away the snow with their snowshoes, or with shovels which they make and carry expressly for this purpose. Imagine now a great ring or square in the snow, two, three or four feet deep, according to the weather or the place where they encamp. This depth of snow makes a white wall for us, which surrounds us on all sides, except the end where it is broken through to form the door. The framework having been brought, which consists of twenty or thirty poles, more or less, according to the size of the cabin, it is planted, not upon the ground but upon the snow; then they throw upon these poles, which converge a little at the top, two or three rolls of bark sewed together, beginning at the bottom, and behold, the house is made. The ground inside, as well as the wall of snow which extends all around the cabin, is covered with little branches of fir; and, as a finishing touch, a wretched skin is fastened to two poles to serve as a door, the doorposts being the snow itself. . . .

You cannot stand upright in this house, as much on account of its low roof as the suffocating smoke; and consequently you must always lie down, or sit flat upon the ground, the usual posture of the Savages. When you go out, the cold, the snow, and the danger of getting lost in these great woods drive you in again more quickly than the wind, and keep you a prisoner in a dungeon which has neither lock nor key.

This prison, in addition to the uncomfortable position that one must occupy upon a bed of earth, has four other great discomforts,—cold, heat, smoke, and dogs. As to the cold, you have the snow at your head with only a pine branch between, often nothing but your hat, and the winds are free to enter in a thousand places. . . . When I lay down at night I could study through this opening both the Stars and the Moon as easily as if I had been in the open fields.

Nevertheless, the cold did not annoy me as much as the heat from the fire. A little place like their cabins is easily heated by a good fire, which sometimes roasted and broiled me on all sides, for the cabin was so narrow that I could not protect myself against the heat. You cannot move to right or left, for the Savages, your neighbors, are at your elbows; you cannot withdraw to the rear, for you encounter the wall of snow, or the bark of the cabin which shuts you in. I did not know what position to take. Had I stretched myself out, the place was so narrow that my legs would have been halfway in the fire; to roll myself up in a ball, and crouch down in their way, was a position I could not retain as long as they could; my clothes were all scorched and burned. You will ask me perhaps if the snow at our backs did not melt under so much heat. I answer, "no;" that if sometimes the heat softened it in the least, the cold immediately turned it into ice. I will say, however, that both the cold and the heat are endurable, and that some remedy may be found for these two evils.

But, as to the smoke, I confess to you that it is martyrdom. It almost killed me, and made me weep continually, although I had neither grief nor sadness in my heart. It sometimes grounded all of us who were in the cabin; that is, it caused us to place our mouths against the earth in order to breathe. For, although the Savages were accustomed to this torment, yet occasionally it became so dense that they, as well as I, were compelled to prostrate themselves, and as it were to eat the earth, so as not to drink the smoke. I have sometimes remained several hours in this position, especially during the most severe cold and when it snowed; for it was then the smoke assailed us with the greatest fury, seizing us by the throat, nose, and eyes...

As to the dogs, which I have mentioned as one of the discomforts of the Savages' houses, I do not know that I ought to blame them, for they have sometimes rendered me good service.... These poor beasts, not being able to live outdoors, came and lay down sometimes upon my shoulders, sometimes upon my feet, and as I only had one blanket to serve both as covering and mattress, I was not sorry for this protection, willingly restoring to them a part of the heat which I drew from them. It is true that, as they were large and numerous, they occasionally crowded and annoyed me so much, that in giving me a little heat they robbed me of my sleep, so that I very often drove them away....

JOHN SMITH

# 6 Description of Virginia

*Captain John Smith (1580–1631) fought the Turks in eastern Europe before his adventures in Virginia began. His life was full of high adventure and the exploration of unknown lands, but his writing is a bit more colorful than it is truthful.*

*Smith was one of the original settlers of Jamestown, Virginia, in 1607, and he took part in governing the colony and managing relations with the native Americans. According to legend, he was saved from death at the native Americans' hands by the friendly intervention of the chief's daughter, Pocahontas. (Most historians doubt the veracity of this and many other Smith anecdotes.)*

*Smith returned with Pocahontas to England in 1609. His later years were given over to promoting both himself and the settlement of the New World he had helped to colonize. His description of Virginia as a land of opportunity, like Columbus's description of the Americas, is an early example of the boosterism and exaggerated advertising that can be found throughout American history. Smith's description of the native Americans, with its mixture of admiration, distrust, and contempt for their failure to behave like Europeans, also set a pattern that continued for centuries.*

## THE COMMODITIES IN VIRGINIA OR THAT MAY BE HAD BY INDUSTRIE.

The mildnesse of the aire, the fertilitie of the soile, and the situation of the rivers are so propitious to the nature and use of man as no place is more convenient for pleasure, profit, and mans sustenance. Under that latitude or climat, here will live any beasts, as horses, goats, sheep, asses, hens, &c. as appeared by them that were carried thither. The waters, Isles, and shoales, are full of safe harbours for ships of warre or marchandize, for boats of all sortes, for transportation or fishing, &c.

The Bay and rivers have much marchandable fish and places fit for Salt coats, building of ships, making of iron, &c.

*Muscovia* and *Polonia* doe yearely receave many thousands, for pitch, tarre, sope ashes, Rosen, Flax, Cordage, Sturgeon, masts, yards, wainscot, Firres, glasse, and such like; also *Swethland* for iron and copper. *France* in like manner, for Wine, Canvas, and Salt, *Spaine* asmuch for Iron, Steele, Figges, Reasons, and Sackes. *Italy* with Silkes and Velvets, consumes our chiefe commodities. *Hol[l]and* maintaines it selfe by fishing and trading at our owne doores. All these temporize with other for necessities, but all as uncertaine as peace or warres: besides the charge, travell, and danger in transporting them, by seas, lands, stormes, and Pyrats. Then how much hath Virginia the prerogative of all those flourishing kingdomes for the benefit of our land, whenas within one hundred miles all those are to bee had, either ready provided by nature, or else to bee prepared, were there but industrious men to labour. Only of Copper wee may doubt is wanting, but there is good probabilitie that both copper and better munerals are there to be had for their labor. Other Countries have it. So then here is a place a nurse for souldiers, a practise for marriners, a trade for marchants, a reward for the good, and that which is most of all, a businesse (most acceptable to God) to bring such poore infidels to the true knowledge of God and his holy Gospell.

## *OF THE NATURALL INHABITANTS OF VIRGINIA.*

The land is not populous, for the men be fewe; their far greater number is of women and children. Within 60 miles of *James* Towne there are about some 5000 people, but of able men fit for their warres scarse 1500. To nourish so many together they have yet no means, because they make so small a benefit of their land, be it never so fertill.

6 or 700 have beene the most [that] hath beene seene together, when they gathered themselves to have surprised *Captaine Smyth at Pamaunke,* having but 15 to withstand the worst of their furie. As small as the proportion of ground that hath yet beene discoverd, is in comparison of that yet unknowne. The people differ very much in stature, especially in language, as before is expressed.

Since being very great as the *Sesquesahamocks,* others very little as the *Wighcocomocoes:* but generally tall and straight, of a comely proportion, and of a colour browne, when they are of any age, but they are borne white. Their haire is generally black; but few have any beards. The men weare halfe their heads shaven, the other halfe long. For Barbers they use their women, who with 2 shels will grate away the haire, of any fashion they please. The women are cut in many fashions agreeable to their yeares, but ever some part remaineth long.

They are very strong, of an able body and full of agilitie, able to endure to lie in the woods under a tree by the fire, in the worst of winter, or in the weedes and grasse, in *Ambuscado* in the Sommer.

They are inconstant in everie thing, but what feare constraineth them to keepe. Craftie, timerous, quicke of apprehension and very ingenious. Some are of disposition feareful, some bold, most cautelous, all *Savage*. Generally covetous of copper, beads, and such like trash. They are soone moved to anger, and so malitious, that they seldome forget an injury: they seldome steale one from another, least their conjurors should reveale it, and so they be pursued and punished. That they are thus feared is certaine, but that any can reveale their offences by conjuration I am doubtful. Their women are carefull not to bee suspected of dishonesty without the leave of their husbands.

Each household knoweth their owne lands and gardens, and most live of their owne labours.

For their apparell, they are some time covered with the skinnes of wilde beasts, which in winter are dressed with the haire, but in sommer without. The better sort use large mantels of deare skins not much differing in fashion from the Irish mantels. Some imbrodered with white beads, some with copper, other painted after their manner. But the common sort have scarce to cover their nakednesse but with grasse, the leaves of trees, or such like. We have seen some use mantels made of Turkey feathers, so prettily wrought and woven with threeds that nothing could bee discerned but the feathers, that was exceeding warme and very handsome. But the women are alwaies covered about their midles with a skin and very shamefast to be seene bare.

They adorne themselves most with copper beads and paintings. Their women some have their legs, hands, breasts and face cunningly imbrodered with diverse workes, as beasts, serpentes, artificially wrought into their flesh with blacke spots. In each eare commonly they have 3 great holes, whereat they hange chaines, bracelets, or copper. Some of their men weare in those holes, a smal greene and yellow coloured snake, neare halfe a yard in length, which crawling and lapping her selfe about his necke often times familiarly would kiss his lips. Others wear a dead Rat tied by the tail. Some on their heads weare the wing of a bird or some large feather, with a Rattell. Those Rattels are somewhat like the chape of a Rapier but lesse, which they take from the taile of a snake. Many have the whole skinne of a hawke or some strange fowle, stuffed with the wings abroad. Others a broad peece of copper, and some the hand of their enemy dryed. Their heads and shoulders are painted red with the roote *Pocone* braied to powder mixed with oyle; this they hold in somer to preserve them from the heate, and in winter from the cold. Many other formes of paintings they use, but he is the most gallant that is the most monstrous to behould.

Their buildings and habitations are for the most part by the rivers or not farre distant from some fresh spring. Their houses are built like our Arbors of small young springs bowed and tyed, and so close covered with mats or the barkes of trees very handsomely, that notwithstanding either winde raine or weather, they are as warme as stooves, but very smoaky, yet at the toppe of the house there is a hole made for the smoake to goe into right over the fire.

Against the fire they lie on little hurdles of Reedes covered with a mat, borne from the ground a foote and more by a hurdle of wood. On these round about the house, they lie heads and points one by thother against the fire: some covered with mats, some with skins, and some starke naked lie on the ground, from 6 to 20 in a house.

Their houses are in the midst of their fields or gardens; which are smal plots of ground, some 20, some 40, some 100, some 200, some more, some lesse. Some times from 2 to 100 of these houses [are] togither, or but a little separated by groves of trees. Neare their habitations is little small wood, or old trees on the ground, by reason of their burning of them for fire. So that a man may gallop a horse amongst these woods any waie, but where the creekes or Rivers shall hinder.

Men women and children have their severall names according to the severall humor of their Parents. Their women (they say) are easilie delivered of childe, yet doe they love children verie dearly. To make them hardy, in the coldest mornings they wash them in the rivers, and by painting and ointments so tanne their skins, that after year or two, no weather will hurt them.

The men bestowe their times in fishing, hunting, wars, and such manlike exercises, scorning to be seene in any woman like exercise, which is the cause that the women be verie painefull and the men often idle. The women and children do the rest of the worke. They make mats, baskets, pots, morters, pound their corne, make their bread, prepare their victuals, plant their corne, gather their corne, beare all kind of burdens, and such like. . . .

*TO WILLIAM POND*

# 7 | *A Letter from Massachusetts Bay*

*The Massachusetts Bay Colony, begun in 1630, was a far larger undertaking than the earlier English settlements at Jamestown and Plymouth. As a result of harsh and lasting religious strife in England, immigration to the colony remained substantial for a decade after 1630, with perhaps 20,000 settlers arriving in New England.*

*But as in the prior settlements, the colonists of early Massachusetts Bay experienced intense suffering. The letter below is addressed to William Pond, a well-to-do farmer who lived near Groton Manor in England. Pond had been advanced money from Governor Winthrop of Massachusetts Bay so that he might send two of his sons to the new colony. Unfortunately, we do not know which of the two sons, Robert or John Pond, was responsible for the unsigned letter. The junior Pond speaks of continuing dependency on "old England," and an inability to gain access to the many resources available in a sparsely settled land. Even with death all around him, the younger Pond was willing to try to make a new home in the New World.*

Most loving and kind father and mother,—My humble duty remembered unto you, trusting in God you are in good health, and I pray remember my love unto my brother Joseph and thank him for his kindness that I have had at his hand at London. . . . My writing unto you is to let you understand what a country this New England is where we live. Here are but a few [Indians], a great part of them died this winter, it was thought a case of the plague. They are a crafty people and will cozen and cheat, and they are a subtle people, and whereas we did expect great store of beaver here is little or none to be found. They are proper men . . . and many of them go naked with a skin about their loins, but now some of them get Englishmen's apparel; and the country is hilly and rocky and some . . . soil is very flat and here is some good ground and marshy ground, but here is no Myckellmes.[1] Spring cattle thrive well here, but they give small amount of milk. The best

1. Refers to the old English custom of eating roast goose on Michaelmas, the Feast of St. Michael, on the 29th of September.

cattle for profit is swines . . . Here is timber good store and acorns good store, and here is good store of fish if we had boats to go for and lines to serve to do fishing. Here are a good store of wild fowl, but they are hard to come by. It is harder to get a shoot then it is in old England and people here are subjects to disease, for here [many] have died of scurvy and of burning fever, near two hundred . . . beside as many lay lame and all Sudbury men are dead but three and three women and some children. . . . If this ship had not come in when it did we would had been put to a wonderful [terrible] strait but thanks be to God for sending it in. I received from the ship a hogshead of meal, and the Governor told me of a hundred weight of cheese the which I have reserved parts of it. I humbly thank you for it. I did expect two cows, the which I had none, nor did I earnestly desire that you should send me any, because the country is not so as we did expect it. Therefore, loving father, I would entreat you that you would send me . . . butter and a hogshead of malt unground, for we drink nothing but water. . . . For the freight, if you of your love will send them I will pay the freight, for here is nothing to be got without commodities to up to the . . . parties amongst the Indians to [trade], for here where we live there is no beaver. Here is no cloth to be had to make no apparel. So I pray, father, send me four or five yards of cloth to make some apparel, and loving father, though I be far distant from you yet I pray you remember me as your child, and we do not know how long we may subsist, for we can not live here without provisions from old England. Therefore, I pray do not put away your shop stuff, for we do not know how long this plantation will stand, for some of the magnates that did uphold it have turned off their men and have given it over. Besides, God had taken away . . . Mr. Johnson and Lady Arabella his wife, which was the chiefest man of estate in the land and the one who could have done the most good.

. . . So here we may live if we have supplies every year from old England, otherwise we can not subsist. I may, as I will, work hard, set an acorn of Eindey wheat. . . . So father, I pray, consider my cause, for here will be but a very poor being, no being without, loving father, your help with provisions from old England. I had thought to come home on this ship, for my provisions are almost all spent, but that I humbly thank you for your great love and kindness in sending me some provisions, or else I should . . . have famished, but now I will, if it please God that I have my health, I will plant what corn I have, and if provisions be not cheaper between this and Myckellmes and that I do not hear from you what I was best to do, I propose to come home at Myckellmes.

My wife remembers her humble duty to you and to my mother, and my love to my brother Joseph and to Sarah Myler. Thus I leave you to the protection of Almighty God.

From Watertown in New England the 15 of March, 1630.[2]

[Unsigned]

We were wonderful sick as we came at sea, with the smallpox. No man thought that I and my little child would have lived. My boy is lame and my girl too, and there died on the ship that I came in 14 persons.

2. Pond dated his letter March 15, 1630. However, a portion of the letter (deleted here) refers to an arrival of a ship that, according to other records, arrived in port in 1631.

COTTON MATHER ET AL.

# 8 Children in Colonial America

*Any age reflects its best and worst qualities in its treatment of children. Seventeenth-century English people and colonists showed the same range of behaviors as we do today.*

*Many scholars believe that children were accused of witchcraft for engaging in behaviors that today would be associated with typical adolescent rebellion. Although the close observation of children's behavior in colonial America focused much attention on their moral development, it produced hideous cycles of punishment and retribution among both children and adults.*

*From the perspective we now have on adolescent growth and social development, it is easier to understand the group hysteria of restless youths than the unbalanced response of their elders who hanged suspects on the evidence of testimony that legal traditions of the era rightly rejected. An examination of the full range of tensions in Massachusetts Bay in the 1690s—the constitutional, political, economic, and religious transition of the colony—puts this overreaction into perspective.*

*In the seventeenth century, selling children as servants or apprentices, even sending them overseas, was all too common. In modern times there has been considerably more social concern with the exploitation of children. Some parallels, however, still remain: in both past and present, society tends to worry much less about the children of the poor than it does about those of the rich.*

*The following pages contain selections from many sources about children in colonial America.*

*The Puritans believed in the existence of witchcraft and found in it a logical explanation for the strange behavior of children. Following are two readings on witchcraft. The first is a newspaper report about a young girl accused of being a witch. The second is a 1689 account of an entire family of witches, written by the famous Puritan divine, Cotton Mather. Such tales occasionally led these religious people to overreact. Many of the adults accused of witchcraft were hanged.*

## SAMUEL WILLARD TO COTTON MATHER

It was not many days ere she was hurried again into violent fits after a different manner, being taken again speechless, and using all endeavors to make away with herself, and do mischief unto others: striking those that held her, spitting in their faces, and if at any time she had done any harm or frightened them, she would laugh immediately, which fits held her sometimes longer, sometimes shorter. Few occasions she had of speech, but when she could speak, she complained of a hard heart, counselled some to beware of sin, for that had brought her to this, bewailed that so many prayers had been put up for her, and she still so hard hearted, and no more good wrought upon her. But being asked whether she were willing to repent, shaked her head and said nothing. Thus she continued till the next sabbath in the afternoon, on which day, in the morning, being somewhat better than at other times, she had but little company tarried with her in the afternoon, when the Devil began to make more full discovery of himself. It had been a question before whether she might properly be called a Demoniac, a person possessed of the Devil, but it was then put out of question. He began (as the persons with her testify) by drawing her tongue out of her mouth most frightfully to an extraordinary length and greatness, and many amazing postures of her body; and then by speaking vocally in her. Whereupon her father and another neighbor were called from the meeting, on whom (as soon as they came in), he railed, calling them rogues, charging them for folly in going to hear a black rogue who told them nothing but a parcel of lies, and deceived them, and many like expressions. After exercise I was called, but understood not the occasion till I came and heard the same voice, a grim, low, yet audible voice it was. The first salutation I had was, Oh! You are a great rogue. I was at the first something daunted and amazed, and many reluctances I had upon my spirits, which brought me to a silence and amazement in my spirits, till at last God heard my groans and gave me both refreshment in Christ and courage. I then called for a light to see whether it might not appear a counterfeit, and observed not any of her organs to move. The voice was hollow, as if it issued out of her throat. He then again called me great black rogue. I challenged him to make it appear. But all the answer was, You tell your people a company of lies. I reflected on myself, and could not but magnify the goodness of God not to suffer Satan to be-spatter the names of his people with those sins which he himself hath pardoned in the blood of Christ. I answered, Satan, thou art a liar and deceiver, and God will vindicate his own truth one day. He answered nothing directly, but said, I am not Satan. I am a pretty black boy; this is my pretty girl. I have been here a great while. I sat still and answered nothing to these expressions. But when he directed himself to me again, Oh! You black rogue, I do not love you, I replied through God's grace, I hate thee. . . . On Friday in the evening she was taken again violently, and then the former voice . . . was heard in her again, not speaking, but imitating the crowing of a cock, accompanied with many other gestures, some violent, some ridiculous, which occasioned my going to her, where by signs she signified that the Devil threatened to carry her away that night. God was again then sought for her. And when in prayer that expression was used, that God had proved Satan a liar, in preserving her once when he had threatened to carry her away that night, and was entreated so to do again, the same voice, which had ceased two days before, was again heard by the by-standers five times distinctly to cry out, Oh! You are a rogue, and then ceased. But the whole time of prayer, sometimes by violence of fits, sometimes by noises she made, she drowned her own hearing from receiving our petition, as she afterwards confessed. Since that time she hath continued for the most part speechless, her fits coming upon her sometimes often, sometimes with greater intermission, and with great varieties in the manner of them, sometimes by violence, sometimes by making her sick, but (through God's goodness) so abated in violence that now one person can as well rule her as formerly four or five. She is observed always to fall into her fits when any strangers go to visit her, and the more go the more violent are her fits.

## *COTTON MATHER: WITCHCRAFTS AND POSSESSIONS. THE FIRST EXAMPLE.*

There dwells at this time, in the south part of Boston, a sober and pious man, whose Name is John Goodwin, whose Trade is that of a Mason, and whose Wife (to which a Good Report gives a share with him in all the Characters of Vertue) has made him the Father of six (now living) Children. Of these Children, all but the Eldest, who works with his Father at his Calling, and the Youngest, who lives yet upon the Breast of its mother, have laboured under the direful effects of a . . . stupendous *Witchcraft*. . . .

The four Children [ages 13, 11, 7, and 5 years old] had enjoyed a Religious Education, and answered it with a very towardly [promise]. They had an observable Affection unto Divine and Sacred things; and those of them that were capable of it, seem'd to have such a [feeling] of their eternal Concernments as is not altogether usual. Their Parents also kept them to a continual Employment, which did more than deliver them from the Temptations of Idleness, and as young as they were, they took a delight in it, it may be as much as they should have done. In a word, Such was the whole Temper and Carriage of the Children, that there cannot easily be any thing more unreasonable, than to imagine that a Design to Dissemble could cause them to fall into any of their odd Fits; though there should not have happened, as there did, a thousand Things, wherein it was perfectly impossible for any Dissimulation of theirs to produce what scores of spectators were amazed at.

About Midsummer, in the year 1688, the Eldest of these Children, who is a Daughter, saw cause to examine their Washerwoman, upon their missing of some Linnen, which twas fear'd she had stollen from them. . . . This Laundress was the Daughter of an ignorant and a scandalous old Woman in the Neighborhood; whose miserable Husband before he died, had sometimes complained of her, that she was undoubtedly a Witch. . . . This Woman in her daughters Defence bestow'd very bad Language upon the Girl that put her to the Question; immediately upon which, the poor child became variously indisposed in her health, and visited with strange Fits, beyond those that attend an Epilepsy, or a Catalepsy, or those that they call The Disease of Astonishment.[1]

It was not long before one of her Sisters, and two of her Brothers, were seized, in Order one after another. . . . Within a few weeks, they were all four tortured every where in a manner so very grievous, that it would have broke an heart of stone to have seen their Agonies. Skilful Physicians were consulted for their Help, and particularly our worthy and prudent Friend Dr. Thoms Oakes, who found himself so [dumbfounded] by the Distempers of the children, he concluded nothing but an hellish Witchcraft could be the [origin] of these maladies. And that which yet more confirmed such Apprehension was, That for one good while, the children were tormented just in the same part of their bodies all at the same time together; and tho they saw and heard not one anothers complaints, tho likewise their pains and sprains were swift like Lightening, yet when (suppose) the Neck, or the Hand, or the Back of one was Rack't, so it was at that instant with t'other too.

The variety of their tortures increased continually. . . . Sometimes they would be Deaf, sometimes Dumb, and sometimes Blind, and often, all this at once. One while their Tongues would be drawn down their Throats; another-while they would be pull'd out upon their Chins, to a prodigious length. They would have their Mouths opened unto such a Wideness, that their Jaws went out of joint; and anon they would clap together again with a Force like that of a strong Spring-Lock. The same would happen to their Shoulder-Blades, and their Elbows, and Handwrists, and several of their joints. . . . They would make most pitteous out-cries, that they were cut with Knives, and struck with Blows that they could not bear. Their Necks would be broken, so that their Neckbone would seem dissolved unto them that felt after it; and yet on the sudden, it would become again so stiff that there was no stirring of their Heads; yea, their Heads would be twisted almost round. . . . Thus they lay some weeks most pittiful Spectacles; and this while as a further Demonstration of Witchcraft in these horrid Effects, when I went to Prayer by one of them, that was very desireous to hear what I said, the Child utterly lost her Hearing till our Prayer was over.

It was a Religious Family that these Afflictions happened unto; and none but a Religious Contrivance to obtain Releef, would have been

1. I.e., stupefaction: diseases that rob people of their wits.

welcome to them. . . . Accordingly they requested the four Ministers of Boston, with the Minister of Charlstown, to keep a Day of Prayer at their thus haunted house; which they did in the Company of some devout people there. Immediately upon this Day, the youngest of the four children was delivered, and never felt any trouble as afore. But there was yet a greater Effect of these our Applications unto our God!

The Report of the Calamities of the Family for which we were thus concerned, arrived now unto the ears of the magistrates, who presently and prudently apply'd themselves, with a just vigour, to enquire into the story. The Father of the Children complained of his Neighbour, the suspected ill woman, . . . and she being sent for by the Justices, gave such a wretched Account of her self, that they saw cause to commit her unto the Gaolers Custody. Goodwin had no proof that could have done her any Hurt; but the Hag had not power to deny her interest in the Enchantment of the Children; and when she was asked, Whether she believed there was a God? her Answer was too blasphemous and horrible for any Pen of mine to mention. An Experiment was made, Whether she could recite the Lord's Prayer; and it was found, that tho clause after clause was most carefully repeated unto her, yet when she said it after them that prompted her, she could not possibly avoid making Nonsense of it, with some ridiculous Depravations. This Experiment I had the curiosity since to see made upon two more, and it had the same Event. Upon the Commitment of this extraordinary Woman, all the Children had some present ease; until one (related unto her) accidentally meeting one or two of them, entertain'd them with her Blessing, that is, Railing; upon which Three of them fell ill again, as they were before. . . .

*Children were often sent to the colonies as apprentices. The next selection is a statement of the conditions of the Virginia Company that accepted child apprentices.*

The Treasurer, Council, and Company of Virginia assembled in their great and general Court the 17th of November 1619 have taken into Consideration the continual great forwardness of his honorable City in advancing the Plantation of Virginia and particularly in furnishing out one hundred Children this last year, which by the goodness of God there safely Arrived, (save such as died in the way) and are well pleased we doubt not for their benefit, for which your bountiful assistance, we in the name of the whole plantation do yield unto you due and deserved thanks.

And forasmuch as we have now resolved to send this next Spring very large supplies for the strength and increasing of the Colony, styled by the name of the London Colony, and find that the sending of those Children to be apprentices has both been very grateful to the people: We pray your Lord and the rest in pursuit of your former so pious Actions to renew your like favors and furnish us again with one hundreth more for the next sprint; Our desire is that we may have them of Twelve years old and upward with allowance of Three pounds apiece for their Transportation and forty shillings apiece for their apparel as was formerly granted. They shall be Apprentices the boys till they come to 21 years of Age; the Girls till the like Age or till they be married and afterwards they shall be placed as Tenants upon the public Land with best Conditions where they shall have houses with stock of Corn and Cattle to begin with, and afterward the moiety of all increase and profit whatsoever. And so we leave this motion to your honorable and grave Consideration.

*Sometimes parents actually sold children to entrepreneurs, thereby partially fulfilling the desperate need for labor in the colonies. The following piece protests such practices.*

I have inquired after the child that was lost, and have spoken with the parents. His name was John Brookes. The last night he was after much trouble and charge freed again, and he relates that there are divers other children in the ship crying, that were enticed away from their parents, that are kept and detained in the ship. The name of the ship is the Seven Brothers and as I hear bound for Virginia; and she is now fallen down to Gravesend, and, if a speedy course be not taken to stop her she will be gone. I heard of two other ships in the river that are at the same work, although the parents of the children see their children in the ship, yet without money they will not let them have them. The woman and child will wait on you, where you approach and when to give you this relation and 'tis believed there are divers people and others carried away that are strangers come from other parts, so that it were good to get the ships searched, and to see who are against their wills carried away. Pray you move it in the House to have a law to make it death. I am confident your mercy to these innocent children will ground a blessing on yourself your own. Pray let not your great affairs put this good work out of your head to stop the ships and discharge the children.

Your most humble servant

George

*Many children were sold in transactions that were part of the African slave trade, as evidenced by the following readings.*

*I*

Henry Carpenter and Robert Helmes to the Royal African Company, 1681:

On the 3rd instant in the Evening, Capt. Cope in the *George and Betty* arrived in this Road with 415 Negroes, most women, amongst which [were] about 40 children under the ages of 8 years to our best Judgment, which we told him was contrary to his Charter Party, who answered that they could not buy so many men and women without [also taking] that number of Children, but we believe something else in it which we hope in Little time to discover . . .

Edwin Stede and Stephen Gascoigne to the Royal African Company, 1683:

And about one third part of those he did bring were very small, most of them no better than sucking children, nay many of them did suck their mothers that were on board . . . some of [the] mothers we believe died on board of ship, and the most part of those small ones [were] not worth above £5 per head. We told Agent White we wondered to see so many small children brought by him, for that they were not worth their freight, to which he replied they cost not much, and the ship as good bring them as nothing, she being paid by the month . . . .

*II*

I also remember that I once, among my several runs along that coast, happened to have aboard a whole family, man, wife, three young boys, and a girl, bought here one after another at several places; and cannot but observe here what mighty satisfaction those poor creatures expressed to be so come together again, though in bondage. For several days successively they could not forbear shedding tears of joy, and continually embracing and caressing one another; which moving me to compassion, I ordered they should be better treated aboard than commonly we can afford to do it, where they are four or five hundred in a ship. And at Martinico, I sold them all together to a considerable planter, at a cheaper rate than I might have expected had they been disposed of severally, being informed of that gentleman's good nature, and having taken his word that he would use that family as well as their circumstances would permit, and settle them in some part by themselves.

*The outlook for children in Europe deeply influenced the Pilgrims' decision to migrate to the New World. William Bradford writes of the Pilgrims' experience in Holland.*

As necessity was a taskmaster over them, so they were forced to be such, not only to their servants (but in a sort) to their dearest children; the which as it did not a little wound the tender hearts of many a loving father and mother, so it produced likewise sundry sad and sorrowful effects. For many of their children that were of best dispositions and gracious inclinations (having learned to bear the yoke in their youth) and willing to bear part of their parents' burden, were (often times) so oppressed with their heavy labors, that though their minds were free and willing, yet their bodies bowed under the weight of the same, and became decrepit in their early youth, the vigor of nature being consumed in the very bud as it were. But that which was more lamentable, and of all sorrows most heavy to be borne, was that many of their children, by these occasions, and the great licentiousness of youth in that country, and the manifold temptations of the place, were drawn away by evil examples into extravagant and dangerous courses, getting the reins off their necks and departing from their parents. Some became soldiers, others took upon them far voyages by sea, and others some worse courses, tending to dissoluteness and the danger of their souls, to the great grief of their parents and dishonor of God. So that they saw their posterity would be in danger to degenerate and be corrupted.

Lastly, (and which was not least) a great hope, and inward zeal they had of laying some good foundation, (or at least to make some way thereunto) for the propagating and advancing the gospel of the kingdom of Christ in those remote parts of the world; yea, though they should be but even as stepping-stones unto others for the performing of so great a work.

*Advice to parents has never been in short supply. Here Benjamin Wadsworth, a Boston clergyman, prescribes rules for rearing children.*

*They should love their children and carefully provide for their outward supply and comfort while unable to provide for themselves* . . . Parents should nourish in themselves a very tender love and affection to their children, and should manifest it by suitably providing for their outward comforts.

Here I might say, as soon as the mother perceives herself with child, she should be careful not to do any thing injurious to herself or to the child God has formed in her. A conscientious regard to the Sixth Commandment (which is, *Thou shalt not kill*) should make her thus careful. If any purposely endeavor to destroy the fruit of their womb (whether they actually do it or not) they're guilty of murder in God's account. Further, before the child is born, provision should be made for its comfort when born. Some observe concerning our Saviour's Mother (the Virgin Mary) that though she was very poor and low and far from home when delivered of her Son, yet she had provided swaddling clothes to wrap her Son in. Mothers also, if able, should suckle their children. . . . Those mothers who have milk and are so healthy as to be able to suckle their children, and yet through sloth or niceness neglect to suckle them, seem very criminal and blameworthy. They seem to dislike and reject that method of nourishing their children which God's wise bountiful Providence has provided as most suitable. Having given these hints about mothers, I may say of parents (comprehending both father and mother) they should provide for the outward supply and comfort of their children. They should nourish and bring them up. . . . They should endeavor that their children may have food suitable for quality and quantity, suitable *raiment* and *lodging*. In case of sickness, lameness, or other distress on children, parents should do all they can for their health or relief. *He that provides not for his own, especially those of his own house, hath denied the faith, and is worse than an infidel* I Tim. 8. . . . Therefore, if they can help it, they should not suffer their children to want any thing that's really good, comfortable, and suitable for them, even as to their outward man. Yet by way of caution I might say, let wisdom and prudence sway, more than fond indulgent fancy, in feeding and clothing your children. Too much niceness and delicateness in these things is not good; it tends not to make them healthy in their bodies, nor serviceable and useful in their generation, but rather the contrary. Let not your children (especially while young and unable to provide for themselves) want any thing needful for their outward comfort.

/ / /

*Parents should govern their children well, restrain, reprove, correct them, as there is occasion.* A Christian householder should rule well his own house. . . . Children should not be left to themselves, to a loose end, to do as they please; but should be under tutors and governors, *not being fit to govern* themselves. . . . Children being bid to obey their parents in all things . . . plainly implies that parents should give suitable precepts to, and maintain a wise government over their children; so carry it, as their children may both fear and love them. You should restrain your children from sin as much as possible. . . . You should reprove them for their faults; yea, if need be, correct them too. . . . Divine precepts plainly show that, as there is occasion, you should chasten and correct your children; you dishonor God and hurt them if you neglect it. Yet, on the other hand, a father should pity his children. . . . You should by no means carry it ill to them; you should not frown, be harsh, morose, faulting and blaming them when they don't deserve it, but do behave themselves well. If you fault and blame your children, show yourself displeased and discontent when they do their best to please you, this is the way to provoke them to wrath and anger, and to discourage them; therefore you should carefully avoid such ill carriage to them. Nor should you ever correct them upon uncertainties, without sufficient evidence of their fault. Neither should you correct them in a rage or passion, but should deliberately endeavor to convince them of their fault, their sin; and that 'tis out of love to God's honor and their good (if they're capable of considering such things) that you correct them. Again, you should never be cruel nor barbarous in your corrections, and if milder ones will reform them, more severe ones should never be used. Under this head of government I might further say, you should refrain your children from bad company as far as possibly you can. . . . If you would not have your sons and daughters destroyed, then keep them from ill company as much as may be. . . . You should not suffer your children needlessly to frequent taverns, nor to be abroad unseasonably on nights, lest they're drawn into numberless hazards and mischiefs thereby. You can't be too careful in these matters.

/ / /

*In Puritan Massachusetts Bay, respect for parents was legally enforced as was the obligation of the parents for the nurture and education of their children.*

*I*

[1646]. If any child[ren] above sixteen years old and of sufficient understanding shall curse or smite their natural father or mother, they shall be put to death, unless it can be sufficiently testified that the parents have been very unchristianly negligent in the education of such children, or so provoked them by extreme and cruel correction that they have been forced thereunto to preserve themselves from death or maiming. . . .

If a man have a stubborn or rebellious son of sufficient years of understanding, viz. sixteen, which will not obey the voice of his father or the voice of his mother, and that when they have chastened him will not harken unto them, then shall his father and mother, being his natural parents, lay hold on him and bring him to the magistrates assembled in Court, and testify to them by sufficient evidence that this their son is stubborn and rebellious and will not obey their voice and chastisement, but lives in sundry notorious crimes. Such a son shall be put to death.

*II*

[1670]. Ordered that John Edy, Senior, shall go to John Fisk's house and to George Lawrence's and William Priest's houses to inquire about their children, whether they be learned to read the English tongue and in case they be defective to warn in the said John, George, and William to the next meeting of the Selectmen.

/ / /

William Priest, John Fisk, and George Lawrence, being warned to a meeting of the Selectmen at John Bigulah's house, they making their appearance and being found defective, were admonished for not learning their children to read the English tongue: were convinced, did acknowledge their neglects, and did promise amendment.

/ / /

[1674]. Agreed that Thomas Fleg, John Whitney, and Joseph Bemus should go about the town to see that children were taught to read the English tongue and that they were taught some orthodox catechism and to see that each man has in his house a copy of the capital laws. For which end the Selectmen agreed there should be copies procured by Captain Mason at the printers and they to be paid for out of the town rate and the men above mentioned to carry them along with them to such of the inhabitants as have none.

/ / /

Thomas Fleg, John Whitney, and Joseph Bemus gave in an account of what they had found concerning children's education and John Fisk being found wholly negligent of educating his children as to reading or catechizing, the Selectmen agreed that Joseph Bemus should warn him into answer for his neglect at the next meeting of the Selectmen.

/ / /

[1676]. Ordered that Captain Mason and Simon Stone shall go to John Fisk to see if his children be taught to read English and their catechism.

*III*

[1675]. William Scant of Braintree being bound over to this court to answer for his not ordering and disposing of his children as may be for their good education, and for refusing to consent to the Selectmen of Braintree in the putting of them forth to service as the law directs; the court having duly weighed and considered what was alleged by him and the state of his family do[th] leave it to the prudence of the Selectmen of Braintree to dispose of his children to service so far forth as the necessity of his family will give leave.

[1678]. Robert Styles of Dorchester presented for not attending the public worship of God, negligence in his calling, and not submitting to authority, testified upon the oaths of Thomas Davenport and Isaac Jones, grandjurymen. Sentenced to be admonished, and order[ed] that he put forth his children, or otherwise the selectmen are hereby empowered to do it according to Law.

# *Questions for Part I*

1. What image of Columbus does Colón's account of his father's venture create? What other perceptions of Columbus's enterprise does your textbook offer?
2. What does Las Casas's account of the Spanish Empire tell us about the *conquistadores'* view of the native Americans? How did the treatment of native Americans reflect the European culture from which the *conquistadores* came?
3. What cultural values can you find expressed in the legend of the Iroquois Confederacy?
4. How did the people of the Roanoke colony solve their initial problems with the native Americans? Be specific.
5. How does Father Le Jeune perceive native American religion? What does he say about the native Americans' character and morality? What are the origins of his observations?
6. Compare John Smith's view of the native Americans with those of Father Le Jeune and Columbus. What do the three views have in common? How do they differ?
7. What difficulties did Pond mention in his letter?
8. Why do you think the adults in Salem believed the young women's stories about witchcraft? What does the witchcraft phenomenon suggest about their religion and society?

# PART II | FROM COLONIES TO REPUBLIC

*The colonial America of the eighteenth century is celebrated by the Daughters of the American Revolution and the illustrators of many American history textbooks. It is the world of Benjamin Franklin, maple furniture, and Mount Vernon.*

*In fact, colonial America consisted of many different societies and many different experiences. Some colonists, including those described by Gottlieb Mittelberger, came to the New World as indentured servants. The status of such persons was difficult and painful, yet some nonetheless advanced to higher stations in life. The African slaves, whose brutal transit to the New World Olaudah Equiano recounts, lacked such opportunities.*

*Life held some astonishing surprises for Mary Jemison, a white woman who was taken captive and assimilated into native American culture. Jemison's account of her captivity provides interesting details about native American life and the attitude of whites toward native Americans.*

*The generation that guided the nation's destinies through the revolutionary era was welded together, despite the remarkable differences among colonies and their peoples, by a common commitment to American nationality. The French-born Crèvecoeur describes the emergence of the new American out of this complex mixture of people. This new American was accustomed to considerable self-government. When, after 1763, the English developed restrictive colonial policies to raise revenues for the administration of an enlarged empire that included India and Canada, the colonists almost instantly perceived threats to their traditional liberties. So did many English critics of the mother country's political system, such as the cartoonists whose work appears in this section.*

*The lengthy quarrel with England revealed many stresses in colonial society that set it on the way to revolution. The struggle for independence had many facets. It was part of a radical change in European diplomacy; it was a revolution in national identity; and it was a challenge to traditional assumptions about the distribution of power within a society.*

*The American Revolution challenged long-held theories of human nature, for many denied the capacity of human beings to use their reason in creating a new form of government. Such leaders as Captain Preston discovered how the rules of order had changed. Plain people like shoemaker George R. T. Hewes, who played a role in both the Boston Massacre and the Boston Tea Party, and Joseph Martin, who fought throughout the long war, developed new visions of their position in society. More than anyone else, Thomas Paine captures the dominant themes of the era, recognizing that the American Revolution would, in fact, usher in a vast age of democratic revolutions throughout the world.*

MARY JEMISON

# 9 Captured by the Indians

*Captivity narratives were popular during the entire period in which native Americans were thought to constitute a danger to white settlers on the frontier. Mary Jemison's narrative is perhaps the most famous, having gone through dozens of printings since its initial publication in 1824. Although it is written in the first person, it is not really an autobiography. Mrs. Jemison was eighty years old and illiterate when James E. Seaver interviewed her and wrote the* Narrative. *By then she was long famous in western New York as the "white woman of the Genesee" who had lived her entire life since her abduction—probably in 1758 at the age of 15—among the Senecas. The* Narrative *is an important source for descriptions of New York native American life and culture, as well as a fascinating account of a white American's assimilation into that culture.*

## CHAPTER III.

The night was spent in gloomy forebodings. What the result of our captivity would be, it was out of our power to determine, or even imagine. At times, we could almost realize the approach of our masters to butcher and scalp us; again, we could nearly see the pile of wood kindled on which we were to be roasted; and then we would imagine ourselves at liberty, alone and defenseless in the forest, surrounded by wild beasts that were ready to devour us. The anxiety of our minds drove sleep from our eyelids; and it was with a dreadful hope and painful impatience that we waited for the morning to determine our fate.

The morning at length arrived, and our masters came early and let us out of the house, and gave the young man and boy to the French, who immediately took them away. Their fate I never learned, as I have not seen nor heard of them since.

I was now left alone in the fort, deprived of my former companions, and of every thing that was near or dear to me but life. But it was not long before I was in some measure relieved by the appearance of two pleasant-looking squaws, of the Seneca tribe, who came and examined me attentively for a short time, and then went out. After a few minutes' absence, they returned in company with my former masters, who gave me to the squaws to dispose of as they pleased.

The Indians by whom I was taken were a party of Shawnees, if I remember right, that lived, when at home, a long distance down the Ohio.

My former Indian masters and the two squaws were soon ready to leave the fort, and accordingly embarked—the Indians in a large canoe, and the two squaws and myself in a small one—and went down the Ohio. When we set off, an Indian in the forward canoe took the scalps of my former friends, strung them on a pole that he placed upon his shoulder, and in that manner carried them, standing in the stern of the canoe directly before us, as we sailed down the river, to the town where the two squaws resided.

On the way we passed a Shawnee town, where I saw a number of heads, arms, legs, and other fragments of the bodies of some white people who had just been burned. The parts that remained were hanging on a pole, which was supported at each end by a crotch stuck in the ground, and were roasted or burnt black as a coal. The fire was yet burning; and the whole appearance afforded a spectacle so shocking that even to this day the blood almost curdles in my veins when I think of them.

At night we arrived at a small Seneca Indian town, at the mouth of a small river that was called by the Indians, in the Seneca language, She-nan-jee, about eighty miles by water from the fort, where the two squaws to whom I belonged resided. There we landed, and the Indians went on; which was the last I ever saw of them.

Having made fast to the shore, the squaws left me in the canoe while they went to their wigwam or house in the town, and returned with a suit of Indian clothing, all new, and very clean and nice. My clothes, though whole and good when I was taken, were now torn in pieces, so that I was almost naked. They first undressed me, and threw my rags into the river; then washed me clean and dressed me in the new suit they had just brought, in complete Indian style; and then led me home and seated me in the center of their wigwam.

I had been in that situation but a few minutes before all the squaws in the town came in to see me. I was soon surrounded by them, and they immediately set up a most dismal howling, crying bitterly, and wringing their hands in all the agonies of grief for a deceased relative.

Their tears flowed freely, and they exhibited all the signs of real mourning. At the commencement of this scene, one of their number began, in a voice somewhat between speaking and singing, to recite some words to the following purport, and continued the recitation till the ceremony was ended; the company at the same time varying the appearance of their countenances, gestures, and tone of voice, so as to correspond with the sentiments expressed by their leader.

"Oh, our brother! alas! he is dead—he has gone; he will never return! Friendless he died on the field of the slain, where his bones are yet lying unburied! Oh! who will not mourn his sad fate? No tears dropped around him: oh, no! No tears of his sisters were there! He fell in his prime, when his arm was most needed to keep us from danger! Alas! he has gone, and left us in sorrow, his loss to bewail! Oh, where is his spirit? His spirit went naked, and hungry it wanders, and thirsty and wounded, it groans to return! Oh, helpless and wretched, our brother has gone! No blanket nor food to nourish and warm him; nor candles to light him, nor weapons of war! Oh, none of those comforts had he! But well we remember his deeds! The deer he could take on the chase! The panther shrunk back at the sight of his strength! His enemies fell at his feet! He was brave and courageous in war! As the fawn, he was harmless; his friendship was ardent; his temper was gentle; his pity was great! Oh! our friend, our companion, is dead! Our brother, our brother! alas, he is gone! But why do we grieve for his loss? In the strength of a warrior, undaunted he left us, to fight by the side of the chiefs! His warwhoop was shrill! His rifle well aimed laid his enemies low: his tomahawk drank of their blood: and his knife flayed their scalps while yet covered with gore! And why do we mourn? Though he fell on the field of the slain, with glory he fell; and his spirit went up to the land of his fathers in war! Then why do we mourn? With transports of joy, they received him, and fed him, and clothed him, and welcomed him there! Oh, friends, he is happy; then dry up your tears! His spirit has seen our distress, and sent us a helper whom with pleasure we greet. Deh-he-wä-mis has come: then let us receive her with joy!—she is handsome and pleasant! Oh! she is our sister, and gladly we welcome her here. In the place of our brother she stands in our tribe. With care we will guard her from trouble; and may she be happy till her spirit shall leave us."

In the course of that ceremony, from mourning they became serene,—joy sparkled in their countenances, and they seemed to rejoice over me as over a long-lost child. I was made welcome among them as a sister to the two squaws before mentioned, and was called Deh-he-wä-mis; which, being interpreted, signifies a pretty girl, a handsome girl, or a pleasant, good thing. That is the name by which I have ever since been called by the Indians.

I afterward learned that the ceremony I at that time passed through was that of adoption. The two squaws had lost a brother in Washington's war, sometime in the year before, and in consequence of his death went up to Fort Du Quesne on the day on which I arrived there, in order to receive a prisoner, or an enemy's scalp, to supply their loss. It is a custom of the Indians, when one of their number is slain or taken prisoner in battle, to give to the nearest relative of the dead or absent a prisoner, if they have chanced to take one; and if not, to give him the scalp of an enemy. On the return of the Indians from the conquest, which is always announced by peculiar shoutings, demonstrations of joy, and the exhibition of some trophy of victory, the mourners come forward and make their claims. If they receive a prisoner, it is at their option either to satiate their vengeance by taking his life in the most cruel manner they can conceive of, or to receive and adopt him into the family, in the place of him whom they have lost. All the prisoners that are taken in battle and carried to the encampment or town by the Indians are given to the bereaved families, till their number is good. And unless the mourners have but just received the news of their bereavement, and are under the operation of a paroxysm of grief, anger, or revenge; or, unless the prisoner is very old, sickly, or homely, they generally save them, and treat them kindly. But if their mental wound is fresh, their loss so great that they deem it irreparable, or if their prisoner or prisoners do not meet their approbation, no torture, let it be ever so cruel, seems sufficient to make them satisfaction. It is family and not national sacrifices among the Indians, that has given them an indelible stamp as barbarians, and identified their character with the idea which is generally formed of unfeeling ferocity and the most barbarous cruelty.

It was my happy lot to be accepted for adoption. At the time of the ceremony I was received by the two squaws to supply the place of their brother in the family; and I was ever considered and treated by them as a real sister, the same as though I had been born of their mother.

During the ceremony of my adoption, I sat motionless, nearly terrified to death at the appearance and actions of the company, expecting every moment to feel their vengeance, and suffer death on the spot. I was, however, happily disappointed; when at the close of the ceremony the company retired, and my sisters commenced employing every means for my consolation and comfort.

Being now settled and provided with a home, I was employed in nursing the children, and doing light work about the house. Occasionally, I was sent out with the Indian hunters, when they went but a short distance, to help them carry their game. My situation was easy; I had no particular hardships to endure. But still, the recollection of my parents, my brothers and sisters, my home, and my own captivity, destroyed my happiness, and made me constantly solitary, lonesome, and gloomy.

My sisters would not allow me to speak English in their hearing; but remembering the charge that my dear mother gave me at the time I left her, whenever I chanced to be alone I made a business of repeating my prayer, catechism, or something I had learned, in order that I might not forget my own language. By practicing in that way, I retained it till I came to Genesee flats, where I soon became acquainted with English people, with whom I have been almost daily in the habit of conversing.

My sisters were very diligent in teaching me their language; and to their great satisfaction, I soon learned so that I could understand it readily, and speak it fluently. I was very fortunate in falling into their hands; for they were kind, good-natured women; peaceable and mild in their dispositions; temperate and decent in their habits, and very tender and gentle toward me. I have great reason to respect them, though they have been dead a great number of years.

/ / /

In the second summer of my living at Wiishto, I had a child, at the time that the kernels of corn first appeared on the cob. When I was taken sick, Sheninjee was absent, and I was sent to a small shed on the bank of the river, which was made of boughs, where I was obliged to stay till my husband returned. My two sisters, who were my only companions, attended me; and on the second day of my confinement my child was born; but it lived only two days. It was a girl; and notwithstanding the shortness of the time that I possessed it, it was a great grief to me to lose it.

After the birth of my child I was very sick, but was not allowed to go into the house for two weeks; when, to my great joy, Sheninjee returned, and I was taken in, and as comfortably provided for as our situation would admit. My disease continued to increase for a number of days; and I became so far reduced that my recovery was despaired of by my friends, and I concluded that my troubles would soon be finished. At length, however, my complaint took a favorable turn, and by the time the corn was ripe I was able to get about. I continued to gain my health, and in the fall was able to go to our winter quarters, on the Saratoga, with the Indians.

From that time nothing remarkable occurred to me till the fourth winter of my captivity, when I had a son born, while I was at Sciota. I had a quick recovery, and my child was healthy. To commemorate the name of my much-lamented father, I called my son Thomas Jemison.

## *CHAPTER IV.*

In the spring, when Thomas was three or four moons (months) old, we returned from Sciota to Wiishto, and soon after set out to go to Fort Pitt, to dispose of our furs and our skins that we had taken in the winter, and procure some necessary articles for the use of our family.

I had then been with the Indians four summers and four winters, and had become so far accustomed to their mode of living, habits, and dispositions, that my anxiety to get away, to be set at liberty and leave them, had almost subsided. With them was my home; my family was there, and there I had many friends to whom I was warmly attached in consideration of the favors, affection, and friendship with which they had uniformly treated me from the time of my adoption. Our labor was not severe; and that of one year was exactly similar in almost every respect to that of the others, without that endless variety that is to be observed in the common labor of the white people. Notwithstanding the Indian women have all the fuel and bread to procure, and the cooking to perform, their task is probably not harder than that of white women, who have those articles provided for them; and their cares certainly are not half as numerous, nor as great. In the summer season, we planted, tended, and harvested our corn, and generally had all our children with us; but had no master to oversee or drive us, so that we could work as leisurely as we pleased. We had no plows on the Ohio, but performed the whole process of planting and hoeing with a small tool that resembled, in some respect, a hoe with a very short handle.

/ / /

Our cooking consisted in pounding our corn into samp or hominy, boiling the hominy, making now and then a cake and baking it in the ashes, and in boiling or roasting our venison. As our cooking and eating utensils consisted of a hominy block and pestle, a small kettle, a knife or two, and a few vessels of bark or wood, it required but little time to keep them in order for use.

Spinning, weaving, sewing, stocking knitting, and the like, are arts which have never been practiced in the Indian tribes generally. After the revolutionary war, I learned to sew, so that I could make my own clothing after a poor fashion; but I have been wholly ignorant of the application of the other domestic arts since my captivity. In the season of hunting, it was our business, in addition to our cooking, to bring home the game that was taken by the Indians, dress it, and carefully preserve the eatable meat, and prepare or dress the skins. Our clothing was fastened together with strings of deerskin, and tied on with the same.

In that manner we lived, without any of those jealousies, quarrels, and revengeful battles between families and individuals, which have been common in the Indian tribes since the introduction of ardent spirits among them.

The use of ardent spirits among the Indians, and a majority of the attempts which have been made to civilize them by the white people, have constantly made them worse and worse; increased their vices, and robbed them of many of their virtues, and will ultimately produce their extermination. I have seen, in a number of instances, the effects of education upon some of our Indians, who were taken, when young, from their families, and placed at school before they had had an opportunity to contract many Indian habits, and there kept till they arrived to manhood; but I have never seen one of those but was an Indian in every respect after he returned. Indians must and will be Indians, in spite of all the means that can be used to instruct them in the arts and sciences.

One thing only marred my happiness while I lived with them on the Ohio, and that was the recollection that I once had tender parents, and a home that I loved. Aside from that recollection, which could not have existed had I been taken in my infancy, I should have been contented in my situation. Notwithstanding all that has been said against the Indians, in consequence of their cruelties to their enemies—cruelties that I have witnessed and had abundant proof of—it is a fact that they are naturally kind, tender, and peaceable toward their friends, and strictly honest; and that those cruelties have been practiced only upon their enemies, according to their idea of justice.

/ / /

GOTTLIEB MITTELBERGER

# 10 On the Misfortune of Indentured Servants

*Indentured, or bonded, servants were an important source of labor in seventeenth- and eighteenth-century America. The term generally refers to immigrants who, in return for passage from Europe to America, had bound themselves to work in America for a number of years, after which time they would become completely free. The practice was closely related to the tradition of apprenticeship, in which a youth was assigned to work for a master in a certain trade and in return was taught the skills of the trade. Convicts were another important source of colonial labor; thousands of English criminals were sentenced to labor in the colonies for a specified period, after which time they were freed.*

*Gottlieb Mittelberger came to Pennsylvania from Germany in 1750. His own fortunes were not so bleak as those of his shipmates. Mittelberger served as a schoolmaster and organist in Philadelphia for three years. He returned to Germany in 1754.*

Both in Rotterdam and in Amsterdam the people are packed densely, like herrings so to say, in the large sea-vessels. One person receives a place of scarcely 2 feet width and 6 feet length in the bedstead, while many a ship carries four to six hundred souls; not to mention the innumerable implements, tools, provisions, water-barrels and other things which likewise occupy much space.

On account of contrary winds it takes the ships sometimes 2, 3 and 4 weeks to make the trip from Holland to . . . England. But when the wind is good, they get there in 8 days or even sooner. Everything is examined there and the custom-duties paid, whence it comes that the ships ride there 8, 10 to 14 days and even longer at anchor, till they have taken in their full cargoes. During that time every one is compelled to spend his last remaining money and to consume his little stock of provisions which had been reserved for the sea; so that most passengers, finding themselves on the ocean where they would be in greater need of them, must greatly suffer from hunger and want. Many suffer want already on the water between Holland and Old England.

When the ships have for the last time weighed their anchors near the city of Kaupp [Cowes] in Old England, the real misery begins with the long voyage. For from there the ships, unless they have good wind, must often sail 8, 9, 10 to 12 weeks before they reach Philadelphia. But even with the best wind the voyage lasts 7 weeks.

But during the voyage there is on board these ships terrible misery, stench, fumes, horror, vomiting, many kinds of sea-sickness, fever, dysentery, headache, heat, constipation, boils, scurvy, cancer, mouth-rot, and the like, all of which come from old and sharply salted food and meat, also from very bad and foul water, so that many die miserably.

Add to this want of provisions, hunger, thirst, frost, heat, dampness, anxiety, want, afflictions and lamentations, together with other trouble, as . . . the lice abound so frightfully, especially on sick people, that they can be scraped off the body. The misery reaches the climax when a gale rages for 2 or 3 nights and days, so that every one believes that the ship will go to the bottom with all human beings on board. In such a visitation the people cry and pray most piteously.

When in such a gale the sea rages and surges, so that the waves rise often like high mountains one above the other, and often tumble over the ship, so that one fears to go down with the ship; when the ship is constantly tossed from side to side by the storm and waves, so that no one can either walk, or sit, or lie, and the closely packed people in the berths are thereby tumbled over each other, both the sick and the well—it will be readily understood that many of these people, none of whom had been prepared for hardships, suffer so terribly from them that they do not survive it.

I myself had to pass through a severe illness at sea, and I best know how I felt at the time. These poor people often long for consolation, and I often entertained and comforted them with singing, praying and exhorting; and whenever it was possible and the winds and waves permitted it, I kept daily prayer-meetings with them on deck. Besides, I baptized five children in distress, because we had no ordained minister on board. I also held divine service every Sunday by reading sermons to the people; and when the dead were sunk in the water, I commended them and our souls to the mercy of God.

Among the healthy, impatience sometimes grows so great and cruel that one curses the other, or himself and the day of his birth, and sometimes come near killing each other. Misery and malice join each other, so that they cheat and rob one another. One always reproaches the other with having persuaded him to undertake the journey. Frequently children cry out against their parents, husbands against their wives and wives against their husbands, brothers and sisters, friends and acquaintances against each other. But most against the soul-traffickers.

Many sigh and cry: "Oh, that I were at home again, and if I had to lie in my pig-sty!" Or they say: "O God, if I only had a piece of good bread, or a good fresh drop of water." Many people whimper, sigh and cry piteously for their homes; most of them get home-sick. Many hundred people necessarily die and perish in such misery, and must be cast into the sea, which drives their relatives, or those who persuaded them to undertake the journey, to such despair that it is almost impossible to pacify and console them. . . .

No one can have an idea of the sufferings which women in confinement have to bear with their innocent children on board these ships. Few of this class escape with their lives; many a mother is cast into the water with her child as soon as she is dead. One day, just as we had a heavy gale, a woman in our ship, who was to give birth and could not give birth under the circumstances, was pushed through a loop-hole [port-hole] in the ship and dropped into the sea, because she was far in the rear of the ship and could not be brought forward.

Children from 1 to 7 years rarely survive the voyage. I witnessed . . . misery in no less than 32 children in our ship, all of whom were thrown into the sea. The parents grieve all the more since their children find no resting-place in the earth, but are devoured by the monsters of the sea.

/ / /

That most of the people get sick is not surprising, because, in addition to all other trials and hardships, warm food is served only three times a week, the rations being very poor and very little. Such meals can hardly be eaten, on account of being so unclean. The water which is served out on the ships is often very black, thick and full of worms, so that one cannot drink it without loathing, even with the greatest thirst. Toward the end we were compelled to eat the ship's biscuit which had been spoiled long ago; though in a whole biscuit there was scarcely a piece the size of a dollar that had not been full of red worms and spiders' nests . . .

At length, when, after a long and tedious voyage, the ships come in sight of land, so that the promontories can be seen, which the people were so eager and anxious to see, all creep from below on deck to see the land from afar, and they weep for joy, and pray and sing, thanking and praising God. The sight of the land makes the people on board the ship, especially the sick and the half dead, alive again, so that their hearts leap within them; they shout and rejoice, and are content to bear their misery in patience, in the hope that they may soon reach the land in safety. But alas!

When the ships have landed at Philadelphia after their long voyage, no one is permitted to leave them except those who pay for their passage or can give good security; the others, who cannot pay, must remain on board the ships till they are purchased, and are released from the ships by their purchasers. The sick always fare the worst, for the healthy are naturally preferred and purchased first; and so the sick and wretched must often remain on board in front of the city for 2 or 3 weeks, and frequently die, whereas many a one, if he could pay his debt and were permitted to leave the ship immediately, might recover and remain alive.

/ / /

The sale of human beings in the market on board the ship is carried on thus: Every day Englishmen, Dutchmen, and High-German people come from the city of Philadelphia and other places, in part from a great distance, say 20, 30, or 40 hours away, and go on board the newly arrived ship that has brought and offers for sale passengers from Europe, and select among the healthy persons such as they deem suitable for their business, and bargain with them how long they will serve for their passage money, which most of them are still in debt for. When they have come to an agreement, it happens that adult persons bind themselves in writing to serve 3, 4, 5, or 6 years for the amount due by them, according to their age and strength. But very young people, from 10 to 15 years, must serve till they are 21 years old.

Many parents must sell and trade away their children like so many head of cattle; for if their children take the debt upon themselves, the parents can leave the ship free and unrestrained; but as the parents often do not know where and to what people their children are going, it often happens that such parents and children, after leaving the ship, do not see each other again for many years, perhaps no more in all their lives.

/ / /

It often happens that whole families, husband, wife, and children, are separated by being sold to different purchasers, especially when they have not paid any part of their passage money.

When a husband or wife has died at sea, when the ship has made more than half of her trip, the survivor must pay or serve not only for himself or herself, but also for the deceased.

When both parents have died over half-way at sea, their children, especially when they are young and have nothing to pawn or to pay, must stand for their own and their parents' passage, and serve till they are 21 years old. When one has served his or her term, he or she is entitled to a new suit of clothes at parting; and if it has been so stipulated, a man gets in addition a horse, a woman, a cow.

When a serf has an opportunity to marry in this country, he or she must pay for each year which he or she would have yet to serve, 5 to 6 pounds. But many a one who has thus purchased and paid for his bride, has subsequently repented his bargain, so that he would gladly have returned his exorbitantly dear ware, and lost the money besides.

If some one in this country runs away from his master, who has treated him harshly, he cannot get far. Good provision has been made for such cases, so that a runaway is soon recovered. He who detains or returns a deserter receives a good reward.

If such a runaway has been away from his master one day, he must serve for it as a punishment a week, for a week a month, and for a month half a year.

/ / /

*OLAUDAH EQUIANO*

# 11 The African Slave Trade

The Interesting Narrative of the Life of Olaudah Equiano, or Gustavus Vassa, the African, Written by Himself *is one of the most important eye-witness accounts of the African slave trade. It is also the pioneering African-American narrative of the passage from slavery to freedom, setting many of the conventions for the more than 6,000 subsequent interviews, essays, and books by which ex-slaves told their dramatic stories. And the book, a bestseller that has gone through many editions since it was first published in London in 1789, is also a remarkable adventure story recounting Equiano's travels in Africa, Europe, and America as well as his part in expeditions to the Arctic and Turkey and his service in the Seven Years' War.*

*Equiano, an Ibo prince kidnapped into slavery when he was eleven years old, was brought first to Barbados and then sent to Virginia. After service in the British navy, he was at last sold to a Quaker merchant who allowed Equiano to purchase his freedom in 1766. In later years he worked to advance the Church of England, his adopted religion, and to abolish the slave trade.*

The first object which saluted my eyes when I arrived on the [Western Africa] coast, was the sea, and a slave ship, which was then riding at anchor, and waiting for its cargo. These filled me with astonishment, which was soon converted into terror, when I was carried on board. I was immediately handled, and tossed up to see if I were sound, by some of the crew; and I was now persuaded that I had gotten into a world of bad spirits, and that they were going to kill me. Their complexions, too, differing so much from ours, their long hair, and the language they spoke, (which was very different from any I had ever heard) united to confirm me in this belief. Indeed, such were the horrors of my views and fears at the moment, that, if ten thousand worlds had been my own, I would have freely parted with them all to have exchanged my condition with that of the meanest slave in my own country. When I looked round the ship too, and saw a large furnace of copper boiling, and a multitude of black people of every description chained together, every one of their countenances expressing dejection and sorrow, I no longer doubted of my fate; and, quite overpowered with horror and anguish, I fell motionless on the deck and fainted. When I recovered a little, I found some black people about me, who I believed were some of those who had brought me on board, and had been receiving their pay; they talked to me in order to cheer me, but all in vain. I asked them if we were not to be eaten by those white men with horrible looks, red faces, and long hair. They told me I was not: and one of the crew brought me a small portion of spirituous liquor in a wine glass, but, being afraid of him, I would not take it out of his hand. One of the blacks, therefore, took it from him and gave it to me, and I took a little down my palate, which, instead of reviving me, as they thought it would, threw me into the greatest consternation at the strange feeling it produced, having never tasted any such liquor before. Soon after this, the blacks who brought me on board went off, and left me abandoned to despair.

I now saw myself deprived of all chance of returning to my native country, or even the least glimpse of hope of gaining the shore, which I now considered as friendly; and I even wished for my former slavery in preference to my present situation, which was filled with horrors of every kind, still heightened by my ignorance of what I was to undergo. I was not long suffered to indulge my grief; I was soon put down under the decks, and there I received such a salutation in my nostrils as I had never experienced in my life: so that, with the loathsomeness of the stench, and crying together, I became so sick and low that I was not able to eat, nor had I the least desire to taste any thing. I now wished for the last friend, death, to relieve me; but soon, to my grief, two of the white men offered me eatables; and, on my refusing to eat, one of them held me fast by the hands, and laid me across, I think the windlass, and tied my feet, while the other flogged me severely. I had never experienced any thing of this kind before, and although not being used to the water, I naturally feared that element the first time I saw it, yet, nevertheless, could I have got over the nettings, I would have jumped over the side, but I could not; and besides, the crew used to watch us very closely who were not chained down to the decks, lest we should leap into the water; and I have seen some of these poor African prisoners most severely cut, for attempting to do so, and hourly whipped for not eating. This indeed was often the case with myself. In a little time after, amongst the poor chained men, I found some of my own nation, which in a small degree gave ease to my mind. I inquired of these what was to be done with us? they gave me to understand, we were to be carried to these white people's country to work for them. I then was a little revived, and thought, if it were no worse than working, my situation was not so desperate; but still I feared I should be put to death, the white people looked and acted, as I thought, in so savage a manner; for I had never seen among any people such instances of brutal cruelty; and this not only shown towards us blacks, but also to some of the whites themselves. One white man in particular I saw, when we were permitted to be on deck, flogged so unmercifully with a large rope near the foremast, that he died in consequence of it; and they tossed him over the side as they would have done a brute. This made me fear these people the more; and I expected nothing less than to be treated in the same manner. I could not help expressing my fears and apprehensions to some of my countrymen; I asked them if these people had no country, but lived in this hollow place? (the ship) they told me they did not, but came from a distant one. "Then," said I, "how comes it in all our country we never heard of them?" They told me because they lived so very far off. I then asked where were their women? had they any like themselves? I was told they had. "And why," said I, "do we not see them?" They answered, because they were left behind. I asked how the vessel could go? they told me they could not tell; but that there was cloth put upon the masts by the help of the ropes I saw, and then the vessel went on; and the white men had some spell or magic they put in the water when they liked, in order to stop the vessel. I was exceedingly amazed at this account, and really thought they were spirits. I therefore wished much to be from amongst them, for I expected they would sacrifice me; but my wishes were vain—for we were so quartered that it was impossible for any of us to make our escape.

While we stayed on the coast I was mostly on deck; and one day, to my great astonishment, I saw one of these vessels coming in with the sails up. As soon as the whites saw it, they gave a great shout, at which we were amazed; and the more so, as the vessel appeared larger by approaching nearer. At last, she came to an anchor in my sight, and when the anchor was let go, I and my countrymen who saw it, were lost in astonishment to observe the vessel stop—and were now convinced it was done by magic. Soon after this the other ship got her boats out, and they came on board of us, and the people of both ships seemed very glad to see each other.—Several of the strangers also shook hands with us black people, and made motions with their hands, signifying I suppose, we were to go to their country, but we did not understand them.

At last, when the ship we were in, had got in all her cargo, they made ready with many fearful noises, and we were all put under deck, so that we could not see how they managed the vessel. But this disappointment was the least of my sorrow. The stench of the hold while we were on the coast was so intolerably loathsome, that it was dangerous to remain there for any time, and some of us had been permitted to stay on the deck for the fresh air; but now that the whole ship's cargo were confined together, it became absolutely pestilential. The closeness of the place, and the heat of the climate, added to the number in the ship, which was so crowded that each had scarcely room to turn himself, almost suffocated us. This produced copious perspirations, so that the air soon became unfit for respiration, from a variety of loathsome smells, and brought on a sickness among the slaves, of which many died—thus falling victims to the improvident avarice, as I may call it, of their purchasers. This wretched situation was again aggravated by the galling of the chains, now became insupportable; and the filth of the necessary tubs, into which the children often fell, and were almost suffocated. The shrieks of the women, and the groans of the dying, rendered the whole a scene of horror almost inconceivable. Happily perhaps, for myself, I was soon reduced so low here that it was thought necessary to keep me almost always on deck; and from my extreme youth I was not put in fetters. In this situation I expected every hour to share the fate of my companions, some of whom were almost daily brought upon deck at the point of death, which I began to hope would soon put an end to my miseries. Often did I think many of the inhabitants of the deep much more happy than myself. I envied them the freedom they enjoyed, and as often wished I could change my condition for theirs. Every circumstance I met with, served only to render my state more painful, and heightened my apprehensions, and my opinion of the cruelty of the whites.

One day they had taken a number of fishes; and when they had killed and satisfied themselves with as many as they thought fit, to our astonishment who were on deck, rather than give any of them to us to eat, as we expected, they tossed the remaining fish into the sea again, although we begged and prayed for some as well as we could, but in vain; and some of my countrymen, being pressed by hunger, took an opportunity, when they thought no one saw them, of trying to get a little privately; but they were discovered, and the attempt procured them some very severe floggings. One day, when we had a smooth sea and moderate wind, two of my wearied countrymen who were chained together, (I was near them at the time,) preferring death to such a life of misery, somehow made through the nettings and jumped into the sea: immediately, another quite dejected fellow, who, on account of his illness, was suffered to be out of irons, also followed their example; and I believe many more would very soon have done the same, if they had not been prevented by the ship's crew, who were instantly alarmed. Those of us that were the most active, were in a moment put down under the deck, and there was such a noise and confusion amongst the people of the ship as I never heard before, to stop her, and get the boat out to go after the slaves. However, two of the wretches were drowned, but they got the other, and afterward flogged him unmercifully, for thus attempting to prefer death to slavery. In this manner we continued to undergo more hardships than I can now relate, hardships which are inseparable from this accursed trade. Many a time we were near suffocation from the want of fresh air, which we were often without for whole days together. This, and the stench of the necessary tubs, carried off many.

During our passage, I first saw flying fishes, which surprised me very much; they used frequently to fly across the ship, and many of them fell on the deck. I also now first saw the use of the quadrant; I had often with astonishment seen the mariners make observations with it, and I could not think what it meant. They at last took notice of my surprise; and one of them, willing to increase it, as well as to gratify my curiosity, made me one day look through it. The clouds appeared to me to be land, which disappeared as they passed along. This heightened my wonder; and I was now more persuaded than ever, that I was in another world, and that every thing about me was magic. At last, we came in sight of the island of Barbadoes, at which the whites on board gave a great shout, and made many signs of joy to us. We did not know what to think of this; but as the vessel drew nearer, we plainly saw the harbor, and other ships of different kinds and sizes, and we soon anchored amongst them, off Bridgetown. Many merchants and planters now came on board, though it was in the evening. They put us in separate parcels, and examined us attentively. They also made us jump, and pointed to the land, signifying we were to go there. We thought by this, we should be eaten by these ugly men, as they appeared to us; and, when soon after we were all put down under the deck again, there was much dread and trembling among us, and nothing but bitter cries to be heard all the night from these apprehensions, insomuch, that at last the white people got some old slaves from the land to pacify us. They told us we were not to be eaten, but to work, and were soon to go on land, where we should see many of our country people. This report eased us much. And sure enough, soon after we were landed, there came to us Africans of all languages.

We were conducted immediately to the merchant's yard, where we were all pent up together, like so many sheep in a fold, without regard to sex or age. As every object was new to me, every thing I saw filled me with surprise. What struck me first, was, that the houses were built with bricks and stories, and in every other respect different from those I had seen in Africa; but I was still more astonished on seeing people on horseback. I did not know what this could mean; and, indeed, I thought these people were full of nothing but magical arts. While I was in this astonishment, one of my fellow-prisoners spoke to a countryman of his, about the horses, who said they were the same kind they had in their country. I understood them, though they were from a distant part of Africa; and I thought it odd I had not seen any horses there; but afterwards, when I came to converse with different Africans, I found they had many horses amongst them, and much larger than those I then saw.

We were not many days in the merchant's custody before we were sold after their usual manner, which is this:—On a signal given, (as the beat of a drum,) the buyers rush at once into the yard where the slaves are confined, and make choice of that parcel they like best. The noise and clamor with which this is attended, and the eagerness visible in the countenances of the buyers, serve not a little to increase the apprehension of terrified Africans, who may well be supposed to consider them as the ministers of that destruction to which they think themselves devoted. In this manner, without scruple, are relations and friends separated, most of them never to see each other again. I remember, in the vessel in which I was brought over, in the men's apartment, there were several brothers, who, in the sale, were sold in different lots; and it was very moving on this occasion, to see and hear their cries at parting. O, ye nominal Christians! might not an African ask you—Learned you this from your God, who says unto you, Do unto all men as you would men should do unto you? Is it not enough that we are torn from our country and friends, to toil for your luxury and lust of gain? Must every tender feeling be likewise sacrificed to your avarice? Are the dearest friends and relations, now rendered more dear by their separation from their kindred, still to be parted from each other, and thus prevented from cheering the gloom of slavery, with the small comfort of being together, and mingling their sufferings and sorrows? Why are parents to lose their children, brothers their sisters, or husbands their wives? Surely, this is a new refinement in cruelty, which, while it has no advantage to atone for it, thus aggravates distress, and adds fresh horrors even to the wretchedness of slavery.

*MICHEL-GUILLAUME-JEAN DE CRÈVECOEUR*

# 12 *What Is an American?*

*Michel Crèvecoeur's* Letters from an American Farmer *was first published in London in 1782. Crèvecoeur was certainly an unusual American farmer. Born in France in 1735, he served with the French against the British in the French and Indian War. From 1783 to 1790 he was the French consul in New York City, but he lived as an "American farmer" in Orange County, New York, from 1769 to 1780.*

*It has been an article of faith for three centuries that moving from Europe to America is a transforming experience, creating a new person from the old. What is American about America is one of the continuing subjects of our history and literature. Few writers have given so persuasive or influential a response as Crèvecoeur to the question, "What is the American, this new man?" Crèvecoeur died in France in 1813. He published his book using an Americanized name: J. Hector St. John.*

## *LETTER III. WHAT IS AN AMERICAN?*

I wish I could be acquainted with the feelings and thoughts which must agitate the heart and present themselves to the mind of an enlightened Englishman, when he first lands on this continent. He must greatly rejoice that he lived at a time to see this fair country discovered and settled; he must necessarily feel a share of national pride, when he views the chain of settlements which embellishes these extended shores. When he says to himself, this is the work of my countrymen, who, when convulsed by factions, afflicted by a variety of miseries and wants, restless and impatient, took refuge here. They brought along with them their national genius, to which they principally owe what liberty they enjoy, and what substances they possess. Here he sees the industry of his native country displayed in a new manner, and traces in their works the embrios of all the arts, sciences, and ingenuity which flourish in Europe. Here he beholds fair cities, substantial villages, extensive fields, an immense country filled with decent houses, good roads, orchards, meadows, and bridges, where an hundred years ago all was wild, woody and uncultivated! What a train of pleasing ideas this fair spectacle must suggest; it is a prospect which must inspire a good citizen with the most heartfelt pleasure. The difficulty consists in the manner of viewing so extensive a scene. He is arrived on a new continent; a modern society offers itself to his contemplation, different from what he had hitherto seen. It is not composed, as in Europe, of great lords who possess every thing, and of a herd of people who have nothing. Here are no aristocratical families, no courts, no kings, no bishops, no ecclesiastical dominion, no invisible power giving to a few a very visible one; no great manufacturers employing thousands, no great refinements of luxury. The rich and the poor are not so far removed from each other as they are in Europe.

/ / /

The next wish of this traveller will be to know whence came all these people? they are a mixture of English, Scotch, Irish, French, Dutch, Germans, and Swedes. From this promiscuous breed, that race now called Americans have arisen. . . .

/ / /

What attachment can a poor European emigrant have for a country where he had nothing? The knowledge of the language, the love of a few kindred as poor as himself, were the only cords that tied him: his country is now that which gives him land, bread, protection, and consequence: *Ubi panis ibi patria* [where I have bread, there is my homeland], is the motto of all emigrants. What then is the American, this new man? He is either an European, or the descendant of an European, hence that strange mixture of blood, which you will find in no other country. I could point out to you a family whose grandfather was an Englishman, whose wife was Dutch, whose son married a French woman, and whose present four sons have now four wives of different nations. *He* is an American, who leaving behind him all his ancient prejudices and manners, receives new ones from the new mode of life he has embraced, the new government he obeys, and the new rank he holds. He becomes an American by being received in the broad lap of our great *Alma Mater.* Here individuals of all nations are melted into a new race of men, whose labours and posterity will one day cause great changes in the world. Americans are the western pilgrims, who are carrying along with them that great mass of arts, sciences, vigour, and industry which began long since in the east; they will finish the great circle. The Americans were once scattered all over Europe; here they are incorporated into one of the finest systems of population which has ever appeared, and which will hereafter become distinct by the power of the different climates they inhabit. The American ought therefore to love this country much better than that wherein either he or his forefathers were born. Here the rewards of his industry follow with equal steps the progress of his labour; his labour is founded on the basis of nature, *self-interest;* can it want a stronger allurement? Wives and children, who before in vain demanded of him a morsel of bread, now, fat and frolicsome, gladly help their father to clear those fields whence exuberant crops are to arise to feed and to clothe them all; without any part being claimed, either by a despotic prince, a rich abbot, or a mighty lord. Here religion demands but little of him; a small voluntary salary to the minister, and gratitude to God; can he refuse these? The American is a new man, who acts upon new principles; he must therefore entertain new ideas, and form new opinions. From involuntary idleness, servile dependence, penury, and useless labour, he has passed to toils of a very different nature, rewarded by ample subsistence.—This is an American.

British America is divided into many provinces, forming a large association, scattered along a coast 1500 miles extent and about 200 wide. This society I would fain examine, at least such as it appears in the middle provinces; if it does not afford that variety of tinges and gradations which may be observed in Europe, we have colours peculiar to ourselves. For instance, it is natural to conceive that those who live near the sea, must be very different from those who live in the woods; the intermediate space will afford a separate and distinct class.

Men are like plants; the goodness and flavour of the fruit proceeds from the peculiar soil and exposition in which they grow. We are nothing but what we derive from the air we breathe, the climate we inhabit, the government we obey, the system of religion we profess, and the nature of our employment. Here you will find but few crimes; these have acquired as yet no root among us. I wish I were able to trace all my ideas; if my ignorance prevents me from describing them properly, I hope I shall be able to delineate a few of the outlines, which are all I propose.

Those who live near the sea, feed more on fish than on flesh, and often encounter that boisterous element. This renders them more bold and enterprising; this leads them to neglect the confined occupations of the land. They see and converse with a variety of people; their intercourse with mankind becomes extensive. The sea inspires them with a love of traffic, a desire of transporting produce from one place to another; and leads them to a variety of resources which supply the place of labour. Those who inhabit the middle settlements, by far the most numerous, must be very different; the simple cultivation of the earth purifies them, but the indulgences of the government, the soft remonstrances of religion, the rank of independent freeholders, must necessarily inspire them with sentiments, very little known in Europe among people of the same class. What do I say? Europe has no such class of men; the early knowledge they acquire, the early bargains they make, give them a great degree of sagacity. As freemen they will be litigious; pride and obstinacy are often the cause of law suits; the nature of our laws and governments may be another. As citizens it is easy to imagine, that they will carefully read the newspapers, enter into every political disquisition, freely blame or censure governors and others. As farmers they will be careful and anxious to get as much as they can, because what they get is their own. As northern men they will love the chearful cup. As Christians, religion curbs them not in their opinions; the general indulgence leaves every one to think for themselves in spiritual matters; the laws inspect our actions, our thoughts are left to God. Industry, good living, selfishness, litigiousness, country politics, the pride of freemen, religious indifference, are their characteristics. If you recede still farther from the sea, you will come into more modern settlements; they exhibit the same strong lineaments, in a ruder appearance. Religion seems to have still less influence, and their manners are less improved.

Now we arrive near the great woods, near the last inhabited districts; there men seem to be placed still farther beyond the reach of government, which in some measure leaves them to themselves. How can it pervade every corner; as they were driven there by misfortunes, necessity of beginnings, desire of acquiring large tracks of land, idleness, frequent want of economy, ancient debts; the re-union of such people does not afford a very pleasing spectacle. When discord, want of unity and friendship; when either drunkenness or idleness prevail in such remote districts; contention, inactivity, and wretchedness must ensue. There are not the same remedies to these evils as in a long established community. The few magistrates they have, are in general little better than the rest; they are often in a perfect state of war; that of man against man, sometimes decided by blows, sometimes by means of the law; that of man against every wild inhabitant of these venerable woods, of which they are come to dispossess them. There men appear to be no better than carnivorous animals of a superior rank, living on the flesh of wild animals when they catch them, and when they are not able, they subsist on grain. He who would wish to see America in its proper light, and have a true idea of its feeble beginnings and barbarous rudiments, must visit our extended line of frontiers where the last settlers dwell, and where he may see the first labours of settlement, the mode of clearing the earth, in all their different appearances; where men are wholly left dependent on their native tempers, and on the spur of uncertain industry, which often fails when not sanctified by the efficacy of a few moral rules. There, remote from the power of example, and check of shame, many families exhibit the most hideous parts of our society. They are a kind of forlorn hope, preceding by ten or twelve years the most respectable army of veterans which come after them. In that space, prosperity will polish some, vice and the law will drive off the rest, who uniting again with others like themselves will recede still farther; making room for more industrious people, who will finish their improvements, convert the loghouse into a convenient habitation, and rejoicing that the first heavy labours are finished, will change in a few years that hitherto barbarous country into a fine fertile, well regulated district. Such is our progress, such is the march of the Europeans toward the interior parts of this continent. In all societies there are offcasts; this impure part serves as our precursors or pioneers; my father himself was one of that class, but he came upon honest principles, and was therefore one of the few who held fast; by good conduct and temperance, he transmitted to me his fair inheritance, when not above one in fourteen of his contemporaries had the same good fortune.

Forty years ago this smiling country was thus inhabited; it is now purged, a general decency of manners prevails throughout, and such has been the fate of our best countries.

Exclusive of those general characteristics, each province has its own, founded on the government, climate, mode of husbandry, customs, and peculiarity of circumstances. Europeans submit insensibly to these great powers, and become, in the course of a few generations, not only Americans in general, but either Pennsylvanians, Virginians, or provincials under some other name. Whoever traverses the continent must easily observe those strong differences, which will grow more evident in time. The inhabitants of Canada, Massachusetts, the middle provinces, the southern ones will be as different as their climates; their only points of unity will be those of religion and language.

As I have endeavoured to shew you how Europeans become Americans; it may not be disagreable to shew you likewise how the various Christian sects introduced, wear out, and how religious indifference becomes prevalent. When any considerable number of a particular sect happen to dwell contiguous to each other, they immediately erect a temple, and there worship the Divinity agreeably to their own peculiar ideas. Nobody disturbs them. If any new sect springs up in Europe, it may happen that many of its professors will come and settle in America. As they bring their zeal with them, they are at liberty to make proselytes if they can, and to build a meeting and to follow the dictates of their consciences; for neither the government nor any other power interferes. If they are peaceable subjects, and are industrious, what is it to their neighbours how and in what manner they think fit to address their prayers to the Supreme Being? But if the sectaries are not settled close together, if they are mixed with other denominations, their zeal will cool for want of fuel, and will be extinguished in a little time. Then the Americans become as to religion, what they are as to country, allied to all. In them the name of Englishman, Frenchman, and European is lost, and in like manner, the strict modes of Christianity as practised in Europe are lost also. This effect will extend itself still farther hereafter, and though this may appear to you as a strange idea, yet it is a very true one. I shall be able perhaps hereafter to explain myself better; in the meanwhile, let the following example serve as my first justification.

Let us suppose you and I to be travelling; we observe that in this house, to the right, lives a Catholic, who prays to God as he has been taught, and believes in transubstantion; he works and raises wheat, he has a large family of children, all hale and robust; his belief, his prayers offend nobody. About one mile farther on the same road, his next neighbour may be a good honest plodding German Lutheran, who addresses himself to the same God, the God of all, agreeably to the modes he has been educated in, and believes in consubstantiation; by so doing he scandalizes nobody; he also works in his fields, embellishes the earth, clears swamps, &c. What has the world to do with his Lutheran principles? He persecutes nobody, and nobody persecutes him, he visits his neighbours, and his neighbours visit him. Next to him lives a seceder, the most enthusiastic of all sectaries; his zeal is hot and fiery, but separated as he is from others of the same complexion, he has no congregation of his own to resort to, where he might cabal and mingle religious pride with worldly obstinacy. He likewise raises good crops, his house is handsomely painted, his orchard is one of the fairest in the neighbourhood. How does it concern the welfare of the country, or of the province at large, what this man's religious sentiments are, or really whether he has any at all? He is a good farmer, he is a sober, peaceable, good citizen: William Penn himself would not wish for more. This is the visible character, the invisible one is only guessed at, and is nobody's business. Next again lives a Low Dutchman, who implicitly believes the rules laid down by the synod of Dort. He conceives no other idea of a clergyman than that of an hired man; if he does his work well he will pay him the stipulated sum; if not he will dismiss him, and do without his sermons, and let his church be shut up for years. But notwithstanding this coarse idea, you will find his house and farm to be the neatest in all the country; and you will judge by his waggon and fat horses, that he thinks more of the affairs of this world than of those of the next. He is sober and laborious, therefore he is all he ought to be as to the affairs of this life; as for those of the next, he must trust to the great Creator. Each of these people instruct their children as well as they can, but these instructions are feeble compared to those which are given to the youth of the poorest class in Europe. Their children will therefore grow up less zealous and more indifferent in matters of religion than their parents. The foolish vanity, or rather the fury of making Proselytes, is unknown here; they have no time, the seasons call for all their attention, and thus in a few years, this mixed neighbourhood will exhibit a strange religious medley, that will be neither pure Catholicism nor pure Calvinism. A very perceptible indifference even in the first generation, will become apparent; and it may happen that the daughter of the Catholic will marry the son of the seceder, and settle by themselves at a distance from their parents. What religious education will they give their children? A very imperfect one. If there happens to be in the neighbourhood any place of worship, we will suppose a Quaker's meeting; rather than not shew their fine clothes, they will go to it, and some of them may perhaps attach themselves to that society. Others will remain in a perfect state of indifference; the children of these zealous parents will not be able to tell what their religious principles are, and their grandchildren still less. The neighbourhood of a place of worship generally leads them to it, and the action of going thither, is the strongest evidence they can give of their attachment to any sect. The Quakers are the only people who retain a fondness for their own mode of worship; for be they ever so far separated from each other, they hold a sort of communion with the society, and seldom depart from its rules, at least in this country. Thus all sects are mixed as well as all nations; thus religious indifference is imperceptibly disseminated from one end of the continent to the other; which is at present one of the strongest characteristics of the Americans. Where this will reach no one can tell, perhaps it may leave a vacuum fit to receive other systems. Persecution, religious pride, the love of contradiction, are the food of what the world commonly calls religion. These motives have ceased here: zeal in Europe is confined; here it evaporates in the great distance it has to travel; there it is a grain of powder inclosed, here it burns away in the open air, and consumes without effect.

But to return to our back settlers. I must tell you, that there is something in the proximity of the woods, which is very singular. It is with men as it is with the plants and animals that grow and live in the forests; they are entirely different from those that live in the plains. I will candidly tell you all my thoughts but you are not to expect that I shall advance any reasons. By living in or near the woods, their actions are regulated by the wildness of the neighbourhood. The deer often come to eat their grain, the wolves to destroy their sheep, the bears to kill their hogs, the foxes to catch their poultry. This surrounding hostility, immediately puts the gun into their hands; they watch these animals, they kill some; and thus by defending their property, they soon become professed hunters; this is the progress; once hunters, farewell to the plough. The chase renders them ferocious, gloomy, and unsociable; a hunter wants no neighbour, he rather hates them, because he dreads the competition. In a little time their success in the woods makes them neglect their tillage. They trust to the natural fecundity of the earth, and therefore do little; carelessness in fencing, often exposes what little they sow to destruction; they are not at home to watch; in order therefore to make up the deficiency, they go oftener to the woods. That new mode of life brings along with it a new set of manners, which I cannot easily describe. These new manners being grafted on the old stock, produce a strange sort of lawless profligacy, the impressions of which are indelible. The manners of the Indian natives are respectable, compared with this European medley. Their wives and children live in sloth and inactivity;

and having no proper pursuits, you may judge what education the latter receive. Their tender minds have nothing else to contemplate but the example of their parents; like them they grow up a mongrel breed, half civilized, half savage, except nature stamps on them some constitutional propensities. That rich, that voluptuous sentiment is gone that struck them so forcibly; the possession of their freeholds no longer conveys to their minds the same pleasure and pride. To all these reasons you must add, their lonely situation, and you cannot imagine what an effect on manners the great distances they live from each other has! Consider one of the last settlements in its first view: of what is it composed? Europeans who have not that sufficient share of knowledge they ought to have, in order to prosper; people who have suddenly passed from oppression, dread of government, and fear of laws, into the unlimited freedom of the woods. This sudden change must have a very great effect on most men, and on that class particularly. Eating of wild meat, whatever you may think, tends to alter their temper: though all the proof I can adduce, is, that I have seen it: and having no place of worship to resort to, what little society this might afford, is denied them.

/ / /

It is in consequence of this straggling situation, and the astonishing power it has on manners, that the back-settlers of both the Carolinas, Virginia, and many other parts, have been long a set of lawless people; it has been even dangerous to travel among them. Government can do nothing in so extensive a country, better it should wink at these irregularities, than that it should use means inconsistent with its usual mildness.

/ / /

THOMAS PRESTON

# 13 An Account of the Boston Massacre

*Historians in recent years have stressed the role of the "crowd" in the coming of the American Revolution. Anonymous colonists taking to the streets in the years after 1763 were an important part of the dynamic of revolution.*

*First-hand accounts of an event do not necessarily make it easy to determine precisely what occurred. In early 1770 British troops were quartered in Boston. Many townspeople resented their presence, and on March 5 a mob of about sixty attacked a small group of soldiers. In the ensuing disturbance, some soldiers, without orders, fired on the mob, killing five people and wounding eight. The incident was taken up and exaggerated by anti-British radicals—the "Patriots"—in Boston, who called it the Boston Massacre. This selection is the account of a British officer who was tried for manslaughter along with several other soldiers. All but two of the accused soldiers were acquitted (John Adams took part in their defense), but the "Massacre" served to inflame anti-British sentiment throughout the colonies.*

## CAPTAIN THOMAS PRESTON'S ACCOUNT OF THE BOSTON MASSACRE (13 MARCH 1770).

It is [a] matter of too great notoriety to need any proofs that the arrival of his Majesty's troops in Boston was extremely obnoxious to its inhabitants. They have ever used all means in their power to weaken the regiments, and to bring them into contempt by promoting and aiding desertions, and with impunity, even where there has been the clearest evidence of the fact, and by grossly and falsely propagating untruths concerning them. On the arrival of the 64th and 65th their ardour seemingly began to abate; it being too expensive to buy off so many, and attempts of that kind rendered too dangerous from the numbers.

/ / /

And [conflict in the streets of Boston] has ever since their departure been breaking out with greater violence after their embarkation. One of their justices, most thoroughly acquainted with the people and their intentions, on the trial of a man of the 14th Regiment, openly and publicly in the hearing of great numbers of people and from the seat of justice, declared "that the soldiers must now take care of themselves, *nor trust too much to their arms,* for they were but a handful; that the inhabitants carried weapons concealed under their clothes, and would destroy them in a moment, *if they pleased.*" This, considering the malicious temper of the people, was an alarming circumstance to the soldiery. Since which several disputes have happened between the townspeople and the soldiers of both regiments, the former being encouraged thereto by the countenance of even some of the magistrates, and by the protection of all the party against government. In general such disputes have been kept too secret from the officers. On the 2d instant two of the 29th going through one Gray's ropewalk, the rope-makers insultingly asked them if they would empty a vault. This unfortunately had the desired effect by provoking the soldiers, and from words they went to blows. Both parties suffered in this affray, and finally the soldiers retired to their quarters. The officers, on the first knowledge of this transaction, took every precaution in their power to prevent any ill consequence. Notwithstanding which, single quarrels could not be prevented, the inhabitants constantly provoking and abusing the soldiery. The insolence as well as utter hatred of the inhabitants to the troops increased daily, insomuch that Monday and Tuesday, the 5th and 6th instant, were privately agreed on for a general engagement, in consequence of which several of the militia came from the country armed to join their friends, menacing to destroy any who should oppose them. This plan has since been discovered.

On Monday night about 8 o'clock two soldiers were attacked and beat. But the party of the townspeople in order to carry matters to the utmost length, broke into two meeting houses and rang the alarm bells, which I supposed was for fire as usual, but was soon undeceived. About 9 some of the guard came to and informed me the town inhabitants were assembling to attack the troops, and that the bells were ringing as the signal for that purpose and not for fire, and the beacon intended to be fired to bring in the distant people of the country. This, as I was captain of the day, occasioned my repairing immediately to the main guard. In my way there I saw the people in great commotion, and heard them use the most cruel and horrid threats against the troops. In a few minutes after I reached the guard, about 100 people passed it and went towards the custom house where the king's money is lodged. They immediately surrounded the sentry posted there, and with clubs and other weapons threatened to execute their vengeance on him. I was soon informed by a townsman their intention was to carry off the soldier from his post and probably murder him. On which I desired him to return for further intelligence, and he soon came back and assured me he heard the mob declare they would murder him. This I feared might be a prelude to their plundering the king's chest. I immediately sent a non-commissioned officer and 12 men to protect both the sentry and the king's money, and very soon followed myself to prevent, if possible, all disorder, fearing lest the officer and soldiers, by the insults and provocations of the rioters, should be thrown off their guard and commit some rash act. They soon rushed through the people, and by charging their bayonets in half-circles, kept them at a little distance. Nay, so far was I from intending the death of any person that I suffered the troops to go to the spot where the unhappy affair took place without any loading in their pieces; nor did I ever give orders for loading them. This remiss conduct in me perhaps merits censure; yet it is evidence, resulting from the nature of things, which is the best and surest that can be offered, that my intention was not to act offensively, but the contrary part, and that not without compulsion. The mob still increased and were more outrageous, striking their clubs or bludgeons one against another, and calling out, come on you rascals, you bloody backs, you lobster scoundrels, fire if you dare, G-d damn you, fire and be damned, we know you dare not, and much more such language was used. At this time I was between the soldiers and the mob, parleying with, and endeavouring all in my power to persuade them to retire peaceably, but to no purpose. They advanced to the points of the bayonets, struck some of them and even the muzzles of the pieces, and seemed to be endeavoring to close with the soldiers. On which some well behaved persons asked me if the guns were charged. I replied yes. They then asked me if I intended to order the men to fire. I answered no, by no means, observing to them that I was advanced before the muzzles of the men's pieces, and must fall a sacrifice if they fired; that the soldiers were upon the half cock and charged bayonets, and my giving the word fire under those circumstances would prove me to be no officer. While I was thus speaking, one of the soldiers having received a severe blow with a stick, stepped a little on one side and instantly fired, on which turning to and asking him why he fired without orders, I was struck with a club on my arm, which for some time deprived me of the use of it, which blow had it been placed on my head, most probably would have destroyed me. On this a general attack was made on the men by a great number of heavy clubs and snowballs being thrown at them, by which all our lives were in imminent danger, some persons at the same time from behind calling out, damn your bloods—why don't you fire. Instantly three or four of the soldiers fired, one after another, and directly after three more in the same confusion and hurry. The mob then ran away, except three unhappy men who instantly expired, in which number was Mr. Gray at whose rope-walk the prior quarrels took place; one more is since dead, three others are dangerously, and four slightly wounded. The whole of this melancholy affair was transacted in almost 20 minutes. On my asking the soldiers why they fired without orders, they said they heard the word fire and supposed it came from me. This might be the case as many of the mob called out fire, fire, but I assured the men that I gave no such order; that my words were, don't fire, stop your firing. In short, it was scarcely possible for the soldiers to know who said fire, or don't fire, or stop your firing. On the people's assembling again to take away the dead bodies, the soldiers supposing them coming to attack them, were making ready to fire again, which I prevented by striking up their firelocks with my hand. Immediately after a townsman came and told me that 4 or 5000 people were assembled in the next street, and had sworn to take my life with every man's with me. On which I judged it unsafe to remain there any longer, and therefore sent the party and sentry to the main guard, where the street is narrow and short, there telling them off into street firings, divided and planted them at each end of the street to secure their rear, momently expecting an attack, as there was a constant cry of the inhabitants to arms, to arms, turn out with your guns; and the town drums beating to arms, I ordered my drums to beat to arms, and being soon after joined by the different companies of the 29th regiment, I formed them as the guard into street firings. The 14th regiment also got under arms but remained at their barracks. I immediately sent a sergeant with a party to Colonel Dalrymple, the commanding officer, to acquaint him with every particular. Several officers going to join their regiment were knocked down by the mob, one very much wounded and his sword taken from him. The lieutenant-governor and Colonel Carr soon after met at the head of the 29th regiment and agreed that the regiment should retire to their barracks, and the people to their houses, but I kept the picket to strengthen the guard. It was with great difficulty that the lieutenant-governor prevailed on the people to be quiet and retire. At last they all went off, excepting about a hundred.

A Council was immediately called, on the breaking up of which three justices met and issued a warrant to apprehend me and eight soldiers. On hearing of this procedure I instantly went to the sheriff and surrendered myself, though for the space of 4 hours I had it in my power to have made my escape, which I most undoubtedly should have attempted and could have easily executed, had I been the least conscious of any guilt. On the examination before the justices, two witnesses swore that I gave the men orders to fire. The one testified he was within two feet of me; the other that I swore at the men for not firing at the first word. Others swore they heard me use the word "fire," but whether do or do not fire, they could not say; others that they heard the word fire, but could not say if it came from me. The next day they got 5 or 6 more to swear I gave the word to fire. So bitter and inveterate are many of the malcontents here that they are industriously using every method to fish out evidence to prove it was a concerted scheme to murder the inhabitants. Others are infusing the utmost malice and revenge into the minds of the people who are to be my jurors by false publications, votes of towns, and all other artifices. That so from a settled rancour against the officers and troops in general, the suddenness of my trial after the affair while the people's minds are all greatly inflamed, I am, though perfectly innocent, under most unhappy circumstances, having nothing in reason to expect but the loss of life in a very ignominious manner, without the interposition of his Majesty's royal goodness.

/ / /

GEORGE ROBERT TWELVES HEWES

# 14 A Patriot Shoemaker

*George Robert Twelves Hewes (1742–1840) was in his nineties when he told the story of his experiences in Revolutionary Boston to James Hawkes in 1833. Hewes claimed not to have read any published account of the happenings there and could "therefore only give the information which I derived from the event[s] of the day." Careful checking by the distinguished labor historian Alfred F. Young has authenticated much of Hewes's account. His story provides a rare opportunity to see an ordinary citizen taking a direct part in great historical events.*

*These experiences had a profound personal effect on Hewes. In the 1760s he had been an awkward young cobbler nervously deferring to his aristocratic customers. A decade later, with these experiences behind him, he would risk his employment and perhaps even a beating for his refusal to take off his hat "for any man." For Hewes, the American Revolution meant that the poor and the ordinary no longer owed the rich and powerful what the eighteenth century called "deference."*

[W]hen I was at the age of twenty-six, I married the daughter of Benjamin Sumner, of Boston. At the time of our intermarriage, the age of my wife was seventeen. We lived together very happily seventy years. She died at the age of eighty-seven.

At the time when the British troops were first stationed at Boston, we had several children, the exact number I do not recollect. By our industry and mutual efforts we were improving our condition.

An account of the massacre of the citizens of Boston, in the year 1770, on the 5th of March, by some of the British troops, has been committed to the record of our history, as one of those interesting events which lead to the revolutionary contest that resulted in our independence. When the various histories of that event were published, no one living at that time could have expected that any one of the actors in that tragical scene, and then, considerably advanced in life, would have lived to revive in our recollection facts relating to it, by the rehearsal of them from his own personal knowledge. But while the public mind has no other source from which it can derive its knowledge of that, and many other interesting events relating to our revolutionary contest, Hewes, with a precision of recollection, perhaps unprecedented in the history of longevity, rehearses many facts relating to them, from his own personal knowledge.

We have been informed by the historians of the revolution, that a series of provocations had excited strong prejudices, and inflamed the passion of the British soldiery against our citizens, previous to the commencement of open hostilities; and prepared their minds to burst out into acts of violence on the application of a single spark of additional excitement, and which finally resulted in the unfortunate massacre of a number of our citizens.

On my inquiring of Hewes what knowledge he had of that event, he replied, that he knew nothing from history, as he had never read any thing relating to it from any publication whatever, and can therefore only give the information which I derived from the event of the day upon which the catastrophe happened. On that day, one of the British officers applied to a barber, to be shaved and dressed; the master of the shop, whose name was Pemont, told his apprentice boy he might serve him, and receive the pay to himself, while Pemont left the shop. The boy accordingly served him, but the officer, for some reason unknown to me, went away from the shop without paying him for his service. After the officer had been gone some time, the boy went to the house where he was, with his account, to demand payment of his bill, but the sentinel, who was before the door, would not give him admittance, nor permit him to see the officer; and as some angry words were interchanged between the sentinel and the boy, a considerable number of the people from the vicinity, soon gathered at the place where they were, which was in King street, and I was soon on the ground among them. The violent agitation of the citizens, not only on account of the abuse offered to the boy, but other causes of excitement, then fresh in the recollection, was such that the sentinel began to be apprehensive of danger, and knocked at the door of the house, where the officers were, and told the servant who came to the door, that he was afraid of his life, and would quit his post unless he was protected. The officers in the house then sent a messenger to the guard-house, to require Captain Preston to come with a sufficient number of his soldiers to defend them from the threatened violence of the people. On receiving the message, he came immediately with a small guard of grenadiers, and paraded them before the custom-house, where the British officers were shut up. Captain Preston then ordered the people to disperse, but they said they would not, they were in the king's highway, and had as good a right to be there as he had. The captain of the guard then said to them, if you do not disperse, I will fire upon you, and then gave orders to his men to make ready, and immediately after gave them orders to fire. Three of our citizens fell dead on the spot, and two, who were wounded, died the next day; and nine others were also wounded. The persons who were killed I well recollect, said Hewes; they were, Gray, a rope maker, Marverick, a young man, Colwell, who was the mate of Captain Colton; Attuck, a mulatto, and Carr, who was an Irishman. Captain Preston then immediately fled with his grenadiers back to the guard-house. The people who were assembled on that occasion, then immediately chose a committee to report to the governor the result of Captain Preston's conduct, and to demand of him satisfaction. The governor told the committee, that if the people would be quiet that night he would give them satisfaction, so far as was in his power; the next morning Captain Preston, and those of his guard who were concerned in the massacre, were, accordingly, by order of the governor, given up, and taken into custody the next morning, and committed to prison.

It is not recollected that the offence given to the barber's boy is mentioned by the historians of the revolution; yet there can be no doubt of its correctness. The account of this single one of the exciting causes of the massacre, related by Hewes, at this time, was in answer to the question of his personal knowledge of that event.

A knowledge of the spirit of those times will easily lead us to conceive, that the manner of the British officers application to the barber, was a little too strongly tinctured with the dictatorial hauteur, to conciliate the views of equality, which at that period were supremely predominant in the minds of those of the whig party, even in his humble occupation; and that the disrespectful notice of his loyal customer, in consigning him to the attention of his apprentice boy, and abruptly leaving his shop, was intended to be treated by the officer with contempt, by so underating the services of his apprentice, as to deem any reward for them beneath his attention. The boy too, may be supposed to have imbibed so much of the spirit which distinguished that period of our history, that he was willing to improve any occasion to contribute his share to the public excitement; to add an additional spark to the fire of political dissention which was enkindling.

When Hewes arrived at the spot where the massacre happened, it appears his attention was principally engaged by the clamours of those who were disposed to aid the boy in avenging the insult offered to him by the British officer, and probably heard nothing, at that time, of any other of the many exciting causes which lead to that disastrous event, though it appeared from his general conversation, his knowledge of them was extensive and accurate.

But to pursue the destiny of Captain Preston, and the guard who fired on the citizens; in about a fortnight after, said Hewes, they were brought to trial and indicted for the crime of murder.

The soldiers were tried first, and acquitted, on the ground, that in firing upon the citizens of Boston, they only acted in proper obedience to the captain's orders. When Preston, their captain, was tried, I was called as one of the witnesses, on the part of the government, and testified, that I believed it was the same man, Captain Preston, that ordered his soldiers to make ready, who also ordered them to fire. Mr. John Adams, former president of the United States, was advocate for the prisoners, and denied the fact, that Captain Preston gave orders to his men to fire; and on his cross examination of me asked whether my position was such, that I could see the captain's lips in motion when the order to fire was given; to which I answered, that I could not. Although the evidence of Preston's having given orders to the soldiers to fire, was thought by the jury sufficient to acquit them, it was not thought to be of weight enough to convict him of a capital offence; he also was acquitted.

Although the excitement which had been occasioned by the wanton massacre of our citizens, had in some measure abated, it was never extinguished until open hostilities commenced, and we had declared our independence. The citizens of Boston continued inflexible in their demand, that every British soldier should be withdrawn from the town, and within four days after the massacre, the whole army decamped. But the measures of the British parliament, which led the American colonies to a separation from that government, were not abandoned. And to carry into execution their favourite project of taxing their American colonies, they employed a number of ships to transport a large quantity of tea into the colonies, of which the American people were apprised, and while resolute measures were taking in all the capital towns, to resist the project of British taxation, the ships arrived, which the people of Boston had long expected.

The particular object of sending this cargo of tea to Boston at that time, and the catastrophe which befell it, have been referred to in the preface. It has also been recorded, among the most important and interesting events in the history of the American revolution; but the rehersal of it at this time, by a witness, and an actor in that tragicomical scene, excites in the recollection of it a novel and extraordinary interest.

On my inquiring of Hewes if he knew who first proposed the project of destroying the tea, to prevent its being landed, he replied that he did not; neither did he know who or what number were to volunteer their services for that purpose. But from the significant allusion of some persons in whom I had confidence, together with the knowledge I had of the spirit of those times, I had no doubt but that a sufficient number of associates would accompany me in that enterprise.

The tea destroyed was contained in three ships, laying near each other, at what was called at that time Griffin's wharf, and were surrounded by armed ships of war; the commanders of which had publicly declared, that if the rebels, as they were pleased to style the Bostonians, should not withdraw their opposition to the landing of the tea before a certain day, the 17th day of December, 1773, they should on that day force it on shore, under the cover of their cannon's mouth. On the day preceding the seventeenth, there was a meeting of the citizens of the county of Suffolk, convened at one of the churches in Boston, for the purpose of consulting on what measures might be considered expedient to prevent the landing of the tea, or secure the people from the collection of the duty. At that meeting a committee was appointed to wait on Governor Hutchinson, and request him to inform them whether he would take any measures to satisfy the people on the object of the meeting. To the first application of this committee, the governor told them he would give them a definite answer by five o'clock in the afternoon. At the hour appointed, the committee again repaired to the governor's house, and on inquiry found he had gone to his country seat at Milton, a distance of about six miles. When the committee returned and informed the meeting of the absence of the governor, there was a confused murmur among the members, and the meeting was immediately dissolved, many of them crying out, Let every man do his duty, and be true to his country; and there was a general huzza for Griffin's wharf. It was now evening, and I immediately dressed myself in the costume of an Indian, equipped with a small hatchet, which I and my associates denominated the tomahawk, with which, and a club, after having painted my face and hands with coal dust in the shop of a blacksmith, I repaired to Griffin's wharf, where the ships lay that contained the tea. When I first appeared in the street, after being thus disguised, I fell in with many who were dressed, equipped and painted as I was, and who fell in with me, and marched in order to the place of our destination. When we arrived at the wharf, there were three of our number who assumed an authority to direct our operations, to which we readily submitted. They divided us into three parties, for the purpose of boarding the three ships which contained the tea at the same time. The name of him who commanded the division to which I was assigned, was Leonard Pitt. The names of the other commanders I never knew. We were immediately ordered by the respective commanders to board all the ships at the same time, which we promptly obeyed. The commander of the division to which I belonged, as soon as we were on board the ship, appointed me boatswain, and ordered me to go to the captain and demand of him the keys to the hatches and a dozen candles. I made the demand accordingly, and the captain promptly replied, and delivered the articles; but requested me at the same time to do no damage to the ship or rigging. We then were ordered by our commander to open the hatches, and take out all the chests of tea and throw them overboard, and we immediately proceeded to execute his orders; first cutting and splitting the chests with our tomahawks, so as thoroughly to expose them to the effects of the water. In about three hours from the time we went on board, we had thus broken and thrown overboard every tea chest to be found in the ship; while those in the other ships were disposing of the tea in the same way, at the same time. We were surrounded by British armed ships, but no attempt was made to resist us. We then quietly retired to our several places of residence, without having any conversation with each other, or taking any measures to discover who were our associates; nor do I recollect of our having had the knowledge of the name of a single individual concerned in that affair, except that of Leonard Pitt, the commander of my division, who I have mentioned. There appeared to be an understanding that each individual should volunteer his services, keep his own secret, and risk the consequences for himself. No disorder took place during that transaction, and it was observed at that time, that the stillest night ensued that Boston had enjoyed for many months.

During the time we were throwing the tea overboard, there were several attempts made by some of the citizens of Boston and its vicinity, to carry off small quantities of it for their family use. To effect that object, they would watch their opportunity to snatch up a handful from the deck, where it became plentifully scattered, and put it into their pockets. One Captain O'Conner, whom I well knew, came on board for that purpose, and when he supposed he was not noticed, filled his pockets, and also the lining of his coat. But I had detected him, and gave information to the captain of what he was doing. We were ordered to take him into custody, and just as he was stepping from the vessel, I seized him by the skirt of his coat, and in attempting to pull him back, I tore it off; but springing forward, by a rapid effort, he made his escape. He had however to run a gauntlet through the crowd upon the wharf; each one, as he passed, giving him a kick or a stroke.

The next day we nailed the skirt of his coat, which I had pulled off, to the whipping post in Charlestown, the place of his residence, with a label upon it, commemorative of the occasion which had thus subjected the proprietor to the popular indignation.

Another attempt was made to save a little tea from the ruins of the cargo, by a tall aged man, who wore a large cocked hat and white wig, which was fashionable at that time. He had slightly slipped a little into his pocket, but being detected, they seized him, and taking his hat and wig from his head, threw them, together with the tea, of which they had emptied his pockets, into the water. In consideration of his advanced age, he was permitted to escape, with now and then a slight kick.

The next morning, after we had cleared the ships of the tea, it was discovered that very considerable quantities of it was floating upon the surface of the water; and to prevent the possibility of any of its being saved for use, a number of small boats were manned by sailors and citizens, who rowed them into those parts of the harbour wherever the tea was visible, and by beating it with oars and paddles, so thoroughly drenched it, as to render its entire destruction inevitable.

# 15 English Cartoonists View the American Revolution

*The English cartoon, or satirical print, was a major form of political commentary in the era of the American Revolution. Then as now, cartoonists scored their highest points with the public by attacking the administration in power, so the English cartoons of the era are surprisingly in agreement with the Americans. They often identify the American cause with English opposition to ministerial corruption, high taxes, and restrictions on political freedom in the mother country. In short, they reflect the same "Republican" tradition that dominated the colonial pamphleteers. Not surprisingly, they were often copied by people on both sides of the Atlantic.*

*Plate I, "The Minister in Surprize"—probably from 1768—satirizes the British government's "surprize" at colonial resistance to the Townshend taxes on glass, paper, painter's lead, and tea.*

*Plate II, "The Fruits of Arbitrary Power; or the Bloody Massacre, Perpetrated in King–street, Boston, by a Party of the XXIXth Regt.," is one of many versions of a celebrated print by Paul Revere depicting the "Boston Massacre" of March 5, 1770. The print was sold separately and also used as the frontispiece of a pamphlet.*

*Plate III, "The able Doctor, or, America Swallowing the Bitter Draught," was published in London in April 1774 and quickly copied in Boston by Paul Revere. It comments on the Boston Port Bill and the imposition of "Military Law" (inscribed on the sword, far right) by means of the figure of Lord North pouring tea down the throat of a hapless symbol of America while England's traditional enemies, France and Spain (far left), look on with great interest.*

*Plate IV, "The Contrast" (date uncertain), calls for conciliation on the part of the British by admonishing the government not to drain the cow (that is, the colonies) of blood, as on the left, but to milk it gently, as on the right.*

*Plate V, "The American Rattlesnake," dated April 12, 1782, has this once common emblem of the Americans encircling British Major General John Burgoyne's army at Saratoga, New York, in 1777 and Lord Cornwallis's at Yorktown in 1781 while preparing "An Apartment" for any further troops the British send. The serpent is saying:*

> *Two British armies I have thus Burgoyne'd*
> *And room for more I've got behind.*

The american Resolves are a Devil of a Dose
New Members
Civil List in Arrears
American Constitution
List of Pensioners
The Minister in Surprize.

*Plate I*

Plate II

Library of Congress

Plate III Library of Congress

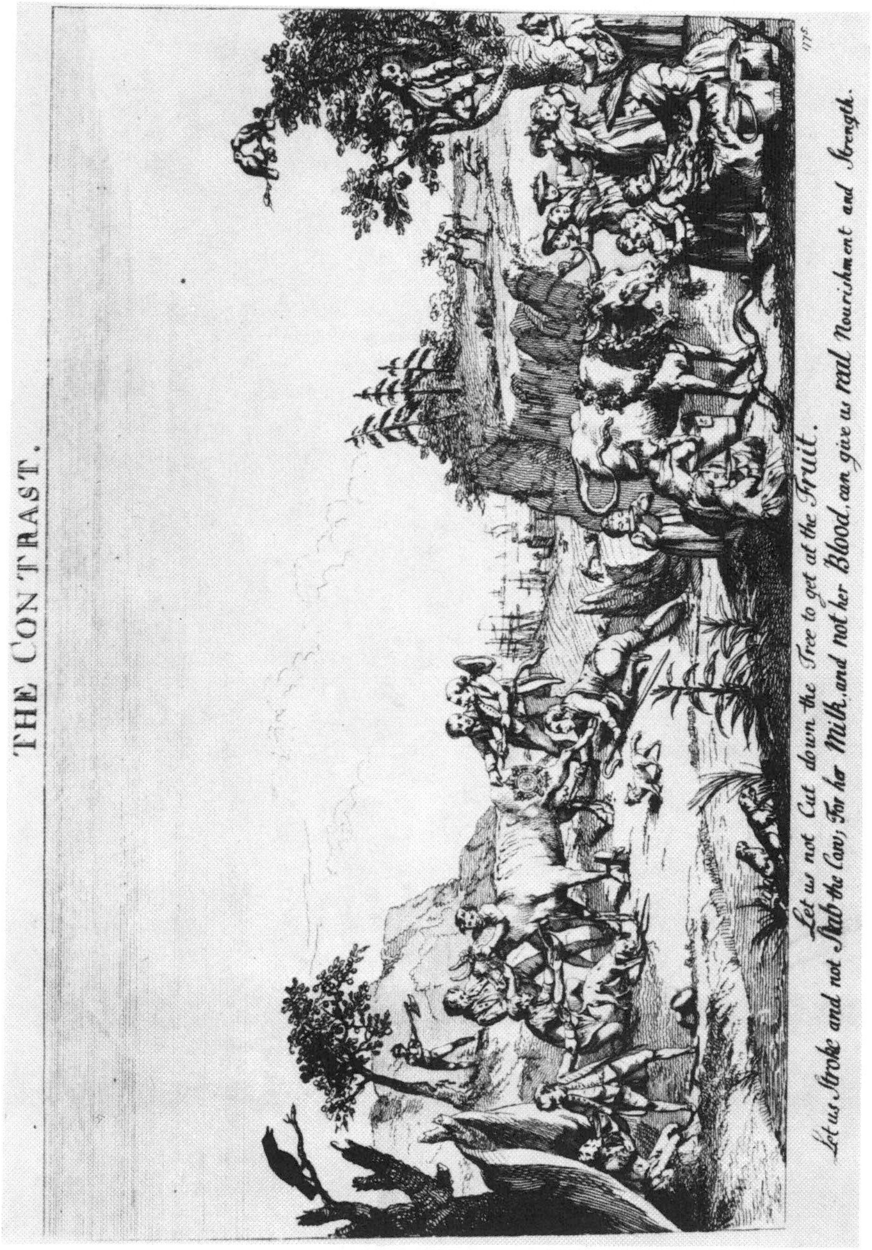

THE CONTRAST.

Let us not Cut down the Tree to get at the Fruit.
Let us Stroke and not Stab the Cow; For her Milk, and not her Blood, can give us real Nourishment and Strength.

1775.

*Plate IV*

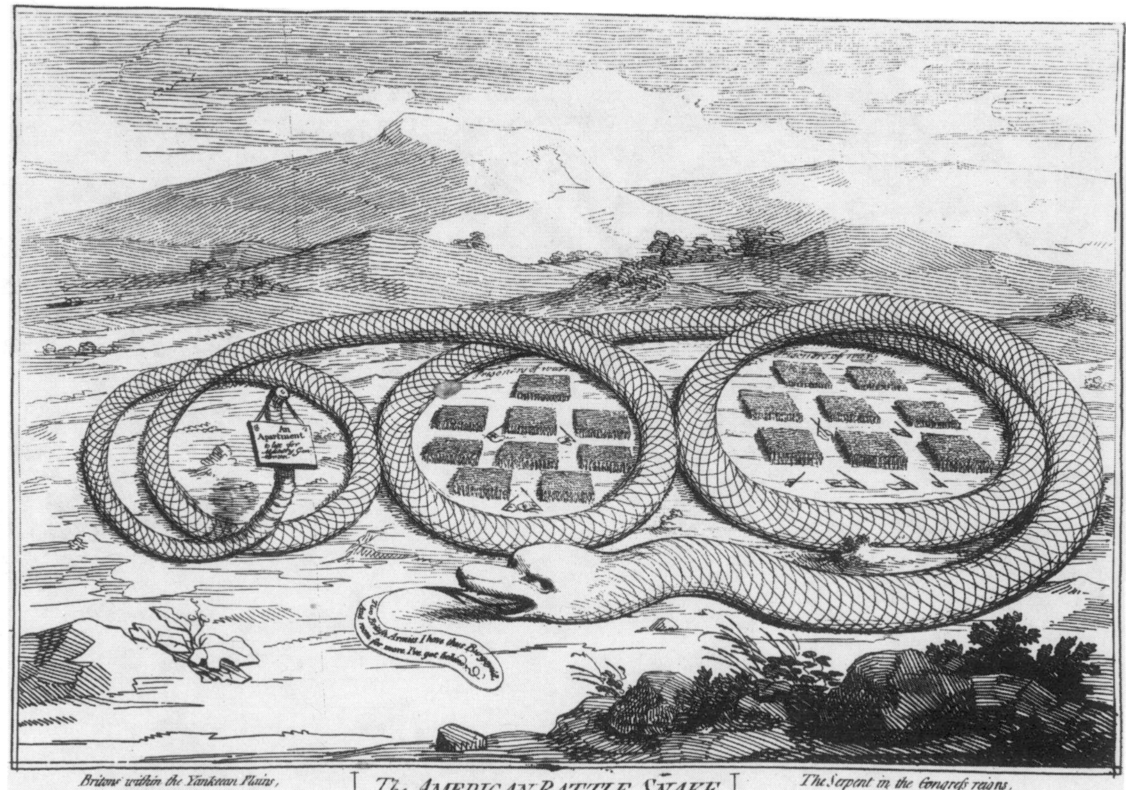


Plate V

Library of Congress

THOMAS PAINE

# 16 *On the Colonial Army's Retreat from New York*

*Thomas Paine (1737–1809) was an international revolutionary who saw the American Revolution as the beginning of an era of democratic revolutions. Born in England, he came to America in 1774. An incomparable publicist, he wrote pamphlets that rallied American public opinion around the patriot cause and articulated an emerging ideology of republicanism that contributed greatly to the willingness to rebel against a king. His widely circulated pamphlet* Common Sense, *published in January 1776, helped prepare American opinion for independence. The first "issue" of* The Crisis*—excerpted below—appeared in late December of 1776 when the patriot army was in retreat from the battle of New York. Fifteen more such pamphlets contributed to the revolutionary cause throughout the lengthy war. Later, Paine returned to England and supported the French Revolution. During that upheaval he was imprisoned in France for a year. Tainted by his support for a violent revolution, Paine died in poverty in the United States, rejected in the very country whose birth he had helped to oversee.*

These are the times that try men's souls. The summer soldier and the sunshine patriot will, in this crisis, shrink from the service of their country; but he that stands it now, deserves the love and thanks of man and woman. Tyranny, like hell, is not easily conquered; yet we have this consolation with us, that the harder the conflict, the more glorious the triumph. What we obtain too cheap, we esteem too lightly: it is dearness only that gives everything its value. Heaven knows how to put a proper price upon its goods; and it would be strange indeed if so celestial an article as FREEDOM should not be highly rated. Britain, with an army to enforce her tyranny, has declared that she has a right (*not only to* TAX) but "*to* BIND *us in* ALL CASES WHATSOEVER," and if being *bound in that manner,* is not slavery, then is there not such a thing as slavery upon earth. Even the expression is impious; for so unlimited a power can belong only to God.

Whether the independence of the continent was declared too soon, or delayed too long, I will not now enter into as an argument; my own simple opinion is, that had it been eight months earlier, it would have been much better. We did not make a proper use of last winter, neither could we, while we were in a dependant state. However, the fault, if it were one, was all our own; we have none to blame but ourselves. But no great deal is lost yet. All that [British General] Howe has been doing for this month past, is rather a ravage than a conquest, which the spirit of the Jerseys, a year ago, would have quickly repulsed, and which time and a little resolution will soon recover.

I have as little superstition in me as any man living, but my secret opinion has ever been, and still is, that God Almighty will not give up a people to military destruction, or leave them unsupportedly to perish, who have so earnestly and so repeatedly sought to avoid the calamities of war, by every decent method which wisdom could invent. Neither have I so much of the infidel in me, as to suppose that He has relinquished the government of the world, and given us up to the care of devils; and as I do not, I cannot see on what grounds the king of Britain can look up to heaven for help against us: a common murderer, a highwayman, or a house-breaker, has as good a pretence as he.

'Tis surprising to see how rapidly a panic will sometimes run through a country. All nations and ages have been subject to them: Britain has trembled like an ague at the report of a French fleet of flat bottomed boats; and in the fourteenth [fifteenth] century the whole English army, after ravaging the kingdom of France, was driven back like men petrified with fear; and this brave exploit was performed by a few broken forces collected and headed by a woman, Joan of Arc. Would that heaven might inspire some Jersey maid to spirit up her countrymen, and save her fair fellow sufferers from ravage and ravishment! Yet panics, in some cases, have their uses; they produce as much good as hurt. Their duration is always short; the mind soon grows through them, and acquires a firmer habit than before. But their peculiar advantage is, that they are the touchstones of sincerity and hypocrisy, and bring things and men to light, which might otherwise have lain forever undiscovered. In fact, they have the same effect on secret traitors, which an imaginary apparition would have upon a private murderer. They sift out the hidden thoughts of man, and hold them up in public to the world. Many a disguised tory has lately shown his head, that shall penitentially solemnize with curses the day on which Howe arrived upon the Delaware.

As I was with the troops at Fort Lee, and marched with them to the edge of Pennsylvania, I am well acquainted with many circumstances, which those who live at a distance know but little or nothing of. Our situation there was exceedingly cramped, the place being a narrow neck of land between the North River and the Hackensack. Our force was inconsiderable, being not one fourth so great as Howe could bring against us. We had no army at hand to have relieved the garrison, had we shut ourselves up and stood on our defence. Our ammunition, light artillery, and the best part of our stores, had been removed, on the apprehension that Howe would endeavor to penetrate the Jerseys, in which case Fort

Lee could be of no use to us; for it must occur to every thinking man, whether in the army or not, that these kind of field forts are only for temporary purposes, and last in use no longer than the enemy directs his force against the particular object, which such forts are raised to defend. Such was our situation and condition at Fort Lee on the morning of the 20th of November, when an officer arrived with information that the enemy with 200 boats had landed about seven miles above: Major General [Nathaniel] Green, who commanded the garrison, immediately ordered them under arms, and sent express to General Washington at the town of Hackensack, distant by the way of the ferry, six miles. Our first object was to secure the bridge over the Hackensack, which laid up the river between the enemy and us, about six miles from us, and three from them. General Washington arrived in about three quarters of an hour, and marched at the head of the troops towards the bridge, which place I expected we should have a brush for; however, they did not choose to dispute it with us, and the greatest part of our troops went over the bridge, the rest over the ferry, except some which passed at a mill on a small creek, between the bridge and the ferry, and made their way through some marshy grounds up to the town of Hackensack, and there passed the river. We brought off as much baggage as the wagons could contain, the rest was lost. The simple object was to bring off the garrison, and march them on till they could be strengthened by the Jersey or Pennsylvania militia, so as to be enabled to make a stand. We staid four days at Newark, collected our out-posts with some of the Jersey militia, and marched out twice to meet the enemy, on being informed that they were advancing, though our numbers were greatly inferior to theirs. Howe, in my little opinion, committed a great error in generalship in not throwing a body of forces off from Staten Island through Amboy, by which means he might have seized all our stores at Brunswick, and intercepted our march into Pennsylvania; but if we believe the power of hell to be limited, we must likewise believe that their agents are under some providential controul.

I shall not now attempt to give all the particulars of our retreat to the Delaware; suffice it for the present to say, that both officers and men, though greatly harassed and fatigued, frequently without rest, covering, or provision, the inevitable consequences of a long retreat, bore it with a manly and martial spirit. All their wishes centred in one, which was, that the country would turn out and help them to drive the enemy back. Voltaire has remarked that King William never appeared to full advantage but in difficulties and in action; the same remark may be made on General Washington, for the character fits him. There is a natural firmness in some minds which cannot be unlocked by trifles, but which, when unlocked, discovers a cabinet of fortitude; and I reckon it among those kind of public blessings, which we do not immediately see, that God hath blessed him with uninterrupted health, and given him a mind that can even flourish upon care.

I shall conclude this paper with some miscellaneous remarks on the state of our affairs; and shall begin with asking the following question, Why is it that the enemy have left the New-England provinces, and made these middle ones the seat of war? The answer is easy: New-England is not infested with tories, and we are. I have been tender in raising the cry against these men, and used numberless arguments to show them their danger, but it will not do to sacrifice a word either to their folly or their baseness. The period is now arrived, in which either they or we must change our sentiments, or one or both must fall. And what is a tory? Good god! what is he? I should not be afraid to go with a hundred whigs against a thousand tories, were they to attempt to get into arms. Every tory is a coward; for servile, slavish, self-interested fear is the foundation of toryism; and a man under such influence, though he may be cruel, never can be brave.

But, before the line of irrecoverable separation be drawn between us, let us reason the matter together: Your conduct is an invitation to the enemy, yet not one in a thousand of you has heart enough to join him. Howe is as much deceived by you as the American cause is injured by you. He expects you will all take up arms, and flock to his standard, with muskets on your shoulders. Your opinions are of no use to him, unless you support him personally, for 'tis soldiers, and not tories, that he wants.

I once felt all that kind of anger, which a man ought to feel, against the mean principles that are held by the tories: a noted one, who kept a tavern at Amboy, was standing at his door, with as pretty a child in his hand, about eight or nine years old, as I ever saw, and after speaking his mind as freely as he thought was prudent, finished with this unfatherly expression, *"Well! give me peace in my day."* Not a man lives on the continent but fully believes that a separation must some time or other finally take place, and a generous parent should have said, *"If there must be trouble, let it be in my day, that my child may have peace,"* and this single reflection, well applied, is sufficient to awaken every man to duty. Not a place upon earth might be so happy as America. Her situation is remote from all the wrangling world, and she has nothing to do but to trade with them. A man can distinguish himself between temper and principle, and I am confident, as I am that God governs the world, that America will never be happy till she gets clear of foreign dominion. Wars, without ceasing, will break out till that period arrives, and the continent must in the end be conqueror; for though the flame of liberty may sometimes cease to shine, the coal can never expire.

America did not, nor does not want force; but she wanted a proper application of that force. Wisdom is not the purchase of a day, and it is no wonder that we should err at the first setting off. From an excess of tenderness, we were unwilling to raise an army, and trusted our cause to the temporary defence of a well-meaning militia. A summer's experience has now taught us better; yet with those troops, while they were collected, we were able to set bounds to the progress of the enemy, and, thank God! they are again assembling. I always considered militia as the best troops in the world for a sudden exertion, but they will not do for a long campaign. Howe, it is probable, will make an attempt on this city; should he fail on this side the Delaware, he is ruined: if he succeeds, our cause is not ruined. He stakes all on his side against a part on ours; admitting he succeeds, the consequence will be, that armies from both ends of the continent will march to assist their suffering friends in the middle states; for he cannot go everywhere, it is impossible. I consider Howe as the greatest enemy the tories have; he is bringing a war into their country, which, had it not been for him and partly for themselves, they had been clear of. Should he now be expelled, I wish with all the devotion of a Christian, that the names of whig and tory may never more be mentioned; but should the tories give him encouragement to come, or assistance if he come, I as sincerely wish that our next year's arms may expel them from the continent, and the congress appropriate their possessions to the relief of those who have suffered in well-doing. A single successful battle next year will settle the whole. America could carry on a two years war by the confiscation of the property of disaffected persons, and be made happy by their expulsion. Say not that this is revenge, call it rather the soft resentment of a suffering people, who, having no object in view but the *good of all*, have staked their *own all* upon a seemingly doubtful event. Yet it is folly to argue against determined hardness; eloquence may strike the ear, and the language of sorrow draw forth the tear of compassion, but nothing can reach the heart that is steeled with prejudice.

Quitting this class of men, I turn with the warm ardor of a friend to those who have nobly stood, and are yet determined to stand the matter out: I call not upon a few, but upon all: not on *this* state or *that* state, but on *every* state: up and help us; lay your shoulder to the wheel; better have too much force than too little, when so great an object is at stake. Let it be told to the future world, that in the depth of winter, when nothing but hope and virtue could survive, that the city and the country, alarmed at one common danger, came forth to meet and to repulse it. Say not that thousands are gone, turn out your tens of thousands; throw not the burden of the day upon Providence, but *"show your faith by your works,"* that God may bless you. It matters not where you live, or what rank of life you hold, the evil or the blessing will reach you all. The far and the near, the home counties and back, the rich and the poor, will suffer or rejoice alike. The heart that feels not now, is dead: the blood of his children will curse his cowardice, who shrinks back at a time when a little might have saved the whole, and made *them* happy. I love the man that can smile in trouble, that can gather strength from distress, and grow brave by reflection. 'Tis the business of little minds to shrink; but he whose heart is firm, and whose conscience approves his conduct, will pursue his principles unto death.

My own line of reasoning is to myself as straight and clear as a ray of light. Not all the treasures of the world, so far as I believe, could have induced me to support an offensive war, for I think it murder; but if a thief breaks into my house, burns and destroys my property, and kills or threatens to kill me, or those that are in it, and to *"bind me in all cases whatsoever"* to his absolute will, am I to suffer it? What signifies it to me, whether he who does it is a king or a common man; my countryman or not my countryman; whether it be done by an individual villain, or an army of them? If we reason to the root of things we shall find no difference; neither can any just cause be assigned why we should punish in the one case and pardon in other. Let them call me rebel, and welcome, I feel no concern from it; but I should suffer the misery of devils, were I to make a whore of my soul by swearing allegiance to one whose character is that of a sottish, stupid, stubborn, worthless, brutish man. I conceive likewise a horrid idea in receiving mercy from a being, who at the last day shall be shrieking to the rocks and mountains to cover him, and fleeing with terror from the orphan, the widow, and the slain of America.

There are cases which cannot be overdone by language, and this is one. There are persons, too, who see not the full extent of the evil which threatens them; they solace themselves with hopes that the enemy, if he succeed, will be merciful. It is the madness of folly, to expect mercy from those who have refused to do justice; and even mercy, where conquest is the object, is only a trick of war; the cunning of the fox is as murderous as the violence of the world, and we ought to guard equally against both. Howe's first object is, partly by threats and partly by promises, to terrify or seduce the people to deliver up their arms and receive mercy. The ministry recommended the same plan to Gage, and this is what the tories call making their peace, *"a peace which passeth all understanding" indeed!* A peace which would be the immediate forerunner of a worse ruin than any we have yet thought of. Ye men of Pennsylvania, do reason upon these things! Were the back counties to give up their arms, they would fall an easy prey to the Indians, who are all armed: this perhaps is what some tories would not be sorry for. Were the home counties to deliver up their arms, they would be exposed to the resentment of the back counties, who would then have it in their power to chastise their defection at pleasure. And were any one state to give up its arms, *that* state must be garrisoned by all Howe's army of Britons and Hessians to preserve it from the anger of the rest. Mutual fear is the principal link in the chain of mutual love, and woe be to that state that breaks the compact. Howe is mercifully inviting you to barbarous destruction, and men must be either rogues or fools that will not see it. I dwell not upon the vapours of imagination: I bring reason to your ears, and, in language as plan as A, B, C, hold up truth to your eyes.

I thank God, that I fear not. I see no real cause for fear. I know our situation well, and can see the way out of it. While our army was collected, Howe dared not risk a battle; and it is no credit to him that he decamped from the White Plains, and waited a mean opportunity to ravage the defenceless Jerseys; but it is great credit to us, that, with a handful of men, we sustained an orderly retreat for near an hundred miles, brought off our ammunition, all our field pieces, the greatest part of our stores, and had four rivers to pass. None can say that our retreat was precipitate, for we were near three weeks in performing it, that the country might have time to come in. Twice we marched back to meet the enemy, and remained out till dark. The sign of fear was not seen in our camp, and had not some of the cowardly and disaffected inhabitants spread false alarms through the country, the Jerseys had never been ravaged. Once more we are again collected and collecting; our new army at both ends of the continent is recruiting fast, and we shall be able to open the next campaign with sixty thousand men, well armed and clothed. This is our situation, and who will may know it. By perseverance and fortitude we have the prospect of a glorious issue; by cowardice and submission, the sad choice of a variety of evils—a ravaged country—a depopulated city—habitations without safety, and slavery without hope—our homes turned into barracks and bawdy-houses for Hessians, and a future race to provide for, whose fathers we shall doubt of. Look on this picture and weep over it! and if there yet remains one thoughtless wretch who believes it not, let him suffer it unlamented.

# *JOSEPH PLUMB MARTIN*

# 17 *A Soldier's View of Victory at Yorktown*

*Joseph Plumb Martin wrote one of the liveliest and most engaging of soldier memoirs,* A Narrative of Some of the Adventures, Dangers and Sufferings of a Revolutionary Soldier, *published in Maine in 1830. Martin's is a good-humored, unvarnished picture of a common soldier, whose major concern is often his next meal or keeping warm through a cold night outdoors.*

*Joseph Martin was born in western Massachusetts in 1760 and became a soldier in the Revolution before his sixteenth birthday. After serving with Connecticut state troops in 1776, he enlisted as a regular in the Continental Army in April 1777 and persevered until the army was demobilized in 1783. During this period he fought with the Light Infantry as well as in the Corps of Sappers and Miners, who built fortifications and dug trenches. Martin's long-suffering loyalty to the Patriot cause and his account of how poorly the soldiers were supported through their years of hardship present a fundamental, realistic view of the Revolutionary War.*

The first of August, I think it was the 1st day of that month, we all of a sudden marched from this ground and directed our course toward King's Ferry near the Highlands, crossed the Hudson, and lay there a few days till the baggage, artillery, &c. had crossed, and then proceeded into New Jersey. We went down to Chatham, where were ovens built for the accommodation of the French troops. We then expected we were to attack New York in that quarter, but after staying here a day or two we again moved off and arrived at Trenton by rapid marches.

It was about sunset when we arrived here and instead of encamping for the night, as we expected, we were ordered immediately on board vessels then lying at the landing place, and a little after sunrise found ourselves at Philadelphia. We, that is the Sappers and Miners, stayed here some days, proving and packing off shells, shot, and other military stores. While we stayed here we drew a few articles of clothing, consisting of a few tow shirts, some overalls and a few pairs of silk-and-oakum stockings. And here or soon after, we each of us received a MONTH'S PAY in specie, borrowed as I was informed by our French officers from the officers in the French army. This was the first that could be called money, which we had received as wages since the year '76, or that we ever did receive till the close of the war, or indeed ever after as wages.

When we had finished our business at Philadelphia, we (the Miners) left the city. A part of our men with myself went down the Delaware in a schooner which had her hold nearly full of gunpowder. We passed Mud Island, where I had experienced such hardships in Nov. '77. It had quite a different appearance to what it had then, much like a fine, fair, warm, and sunny day succeeding a cold, dark, stormy night. Just after passing Mud Island in the afternoon, we had a smart thundershower; I did not feel very agreeably, I confess, during its continuance, with such a quantity of powder under my feet. I was not quite sure that a stroke of the electric fluid might not compel me to leave the vessel sooner than I wished; but no accident happened, and we proceeded down the river to the mouth of Christiana [Christina] Creek, up which we were bound.

We were compelled to anchor here on account of wind and tide. Here we passed an uneasy night from fear of British cruisers, several of which were in the bay. In the morning we got under weigh [way], the wind serving, and proceeded up the creek 14 miles, the creek passing the most of its course through a marsh as crooked as a snake in motion. . . . We went on till the vessel grounded for lack of water. We then lightened her by taking out a part of her cargo, and when the tide came in we got up to the wharves and left her at the disposal of the artillerists.

We then crossed over land to the head of the Elk, or the head, or rather bottom, of Chesapeake Bay. Here we found a *large* fleet of *small* vessels waiting to convey us and other troops, stores, &c. down the bay. We soon embarked, that is such of us as went by water, the greater part of the army having gone on by land. I was in a small schooner called the *Birmingham*. There was but a small number of our corps of Sappers and Miners in this vessel, with a few artillerists, 6 or 8 officers, and a commissary who had a small quantity of stores on board, among which was a hogshead containing 20 or 30 gallons of rum. To prevent the men from getting more than their share of the liquor, the officers (who loved a little of the "good creature" as well as the men) had the bulkhead between the hold and the cabin taken down and placed the hogshead in the cabin, carefully nailing up the partition again, when they thought that they had the exclusive disposal of the precious treasure. But the soldiers were as wily as they, for the very first night after the officers had snugly secured it, as they thought, the head of the cask being crowded against the bulkhead, the soldiers contrived to loosen one of the boards at the lower end, so as to swing it aside, and broached the hogshead on the other head, so that while the officers in the cabin thought they were the sole possessors of its contents, the soldiers in the hold had possession of at least as good a share as themselves.

We passed down the bay making a grand appearance with our mosquito fleet to Annapolis (which I had left about five months before for West Point). Here we stopped, fearing to proceed any further at present, not knowing exactly how matters were going on down the bay. A French cutter was dispatched to procure intelligence. She returned in the course of three or four days, bringing word that the passage was clear; we then proceeded and soon arrived at the mouth of the James River, where were a number of armed French vessels and two or three 50-gun ships. We passed in sight of the French fleet, then lying in Lynnhaven Bay; they resembled a swamp of dry pine trees. We had passed several of their men-of-war higher up the bay.

We were obliged to stay here a day or two on account of a severe northeast rainstorm. . . . After the storm had ceased, we proceeded up the [James] river to a place called Burwell's Ferry, where the fleet all anchored. . . . Soon after landing we marched to Williamsburg, where we joined General Lafayette, and very soon after, our whole army arriving, we prepared to move down and pay our old acquaintance, the British at Yorktown, a visit. I doubt not but their wish was not to have so many of us come at once, as their accommodations were rather scanty. They thought, "The fewer the better cheer." We thought, "The more the merrier." We had come a long way to see them and were unwilling to be put off with excuses; we thought the present time quite as convenient (at least for us) as any future time could be, and we accordingly persisted, hoping that, as they pretended to be a very courtly people, they would have the politeness to come out and meet us, which would greatly shorten the time to be spent in the visit, and save themselves and us much labor and trouble; but they were too impolite at this time to do so.

We marched from Williamsburg the last of September. It was a warm day; when we had proceeded about halfway to Yorktown we halted and rested two or three hours. Being about to cook some victuals, I saw a fire which some of the Pennsylvania troops had kindled a short distance off. I went to get some fire while some of my messmates made other preparations. . . . I had taken off my coat and unbuttoned my waistcoat, it being (as I said before) very warm; my pocketbook containing about five dollars in money and some other articles, in all about seven dollars, was in my waistcoat pocket. When I came among the strangers, they appeared to be uncommonly complaisant, asking many questions, helping me to fire, and chatting very familiarly. I took my fire and returned, but it was not long before I perceived that those kindhearted helpers had helped themselves to my pocketbook and its whole contents. I felt mortally chagrined, but there was no plaster for my sore but patience, and my plaster of that at this time, I am sure, was very small and very thinly spread, for it never covered the wound.

Here, or about this time, we had orders from the Commander in Chief that, in case the enemy should come out to meet us, we should exchange but one round with them and then decide the conflict with the bayonet, as they valued themselves at that instrument. The French forces could play their part at it, and the Americans were never backward at trying its virtue. The British, however, did not think fit at that time to give us an opportunity to soil our bayonets in their carcasses, but why they did not we could never conjecture; we as much expected it as we expected to find them there.

We went on and soon arrived and encamped in their neighborhood, without . . . molestation. Our Miners lay about a mile and a half from their works in open view of them. Here again we encountered our old associate, hunger. Affairs, as they respected provisions, &c. were not yet regulated. No eatable stores had arrived, nor could we expect they should until we knew what reception the enemy would give us. We were, therefore, compelled to try our hands at foraging again. We, that is, our corps of Miners, were encamped near a large wood. There was a plenty of shoats [young hogs] all about this wood, fat and plump, weighing generally from 50 to 100 pounds apiece. We soon found some of them, and as no owner appeared to be at hand and the hogs not understanding our inquiries (if we made any) sufficiently to inform us to whom they belonged, we made free with some of them to satisfy the calls of nature till we could be better supplied, if better we could be. Our officers countenanced us and that was all the permission we wanted; and many of us did not want even that.

We now began to make preparations for laying close siege to the enemy. We had holed him, and nothing remained but to dig him out. Accordingly, after taking every precaution to prevent his escape, [we] settled our guards, provided fascines and gabions, made platforms for the batteries to be laid down when needed, brought on our battering pieces, ammunition, &c; on the 5th of October we began to put our plans into execution.

One-third part of all the troops were put in requisition to be employed in opening the trenches. A third part of our Sappers and Miners were ordered out this night to assist the engineers in laying out the works. It was a very dark and rainy night. However, we repaired to the place and began by following the engineers and laying laths [narrow strips] of pine wood end-to-end upon the line marked out by the officers for the trenches. We had not proceeded far in the business before the engineers ordered us to desist and remain where we were, and be sure not to straggle a foot from the spot while they were absent from us. In a few minutes after their departure, there came a man alone to us having on a surtout [long overcoat], as we conjectured (it being exceeding dark), and inquired for the engineers. We now began to be a little jealous for our safety, being alone and without arms, and within 40 rods of the British trenches. The stranger inquired what troops we were, talked familiarly with us a few minutes, when being informed which way the officers had gone, he went off in the same direction, after strictly charging us, in case we should be taken prisoners, not to discover to the enemy what troops we were. We were obliged to him for his kind advice, but we considered ourselves as standing in no great need of it; for we knew as well as he did that Sappers and Miners were allowed no quarters, at least are entitled to none by the laws of warfare, and of course should take care, if taken and the enemy did not find us out, not to betray our own secret.

In a short time the engineers returned and the afore-mentioned stranger with them. They discoursed together some time when, by the officers often calling him "Your Excellency," we discovered that it was General Washington. Had we dared, we might have cautioned him for exposing himself too carelessly to danger at such a time, and doubtless he would have taken it in good part if we had. But nothing ill happened to either him or ourselves.

It coming on to rain hard, we were ordered back to our tents, and nothing more was done that night. The next night, which was the 6th of October, the same men were ordered to the lines that had been there the night before. We this night completed laying out the works. The troops of the line were there ready with entrenching tools and began to entrench after General Washington had struck a few blows with a pickax, a mere ceremony that it might be said "General Washington with his own hands first broke ground at the siege of Yorktown." The ground was sandy and soft, and the men employed that night ate no "idle bread" (and I question if they ate any other), so that by daylight they had covered themselves from danger from the enemy's shot, who it appeared never mistrusted that we were so near them the whole night, their attention being directed to another quarter. There was upon the right of their works a marsh; our people had sent to the western side of this marsh a detachment to make a number of fires, by which, and our men often passing before the fires, the British were led to imagine that we were about some secret mischief there, and consequently directed their whole fire to that quarter, while we were entrenching literally under their noses.

As soon as it was day they perceived their mistake and began to fire where they ought to have done sooner. They brought out a fieldpiece or two without their trenches, and discharged several shots at the men who were at work erecting a bomb battery; but their shot had no effect, and they soon gave it over. . . .

I do not remember exactly the number of days we were employed before we got our batteries in readiness to open upon the enemy, but think it was not more than two or three. The French, who were upon our left, had completed their batteries a few hours before us, but were not allowed to discharge their pieces till the American batteries were ready. Our commanding battery was on the near bank of the [York] river and contained 10 heavy guns; the next was a bomb battery of three large mortars; and so on through the whole line. The whole number, American and French, was 92 cannon, mortars and howitzers. Our flagstaff was in the 10-gun battery upon the right of the whole. I was in the trenches the day that the batteries were to be opened. All were upon the tiptoe of expectation and impatience to see the signal given to open the whole line of batteries, which was to be the hoisting of the American flag in the 10-gun battery.

About noon the much-wished-for signal went up. I confess I felt a secret pride swell my heart when I saw the "star-spangled banner" waving majestically in the very faces of our implacable adversaries; it appeared like an omen of success to our enterprise, and so it proved in reality. A simultaneous discharge of all the guns in the line followed, the French troops accompanying it with "Huzza for the Americans!" It was said that the first shell sent from our batteries entered an elegant house formerly owned or occupied by the Secretary of State under the British government, and burned directly over a table surrounded by a large party of British officers at dinner, killing and wounding a number of them. This was a warm day to the British.

The siege was carried on warmly for several days, when most of the guns in the enemy's works were silenced. We now began our second parallel, about halfway between our works and theirs. There were two strong redoubts held by the British on their left. It was necessary for us to possess those redoubts before we could complete our trenches. One afternoon, I, with the rest of our corps that had been on duty in the trenches the night but one before, were ordered to the lines. I mistrusted something extraordinary, serious, or comical was going forward, but what I could not easily conjecture.

We arrived at the trenches a little before sunset. I saw several officers fixing bayonets on long staves. I then concluded we were about to make a general assault upon the enemy's works, but before dark I was informed of the whole plan, which was to storm the redoubts, the one by the Americans and the other by the French. The Sappers and Miners were furnished with axes and were to proceed in front and cut a passage for the troops through the abatis, which are composed of the tops of trees, the small branches cut off with a slanting stroke which renders them as sharp as spikes. These trees are then laid at a small distance from the trench or ditch, pointing outwards, and the butts fastened to the ground in such a manner that they cannot be removed by those on the outside of them; it is almost impossible to get through them. Through these we were to cut a passage before we or the other assailants could enter.

At dark the detachment was formed and advanced beyond the trenches and lay down on the ground to await the signal for advancing to the attack, which was to be three shells from a certain battery near where we were lying. All the batteries in our line were silent, and we lay anxiously waiting for the signal. The two brilliant planets, Jupiter and Venus, were in close contact in the western hemisphere (the same direction that the signal was to be made in). When I happened to cast my eyes to that quarter, which was often, and I caught a glance of them, I was ready to spring on my feet, thinking they were the signal for starting. Our watchword was "Rochambeau," the commander of the French forces' name, a good watchword, for being pronounced *Ro-sham-bow,* it sounded, when pronounced quick, like *rush-on-boys.*

We had not lain here long before the expected signal was given, for us and the French, who were to storm the other redoubt, by the three shells with their fiery trains mounting the air in quick succession. The word up, up, was then reiterated through the detachment. We immediately moved silently on toward the redoubt we were to attack with unloaded muskets. Just as we arrived at the abatis, the enemy discovered us and directly opened a sharp fire upon us. We were now at a place where many of our large shells had burst in the ground, making holes sufficient to bury an ox in; the men having their eyes fixed upon what was transacting before them, were every now and then falling into these holes. I thought the British were killing us off at a great rate. At length one of the holes happening to pick me up, I found out the mystery of the huge slaughter.

As soon as the firing began, our people began to cry, "The fort's our own!" and it was "Rush on boys." The Sappers and Miners soon cleared a passage for the infantry, who entered it rapidly. Our Miners were ordered not to enter the fort, but there was no stopping them. "We will go," said they. "Then go to the d- - -l," said the commanding officer of our corps, "if you will." I could not pass at the entrance we had made, it was so crowded; I therefore forced a passage at a place where I saw our shot had cut away some of the abatis. Several others entered at the same place.

While passing, a man at my side received a ball in his head and fell under my feet, crying out bitterly. While crossing the trench, the enemy threw hand grenades (small shells) into it; they were so thick that I at first thought them cartridge papers on fire, but was soon undeceived by their cracking. As I mounted the breastwork, I met an old associate hitching himself down into the trench. I knew him by the light of the enemy's musketry, it was so vivid. The fort was taken and all quiet in a very short time. Immediately after the firing ceased, I went out to see what had become of my wounded friend and the other that fell in the passage; they were both dead. In the heat of the action I saw a British soldier jump over the walls of the fort next the river and go down the bank, which was almost perpendicular and 20 or 30 feet high. When he came to the beach he made off for the town, and if he did not make good use of his legs I never saw a man that did.

All that were in the action of storming the redoubt were exempted from further duty that night. We laid down upon the ground and rested the remainder of the night as well as a constant discharge of grape and canister shot would permit us to do, while those who were on duty for the day completed the second parallel by including the captured redoubts within it. We returned to camp early in the morning, all safe and sound, except one of our lieutenants, who had received a slight wound on the top of the shoulder by a musket shot. Seven or eight men belonging to the infantry were killed, and a number wounded. . . .

We were on duty in the trenches 24 hours, and 48 hours in camp. The invalids did the camp duty, and we had nothing else to do but to attend morning and evening roll calls and recreate ourselves as we pleased the rest of the time, till we were called upon to take our turns on duty in the trenches again. The greatest inconvenience we felt was the want of good water, there being none near our camp but nasty frog ponds where all the horses in the neighborhood were watered, and we were forced to wade through the water in the skirts of the ponds, thick with mud and filth, to get at water in any wise fit for use, and that full of frogs. All the springs about the country, although they looked well, tasted like copperas water or like water that had been standing in iron or copper vessels.

I was one day rambling alone in the woods when I came across a small brook of very good water about a mile from our tents. We used this water daily to drink, or we should almost have suffered. But it was "the fortune of war." I was one night in the trenches, erecting a bomb battery; the enemy (it being very dark) were directed in their firing by a large tree. I was ordered by our officers to take two or three men and fell the tree with some old axes as dull as hoes; the tree was very large, and we were two hours in cutting it, although we took Solomon's advice in handling dull tools by "putting to the more strength," the British all the time urging us to exert ourselves with round and grape shot. They struck the tree a number of times while we were at it, but chanced to do us no harm at all.

In the morning, while the relieves were coming into the trenches, I was sitting on the side of the trench, when some of the New York troops coming in, one of the sergeants stepped up to the breastwork to look about him. The enemy threw a small shell which fell upon the outside of the works; the man turned his face to look at it; at that instant a shot from the enemy . . . passed just by his face without touching him at all. He fell dead into the trench. I put my hand on his forehead and found his skull was shattered all in pieces and the blood flowing from his nose and mouth, but not a particle of skin was broken. I never saw an instance like this among all the men I saw killed during the whole war.

After we had finished our second line of trenches there was but little firing on either side. After Lord Cornwallis had failed to get off, upon the 17th day of October (a rather unlucky day for the British) he requested a cessation of hostilities for, I think, 24 hours when commissioners from both armies met at a house between the lines to agree upon articles of capitulation. We waited with anxiety the termination of the armistice, and as the time drew nearer our anxiety increased. The time at length arrived; it passed, and all remained quiet. And now we concluded that we had obtained what we had taken so much pains for—for which we had encountered so many dangers and had so anxiously wished. Before night we were informed that the British had surrendered and that the siege was ended.

The next day we were ordered to put ourselves in as good order as our circumstances would admit, to see (what was the completion of our present wishes) the British army march out and stack their arms. The trenches, where they crossed the road leading to the town, were leveled and all things put in order for this grand exhibition. After breakfast on the 19th, we were marched onto the ground and paraded on the right-hand side of the road, and the French forces on the left. We waited two or three hours before the British made their appearance; they were not always so dilatory, but they were compelled at last by necessity to appear all armed, with bayonets fixed, drums beating, and faces lengthening.

They were led by General O'Hara, with the American General Lincoln on his right, the Americans and French beating a march as they passed out between them. It was a noble sight to us, and the more so, as it seemed to promise a speedy conclusion to the contest. The British did not make so good an appearance as the German forces; but there was certainly some allowance to be made in their favor. The English felt their honor wounded; the Germans did not greatly care whose hands they were in. The British paid the Americans, seemingly, but little attention as they passed them, but they eyed the French with considerable malice depicted in their countenances. They marched to the place appointed and stacked their arms; they then returned to the town in the same manner they had marched out, except being divested of their arms. After the prisoners were marched off into the country our army separated, the French remaining where they then were and the Americans marching for the Hudson.

# *Questions for Part II*

1 Explain the native-American custom of adoption as Mary Jemison tells it. Why do you think captivity narratives were popular reading?

2 Why do you think the people described by Mittelberger agreed to come to America as indentured servants?

3 What were Equiano's chief reactions to his experience with the slave trade and what perception of Europeans did he acquire from his experience?

4 Briefly summarize Crèvecoeur's answer to the question, "What then is the American, this new man?" How does Crèvecoeur contrast America with Europe? What does he say about the frontiersmen, the "back-settlers"?

5 How accurate or inaccurate do you think Preston's account of the Boston Massacre is? Why?

6 What does Hewes's account of his role in the Boston Tea Party tell you about how the experience of resisting the British changed common people?

7 Are you surprised the English cartoonists took the views they did about events leading to the American Revolution? How can you explain this criticism of their government? What influence would such opinions have in the colonies?

8 What is the main objective of Paine's pamphlet? Are there any phrases in it that you have heard before? What are a "summer soldier" and a "sunshine patriot"? Who were the "Hessians" to whom Paine refers?

9 Why do you think Martin was willing to endure for so many years the hardships of being a soldier in the Revolution?

# PART III THE GROWTH OF A NEW NATION

*The young republic developed a vigorous economic and political life as it established its independent place in the world, extended its borders through the Louisiana Purchase, and began a rapid movement westward led by explorers such as Lewis and Clark. With a vast territory far beyond the Mississippi to exploit, a national identity and governmental structure largely set, and relations with foreign powers on a calm course (after the War of 1812), the minds and energies of Americans were engaged in settling the West, creating wealth, and building religious and cultural institutions in an expanding nation.*

*The selections that follow present restless Americans—some, like John Doyle, newly arrived—wasting natural resources, having their souls saved by preachers such as Peter Cartwright, and founding new industries such as the Lowell textile mills. Like the Cherokee John Ross, some struggle against losing their birthright. Others wage war with Mexico or move relentlessly westward, as did Priscilla Merriman Evans and her family. One selection details the gold rush that provided the impetus for linking California with the rest of the nation, rounding out a transcontinental republic.*

*MERIWETHER LEWIS AND WILLIAM CLARK*

# 18 *Crossing the Great Divide*

*The most famous expedition in American history was the brainchild of Thomas Jefferson. For years Jefferson had dreamed that a party of explorers could search out a passage to the Pacific, win the native Americans to the new republic to the east, and study the geography, plants, and minerals of a vast and unknown territory.*

*Meriwether Lewis and William Clark were two young men willing to follow Jefferson's dream. Their expedition from St. Louis to the mouth of the Columbia River and back is one of the great adventure stories of our history. The journals and notebooks that members of the party kept have been used by historians, geographers, anthropologists, botanists, and zoologists.*

*The selections here present Lewis and Clark crossing the Great Divide in one of the most difficult parts of their journey. The reader can see their careful search for information about the best way west, and their careful observation of native-American ways. The reader will also glimpse the most famous single drama of the expedition: the extraordinary moment when Sacajawea, wife of one of their interpreters, meets a party of Shoshone, her native nation, headed by a chief who is the brother she has not seen since she was a small child. The first excerpt was written by Nicholas Biddle, who was later head of the Bank of the United States. Biddle's descriptions are taken from the notes of various participants in the expedition. They have sometimes been published—incorrectly—as part of the actual journals of Lewis and Clark.*

[Biddle] SATURDAY, AUGUST 17TH 1805.—

Captain Lewis rose very early and despatached Drewyer and the Indian down the river in quest of the boats. Sheilds was sent out at the same time to hunt, while M'Neal prepared a breakfast out of the remainder of the meat. Drewyer had been gone about two hours, and the Indians were all anxiously waiting for some news, when an Indian who had straggled a short distance down the river, returned with a report that he had seen the white men, who were only a short distance below, and were coming on. The Indians were all transported with joy, and the chief in the warmth of his satisfaction renewed his embrace to Capt.

Lewis, who was quite as much delighted as the Indians themselves; the report proved most aggreeably true.

On setting out at seven o'clock, Captain Clarke with Chaboneau and his wife walked on shore, but they had not gone more than a mile before Clarke saw Sacajawea, who was with her husband 100 yards ahead, began to dance and show every mark of the most extravagant joy, turning round him and pointing to several Indians, whom he now saw advancing on horseback, sucking her fingers at the same time to indicate that they were of her native tribe. As they advanced, Captain Clarke discovered among them Drewyer dressed like an Indian, from whom he learnt the situation of the party. While the boats were performing the circuit, he went towards the forks with the Indians, who as they went along, sang aloud with the greatest appearance of delight.

We soon drew near to the camp, and just as we approached it a woman made her way through the crowd towards Sacajawea, and recognising each other, they embraced with the most tender affection. The meeting of these two young women had in it something peculiarly touching, not only in the ardent manner in which their feelings were expressed, but from the real interest of their situation. They had been companions in childhood, in the war with the Minetarees they had both been taken prisoners in the same battle, they had shared and softened the rigours of their captivity, till one of them had escaped from the Minnetarees, with scarce a hope of ever seeing her friend relieved from the hands of her enemies. While Sacajawea was renewing among the women the friendships of former days, Captain Clarke went on, and was received by Captain Lewis and the chief, who after the first embraces and salutations were over, conducted him to a sort of circular tent or shade of willows. Here he was seated on a white robe; and the chief immediately tied in his hair six small shells resembling pearls, an ornament highly valued by these people, who procure them in the course of trade from the sea-coast. The moccasins of the whole party were then taken off, and after much ceremony the smoking began. After this the conference was to be opened, and glad of an opportunity of being able to converse more intelligibly, Sacajawea was sent for; she came into the tent, sat down, and was beginning to interpret, when in the person of Cameahwait she recognised her brother: She instantly jumped up, and ran and embraced him, throwing over him her blanket and weeping profusely: The chief was himself moved, though not in the same degree. After some conversation between them she resumed her seat, and attempted to interpret for us, but her new situation seemed to overpower her, and she was frequently interrupted by her tears. After the council was finished the unfortunate woman learnt that all her family were dead except two brothers, one of whom was absent, and a son of her eldest sister, a small boy, who was immediately adopted by her.

[Lewis] SATURDAY AUGUST 17TH 1805.—

we made them [the Indians] sensible of their dependance on the will of our government for every species of merchandize as well for their defence & comfort; and apprized them of the strength of our government and it's friendly dispositions towards them. we also gave them as a reason why we wished to pe[ne]trate the country as far as the ocean to the west of them was to examine and find out a more direct way to bring merchandize to them. that as no trade could by carryed on with them before our return to our homes that it was mutually advantageous to them as well as to ourselves that they should render us such aids as they had in their power to furnish in order to haisten our voyage and of course our return home. that such were their horses to transport our baggage without which we could not subsist, and that a pilot to conduct us through the mountains was also necessary if we could not decend the river by water. but that we did not ask either their horses or their services without giving a satisfactory compensation in return. that at present we wished them to collect as many horses as were necessary to transport our baggage to their village on the Columbia where we would then trade with them at our leasure for such horses as they could spare us.

the chief thanked us for friendship towards himself and nation & declared his wish to serve us in every rispect. that he was sorry to find that it must yet be some time before they could be furnished with firearms but said they could live as they had done heretofore until we brought them as we had promised. he said they had not horses enough with them at present to remove our baggage to their village over the mountain, but that he would return tomorrow and encourage his people to come over with their horses and that he would bring his own and assist us. this was complying with all we wished at present.

we next enquired who were chiefs among them. Cameahwait pointed out two others whom he said were Chiefs. we gave him a medal of the small size with the likeness of Mr. Jefferson the President of the U' States in releif on one side and clasp hands with a pipe and tomahawk in the other, to the other Chiefs we gave each a small medal which were struck in the Presidency of George Washing[ton] Esqr. we also gave small medals of the last discription two young men whom the 1st Chief informed us wer good young men and much rispected among them. we gave the 1st Chief an uniform coat shirt a pair of scarlet legings a carrot of tobacco and some small articles to each of the others we gave a shi[r]t leging[s] handkerchief a knife some tobacco and a few small articles we also distributed a good quantity paint mockerson awles knives beads looking-glasses &c among the other Indians and gave them a plentifull meal of lyed corn which was the first they had ever eaten in their lives. they were much pleased with it. every article about us appeared to excite astonishment in there minds; the appearance of the men, their arms, the canoes, our manner of working them, the b[l]ack man york and the sagacity of my dog were equally objects of admiration. I also shot my air-gun which was so perfectly incomprehensible that they immediately denominated it the great medicine.

Capt. Clark and myself now concerted measures for our future operations, and it was mutually agreed that he should set out tomorrow morning with eleven men furnished with axes and other necessary tools for making canoes, their arms accoutrements and as much of their baggage as they could carry. also to take the indians, C[h]arbono and the indian woman with him; that on his arrival at the Shoshone camp he was to leave Charbono and the Indian woman to haisten the return of the Indians with their horses to this place, and to proceede himself with the eleven men down the Columbia in order to examine the river and if he found it navigable and could obtain timber to set about making canoes immediately. In the mean time I was to bring the party and baggage to the Shoshone Camp, calculating that by the time I should reach that place that he would have sufficiently informed himself with rispect to the state of the river &c. as to determine us whether to prosicute our journey from thence by land or water. in the former case we should want all the horses which we could perchase, and in the latter only to hire the Indians to transport our baggage to the place at which we made the canoes.

SUNDAY AUGUST 18TH 1805.—

This morning while Capt. Clark was busily engaged in preparing for his rout, I exposed some articles to barter with the Indians for horses as I wished a few at this moment to releive the men who were going with Capt Clark from the labour of carrying their baggage, and also one to keep here in order to pack the meat to camp which the hunters might kill. I soon obtained three very good horses. for which I gave an uniform coat, a pair of legings, a few handkerchiefs, three knives and some other small articles the whole of which did not cost more than about 20$ in the U' States. the Indians seemed quite as well pleased with their bargin as I was. the men also purchased one for an old checked shirt a pair of old legings and a knife. two of those I purchased Capt. C. took on with him. at 10 a.m. Capt. Clark departed with his detachment and all the Indians except 2 men and 2 women who remained with us.

after there departure this morning I had all the stores and baggage of every discription opened and aired. and began the operation of forming the packages in proper parsels for the purpose of transporting them on horseback. the rain in the evening compelled me to desist from my operations. I had the raw hides put in the water in order to cut them in throngs proper for lashing the packages and forming the necessary geer for pack horses, a business which I fortunately had not to learn on this occasion. I had the net arranged and set this evening to catch some trout which we could see in great abundance at the bottom of the river.

MONDAY AUGUST 19TH 1805.—

The Shoshonees may be estimated at about 100 warriors, and about three times that number of woomen and children.* they have more children among them than I expected to have seen among a people who procure subsistence with such difficulty. there are but few very old persons, nor did they appear to treat those with much tenderness or rispect. The man is the sole propryetor of his wives and daughters, and can barter or dispose of either as he thinks proper. a plurality of wives is common among them, but these are not generally sisters as with the Minnitares & Mandans but are purchased of different fathers. The father frequently disposes of his infant daughters in marriage to men who are grown or to men who have sons for whom they think proper to provide wives. the compensation given in such cases usually consists of horses or mules which the father receives at the time of contract and converts to his own uce. the girl remains with her parents untill she is conceived to have obtained the age of puberty which with them is considered to be about the age of 13 or 14 years. the female at this age is surrendered to her soveriegn lord and husband agreeably to contract, and with her is frequently restored by the father quite as much as he received in the first instance in payment for his daughter; but this is discretionary with the father. Sah-car-gar-we-ah had been thus disposed of before she was taken by the Minnetares, or had arrived to the years of puberty. the husband was yet living with this band. he was more than double her age and had two other wives. he claimed her as his wife but said that as she had had a child by another man, who was Charbono, that he did not want her.

They seldom correct their children particularly the boys who soon become masters of their own acts. they give as a reason that it cows and breaks the sperit of the boy to whip him, and that he never recovers his independence of mind after he is grown. They treat their women but with little rispect, and compel them to perform every species of drudgery. they collect the wild fruits and roots, attend to the horses or assist in that duty, cook, dress the skins and make all their apparel, collect wood and make their fires, arrange and form their lodges, and when they travel pack the horses and take charge of all the baggage; in short the man dose little else except attend his horses hunt and fish. the man considers himself degraded if he is compelled to walk any distance; and if he is so unfortunately poor as only to possess two horses he rides the best himself and leavs the woman or women if he has more

*Lewis's figures refer to this band only.

than one, to transport their baggage and children on the other, and to walk if the horse is unable to carry the additional weight of their persons. the chastity of their women is not held in high estimation, and the husband will for a trifle barter the companion of his bead for a night or longer if he conceives the reward adiquate; tho' they are not so importunate that we should caress their women as the siouxs were. and some of their women appear to be held more sacred than in any nation we have seen. I have requested the men to give them no cause of jealousy by having connection with their women without their knowledge, which with them, strange as it may seem is considered as disgracefull to the husband as clandestine connections of a similar kind are among civilized nations. to prevent this mutual exchange of good officies altogether I know it impossible to effect, particularly on the part of our young men whom some months abstanence have made very polite to those tawney damsels. no evil has yet resulted and I hope will not from these connections.

notwithstanding the late loss of horses which this people sustained by the Minnetares the stock of the band may be very safely estimated at seven hundred of which they are perhaps about 40 coalts and half that number of mules. their arms offensive and defensive consist in the bow and arrows shield, some, lances, and a weapon called by the Cippeways who formerly used it, the pog-gar'-mag-gon' [war club]. in fishing they employ wairs, gigs, and fishing hooks. the salmon is the principal object of their pursuit. they snair wolves and foxes.

I was anxious to learn whether these people had the venerial, and made the enquiry through the interpreter and his wife; the information was that they sometimes had it but I could not learn their remedy; they most usually die with it's effects. this seems a strong proof that these disorders bothe ganaraehah and Louis Venerae* are native disorders of America. tho' these people have suffered much by the small pox which is known to be imported and perhaps those other disorders might have been contracted from other indian tribes who by a round of communications might have obtained from the Europeans since it was introduced into that quarter of the globe. but so much detached on the other ha[n]d from all communication with the whites that I think it most probable that those disorders are original with them.

from the middle of May to the first of September these people reside on the waters of the Columbia where they consider themselves in perfect security from their enimies as they have not as yet ever found their way to this retreat; during this season the salmon furnish the principal part of their subsistence and as this fish either perishes or returns about the 1st of September they are compelled at this season in surch of subsistence to resort to the Missouri, in the vallies of which, there is more game even [than] within the mountains. here they move

*Gonorrhea and syphilis.

slowly down the river in order to collect and join other bands either of their own nation or the Flatheads, and having become sufficiently strong as they conceive venture on the Eastern side of the Rocky mountains into the plains, where the buffaloe abound. but they never leave the interior of the mountains while they can obtain a scanty subsistence, and always return as soon as they have acquired a good stock of dryed meat in the plains; when this stock is consumed they venture again into the plains; thus alternately obtaining their food at the risk of their lives and retiring to the mountains, while they consume it. These people are now on the eve of their departure for the Missouri, and inform us that they expect to be joined at or about the three forks by several bands of their own nation, and a band of the Flatheads.

[Clark] AUGUST 19TH MONDAY 1805.—

A very cold morning Forst to be seen we set out a 7 oClock and proceeded on thro a wide level Vallie this Vallie Continues 5 miles & then becoms narrow, we proceeded on up the main branch with a gradial assent to the head and passed over a low mountain and Decended a Steep Decent to a butifull Stream, passed over a Second hill of a verry Steep assent & thro' a hilley Countrey for 8 miles an[d] Encamped on a Small Stream, the Indians with us we wer oblige[d] to feed. one man met me with a mule & Spanish Saddle to ride, I gave him a westcoat a mule is considered of great value among those people we proceeded on over a verry mountainous Countrey across the head of hollows & Springs

[Lewis] TUESDAY AUGUST 20TH 1805.—

I walked down the river about ¾ of a mile and selected a place near the river bank unperceived by the Indians for a cash [cache], which I set three men to make, and directed the centinel to discharge his gun if he perceived any of the Indians going down in that direction which was to be the signal for the men at work on the cash to desist and seperate, least these people should discover our deposit and rob us of the baggage we intend leaving here. by evening the cash was completed unperceived by the Indians, and all our packages made up. the Pack-saddles and harness is not yet complete. in this operation we find ourselves at a loss for nails and boards; for the first we substitute throngs of raw hide which answer verry well, and for the last [had] to cut off the blades of our oars and use the plank of some boxes which have heretofore held other articles and put those articles into sacks of raw hide which I have had made for the purpose. by this means I have obtained as many boards as will make 20 saddles which I suppose will be sufficient for our present exegencies. I made up a small assortment of medicines, together with the specemines of plants, minerals, seeds &c, which, I have collected between this place and the falls of the Missouri which I shall deposit here.

I now prevailed on the Chief to instruct me with rispect to the geography of his country. this he undertook very cheerfully, by delineating the rivers on the ground. but I soon found that his information fell far short of my expectation or wishes. he drew the river on which we now are [the Lemhi] to which he placed two branches just above us, which he shewed me from the openings of the mountains were in view; he next made it discharge itself into a large river which flowed from the S.W. about ten miles below us [the Salmon], then continued this joint stream in the same direction of this valley or N.W. for one days march and then enclined it to the West for 2 more days march. here we placed a number of heaps of sand on each side which he informed me represented the vast mountains of rock eternally covered with snow through which the river passed. that the perpendicular and even juting rocks so closely hemned in the river that there was no possibil[it]y of passing along the shore; that the bed of the river was obstructed by sharp pointed rocks and the rapidity of the stream such that the whole surface of the river was beat into perfect foam as far as the eye could reach. that the mountains were also inaccessible to man or horse. he said that this being the state of the country in that direction that himself nor none of his nation had ever been further down the river than these mountains.

I then enquired the state of the country on either side of the river but he could not inform me. . . . I now asked Cameahwait by what rout the Pierced nosed [Nez Percé] indians, who he informed me inhabited this river below the mountains, came over to the Missouri; this he informed me was to the north, but added that the road was a very bad one as he had been informed by them and that they had suffered excessively with hunger on the rout being obliged to subsist for many days on berries alone as there was no game in that part of the mountains which were broken rockey and so thickly covered with timber that they could scarcely pass. however knowing that Indians had passed, and did pass, at this season on that side of this river to the same below the mountains, my rout was instantly settled in my own mind, p[r]ovided the account of this river should prove true on an investigation of it, which I was determined should be made before we would undertake the rout by land in any direction. I felt perfectly satisfyed, that if the Indians could pass these mountains with their women and Children, that we could also pass them; and that if the nations on this river below the mountains were as numerous as they were stated to be that they must have some means of subsistence which it would be equally in our power to procure in the same country. they informed me that there was no buffaloe on the West side of the mountains; that the game consisted of a few Elk deer and Antelopes, and that the natives subsisted on fish and roots principally.

in this manner I spend the day smoking with them and acquiring what information I could with respect to their country. they informed me that they could pass to the Spaniards by the way of the yellowstone river in 10 days. I can discover that these people are by no means friendly to the Spaniards. their complaint is, that the Spaniards will not let them have fire arms and ammunition, that they put them off by telling them that if they suffer them to have guns they will kill each other, thus leaving them defenceless and an easy prey to their bloodthirsty neighbours to the East of them, who being in possession of fire arms hunt them up and murder them without rispect to sex or age and plunder them of their horses on all occasions. they told me that to avoid their enemies who were eternally harrassing them that they were obliged to remain in the interior of these mountains at least two thirds of the year where the[y] suffered as we then saw great heardships for the want of food sometimes living for weeks without meat and only a little fish roots and berries. but this added Câmeahwait, with his ferce eyes and lank jaws grown meager for the want of food, would not be the case if we had guns, we could then live in the country of buffaloe and eat as our enimies do and not be compelled to hide ourselves in these mountains and live on roots and berries as the bear do. we do not fear our enimies when placed on an equal footing with them. I told them that the Minnetares Mandans . . . had promised us to desist from making war on them & that we would indevour to find the means of making the Minnetares of fort d[e] Prarie or as they call them Pahkees desist from waging war against them also. that after our finally returning to our homes towards the rising sun whitemen would come to them with an abundance of guns and every other article necessary to their defence and comfort, and that they would be enabled to supply themselves with these articles on reasonable terms in exchange for the skins of the beaver Otter and Ermin so abundant in their country. they expressed great pleasure at this information and said they had been long anxious to see the whitemen that traded guns; and that we might rest assured of their friendship and that they would do whatever we wished them.

PETER CARTWRIGHT

# 19 Autobiography of a Circuit Rider

*Peter Cartwright was a pioneer Methodist evangelist who contributed to the great work of the Methodists in bringing evangelical Protestantism to new settlements in the West. Born in Virginia in 1785 and raised in Kentucky, Cartwright rode "circuit" as an itinerant preacher of enthusiastic religion through parts of Kentucky, Tennessee, Indiana, and Ohio. In 1824, because of his hatred of slavery, Cartwright had his circuit transferred to Illinois. Evidently, however, he was less persuasive as a politician than as a revivalist; in 1846 Cartwright lost an election for the United States House of Representatives. The winner was Abraham Lincoln.*

*The circuit riders taught a highly emotional form of religion that emphasized personal morality, civic virtue, and the importance of education. Their contribution to the characteristic culture of the American Middle West quickly came to symbolize all of American life. Cartwright's personal experience of conversion and his subsequent career are highly representative of circuit riders. He wrote his autobiography in 1857.*

## CONVERSION

In 1801, when I was in my sixteenth year, my father, my eldest half brother, and myself, attended a wedding about five miles from home, where there was a great deal of drinking and dancing, which was very common at marriages in those days. I drank little or nothing; my delight was in dancing. After a late hour in the night, we mounted our horses and started for home. I was riding my race-horse.

A few minutes after we had put up the horses, and were sitting by the fire, I began to reflect on the manner in which I had spent the day and evening. I felt guilty and condemned. I rose and walked the floor. My mother was in bed. It seemed to me, all of a sudden, my blood rushed to my head, my heart palpitated, in a few minutes I turned blind; an awful impression rested on my mind that death had come and I was unprepared to die. I fell on my knees and began to ask God to have mercy on me.

My mother sprang from her bed, and was soon on her knees by my side, praying for me, and exhorting me to look to Christ for mercy, and then and there I promised the Lord that if he would spare me, I would seek and serve him; and I never fully broke that promise. My mother prayed for me a long time. At length we lay down, but there was little sleep for me. Next morning I rose, feeling wretched beyond expression. I tried to read in the Testament, and retired many times to secret prayer through the day, but found no relief. I gave up my racehorse to my father, and requested him to sell him. I went and brought my pack of cards, and gave them to mother, who threw them into the fire, and they were consumed. I fasted, watched, and prayed, and engaged in regular reading of the Testament. I was so distressed and miserable, that I was incapable of any regular business.

My father was greatly distressed on my account, thinking I must die, and he would lose his only son. He bade me retire altogether from business, and take care of myself.

Soon it was noised abroad that I was distracted, and many of my associates in wickedness came to see me, to try and divert my mind from those gloomy thoughts of my wretchedness; but all in vain. I exhorted them to desist from the course of wickedness which we had been guilty of together. The class-leader and local preacher were sent for. They tried to point me to the bleeding Lamb, they prayed for me most fervently. Still I found no comfort, and although I had never believed in the doctrine of unconditional election and reprobation, I was sorely tempted to believe I was a reprobate, and doomed, and lost eternally, without any chance of salvation.

At length one day I retired to the horse-lot, and was walking and wringing my hands in great anguish, trying to pray, on the borders of utter despair. It appeared to me that I heard a voice from heaven, saying "Peter, look at me." A feeling of relief flashed over me as quick as an electric shock. It gave me hopeful feelings, and some encouragement to seek mercy, but still my load of guilt remained. I repaired to the house, and told my mother what had happened to me in the horse-lot. Instantly she seemed to understand it, and told me the Lord had done this to encourage me to hope for mercy, and exhorted me to take encouragement, and seek on, and God would bless me with the pardon of my sins at another time.

Some days after this, I retired to a cave on my father's farm to pray in secret. My soul was in an agony; I wept, I prayed, and said, "Now, Lord, if there is mercy for me, let me find it," and it really seemed to me that I could almost lay hold of the Saviour, and realize a reconciled God. All of a sudden, such a fear of the devil fell upon me that it really appeared to me that he was surely personally there, to seize and drag me down to hell, soul and body, and such a horror fell on me that I sprang to my feet and ran to my mother at the house. My mother told me that this was a device of Satan to prevent me from finding the blessing then. Three months rolled away, and still I did not find the blessing of the pardon of my sins.

This year, 1801, the Western Conference [of preachers] existed, and I think there was but one presiding elder's district in it, called the Kentucky District. William M'Kendree (afterward bishop) was appointed to the Kentucky District. Cumberland Circuit, which, perhaps, was six hundred miles round, and lying partly in Kentucky and partly in Tennessee, was one of the circuits of this district. John Page and Thomas Wilkerson were appointed to this circuit.

In the spring of this year, Mr. M'Grady, a minister of the Presbyterian Church, who had a congregation and meeting-house, as we then called them, about three miles north of my father's house, appointed a sacramental meeting in this congregation, and invited the Methodist preachers to attend with them, and especially John Page, who was a powerful Gospel minister, and was very popular among the Presbyterians. Accordingly he came, and preached with great power and success.

There were no camp-meetings in regular form at this time, but as there was a great waking up among the Churches, from the revival that had broken out at Cane Ridge, before mentioned, many flocked to those sacramental meetings. The church would not hold the tenth part of the congregation. Accordingly, the officers of the Church erected a stand in a contiguous shady grove, and prepared seats for a large congregation.

The people crowded to this meeting from far and near. They came in their large wagons, with victuals mostly prepared. The women slept in the wagons, and the men under them. Many stayed on the ground night and day for a number of nights and days together. Others were provided for among the neighbors around. The power of God was wonderfully displayed; scores of sinners fell under the preaching, like men slain in mighty battle; Christians shouted aloud for joy.

To this meeting I repaired, a guilty, wretched sinner. On the Saturday evening of said meeting, I went, with weeping multitudes, and bowed before the stand, and earnestly prayed for mercy. In the midst of a solemn struggle of soul, an impression was made on my mind, as though a voice said to me, "Thy sins are all forgiven thee." Divine light flashed all round me, unspeakable joy sprung up in my soul. I rose to my feet, opened my eyes, and it really seemed as if I was in heaven; the trees, the leaves on them, and everything seemed, and I really thought were, praising God. My mother raised the shout, my Christian friends crowded around me and joined me in praising God; and though I have been since then, in many instances, unfaithful, yet I have never, for one moment, doubted that the Lord did, then and there, forgive my sins and give me religion.

Our meeting lasted without intermission all night, and it was believed by those who had a very good right to know, that over eighty souls were converted to God during its continuance. I went on my way rejoicing for many days.

/ / /

To show the ignorance the early Methodist preachers had to contend with in the Western wilds, I will relate an incident or two that occurred to Wilson Lee in Kentucky. He was one of the early pioneer Methodist preachers sent to the West. He was a very solemn and grave minister. At one of his appointments, at a private house on a certain day, they had a motherless pet lamb. The boys of the family had mischievously learned this lamb to butt. They would go near it, and make motions with their heads, and the lamb would back and then dart forward at them, and they would jump out of the way, so that the sheep would miss them.

A man came into the congregation who had been drinking and frolicking all the night before. He came in late, and took his seat on the end of the bench nearly in the door, and, having slept none the night before, presently he began to nod; and as he nodded and bent forward, the pet lamb came along by the door, and seeing this man nodding and bending forward, he took it as a banter, and straightway backed and then sprang forward, and gave the sleeper a severe jolt right on the head, and over he tilted him, to the no small amusement of the congregation, who all burst out into laughter; and grave as the preacher, Mr. Lee, was, it so excited his risibilities that he almost lost his balance. But recovering himself a little, he went on in a most solemn and impressive strain. His subject was the words of our Lord: "Except a man deny himself, and take up his cross, he cannot be my disciple." He urged on his congregation, with melting voices and tearful eyes, to take up the cross, no matter what it was, take it up.

There were in the congregation a very wicked Dutchman and his wife, both of whom were profoundly ignorant of the Scriptures and the plan of salvation. His wife was a notorious scold, and so much was she given to this practice, that she made her husband unhappy, and kept him almost always in a perfect fret, so that he led a most miserable and uncomfortable life. It pleased God that day to cause the preaching of Mr. Lee to reach their guilty souls and break up the great deep of their hearts. They wept aloud, seeing their lost condition, and they, then and there, resolved to do better, and from that time forward to take up the cross and bear it, be it what it might.

The congregation were generally deeply affected. Mr. Lee exhorted them and prayed for them as long as he consistently could, and, having another appointment some distance off that evening, he dismissed the congregation, got a little refreshment, saddled his horse, mounted, and started for his evening appointment. After riding some distance, he saw, a little ahead of him, a man trudging along, carrying a woman on his back. This greatly surprised Mr. Lee. He very naturally supposed that the woman was a cripple, or had hurt herself in some way, so that she could not walk. The traveller was a small man, and the woman large and heavy.

Before he overtook them Mr. Lee began to cast about in his mind how he could render them assistance. When he came up to them, lo and behold, who should it be but the Dutchman and his wife that had been so affected under his sermon at meeting. Mr. Lee rode up and spoke to them, and inquired of the man what had happened, or what was the matter, that he was carrying his wife.

The Dutchman turned to Mr. Lee and said, "Be sure you did tell us in your sarmon dat we must take up de cross and follow de Saviour, or dat we could not be saved to go to heaven, and I does desire to go to heaven so much as any pody; and dish vife is so pad, she scold and scold all de time, and dish woman is de createst cross I have in de whole world, and I does take her up and pare her, for I must save my soul."

You may be sure Mr. Lee was posed for once, but after a few moments' reflection he told the Dutchman to put his wife down, and he dismounted from his horse. He directed them to sit down on a log by the road side. He held the reins of his horse's bridle and sat down by them, took out his Bible, read to them several passages of Scripture, and explained and expounded to them the way of the Lord more perfectly. He opened to them the nature of the cross of Christ, what it is, how it is to be taken up, and how they were to bear that cross; and after teaching and advising them some time, he prayed for them by the road side, left them deeply affected, mounted his horse, and rode on to his evening appointment.

Long before Mr. Lee came around his circuit to his next appointment the Dutchman and his scolding wife were both powerfully converted to God, and when he came round he took them into the Church. The Dutchman's wife was cured of her scolding. Of course he got clear of this cross. They lived together long and happily, adorning their profession, and giving ample evidence that religion could cure a scolding wife, and that God could and did convert poor ignorant Dutch people.

This Dutchman often told his experience in love-feasts, with thrilling effect, and hardly ever failed to melt the whole congregation into a flood of tears; and on one particular occasion which is vividly printed on my recollection, I believe the whole congregation in the love-feast, which lasted beyond the time allotted for such meetings, broke out into a loud shout.

Thus Brother Lee was the honored instrument in the hand of God of planting Methodism, amid clouds of ignorance and opposition, among the early settlers of the far West. Brother Lee witnessed a good confession to the end. At an early period of his ministry he fell from the walls of Zion with the trump of God in his hand, and has gone to his reward in heaven. Peace to his memory.

## *THE GREAT REVIVAL*

From 1801 for years a blessed revival of religion spread through almost the entire inhabited parts of the West, Kentucky, Tennessee, the Carolinas, and many other parts, especially through the Cumberland country, which was so called from the Cumberland River, which headed and mouthed in Kentucky, but in its great bend circled south through Tennessee, near Nashville. The Presbyterians and Methodists in a great measure united in this work, met together, prayed together, and preached together.

In this revival originated our camp-meetings, and in both these denominations they were held every year, and, indeed, have been ever since, more or less. They would erect their camps with logs or frame them, and cover them with clapboards or shingles. They would also erect a shed, sufficiently large to protect five thousand people from wind and rain, and cover it with boards or shingles; build a large stand, seat the shed, and here they would collect together from forty to fifty miles around, sometimes further than that. Ten, twenty, and sometimes thirty ministers, of different denominations, would come together and preach night and day, four or five days together; and, indeed, I have known these camp-meetings to last three or four weeks, and great good resulted from them. I have seen more than a hundred sinners fall like dead men under one powerful sermon, and I have seen and heard more than five hundred Christians all shouting aloud the high praises of God at once; and I will venture to assert that many happy thousands were awakened and converted to God at these camp-meetings. Some sinners mocked, some of the old dry professors opposed, some of the old starched Presbyterian preachers preached against these exercises, but still the work went on and spread almost in every direction, gathering additional force, until our country seemed all coming home to God.

/ / /

[A] new exercise broke out among us, called the *jerks*, which was overwhelming in its effects upon the bodies and minds of the people. No matter whether they were saints or sinners, they would be taken under a warm song or sermon, and seized with a convulsive jerking all over, which they could not by any possibility avoid, and the more they resisted the more they jerked. If they would not strive against it and pray in good earnest, the jerking would usually abate. I have seen more than five hundred persons jerking at one time in my large congregations. Most usually persons taken with the jerks, to obtain relief, as they said, would rise up and dance. Some would run, but could not get away. Some would resist; on such the jerks were generally very severe.

To see those proud young gentlemen and young ladies, dressed in their silks, jewelry, and prunella, from top to toe, take the *jerks* would often excite my risibilities. The first jerk or so, you would see their fine bonnets, caps, and combs fly; and so sudden would be the jerking of the head that their long loose hair would crack almost as loud as a wagoners whip.

At one of my appointments in 1804 there was a very large congregation turned out to hear the Kentucky boy, as they called me. Among the rest there were two very finely-dressed, fashionable young ladies, attended by two brothers with loaded horsewhips. Although the house was large, it was crowded. The two young ladies, coming in late, took their seats near where I stood, and their two brothers stood in the door. I was a little unwell, and I had a phial of peppermint in my pocket. Before I commenced preaching I took out my phial and swallowed a little of the peppermint. While I was preaching, the congregation was melted into tears. The two young gentlemen moved off to the yard fence, and both the young ladies took the jerks, and they were greatly mortified about it. There was a great stir in the congregation. Some wept, some shouted, and before our meeting closed several were converted.

As I dismissed the assembly a man stepped up to me, and warned me to be on my guard, for he had heard the two brothers swear they would horsewhip me when meeting was out, for giving their sisters the jerks. "Well," said I, "I'll see to that."

I went out and said to the young men that I understood they intended to horsewhip me for giving their sisters the jerks. One replied that he did. I undertook to expostulate with him on the absurdity of the charge against me, but he swore I need not deny it; for he had seen me take out a phial, in which I carried some truck that gave his sisters the jerks. As quick as thought it came into my mind how I would get clear of my whipping, and, jerking out the peppermint phial, said I, "Yes; if I gave your sisters the jerks I'll give them to you." In a moment I saw he was scared. I moved towards him, he backed, I advanced, and he wheeled and ran, warning me not to come near him, or he would kill me. It raised the laugh on him, and I escaped my whipping. I had the pleasure, before the year was out, of seeing all four soundly converted to God, and I took them into the Church.

While I am on this subject I will relate a very serious circumstance which I knew to take place with a man who had the jerks at a camp-meeting, on what was called the Ridge, in William Magee's congregation. There was a great work of religion in the encampment. The jerks were very prevalent. There was a company of drunken rowdies who came to interrupt the meeting. These rowdies were headed by a very large drinking man. They came with their bottles of whisky in their pockets. This large man cursed the jerks, and all religion. Shortly afterward he took the jerks, and he started to run, but he jerked so powerfully he could not get away. He halted among some saplings, and, although he was violently agitated, he took out his bottle of whisky, and swore he would drink the damned jerks to death; but he jerked at such a rate he could not get the bottle to his mouth, though he tried hard. At length he fetched a sudden jerk, and the bottle struck a sapling and was broken to pieces, and spilled his whisky on the ground. There was a great crowd gathered round him, and when he lost his whisky he became very much enraged, and cursed and swore very profanely, his jerks still increasing. At length he fetched a very violent jerk, snapped his neck, fell, and soon expired, with his mouth full of cursing and bitterness.

I always looked upon the jerks as a judgment sent from God, first, to bring sinners to repentance; and, secondly to show professors that God could work with or without means, and that he could work over and above means, and do whatsoever seemeth him good, to the glory of his grace and the salvation of the world.

There is no doubt in my mind that, with weak-minded, ignorant, and superstitious persons, there was a great deal of sympathetic feeling with many that claimed to be under the influence of this jerking exercise; and yet, with many, it was perfectly involuntary. It was, on all occasions, my practice to recommend fervent prayer as a remedy, and it almost universally proved an effectual antidote.

There were many other strange and wild exercises into which the subjects of this revival fell; such, for instance, as what was called the running, jumping, barking exercise. The Methodist preachers generally preached against this extravagant wildness. I did it uniformly in my little ministrations, and sometimes gave great offense; but I feared no consequences when I felt my awful responsibilities to God. From these wild exercises, another great evil arose from the heated and wild imaginations of some. They professed to fall into trances and see visions; they would fall at meetings and sometimes at home, and lay apparently powerless and motionless for days, sometimes for a week at a time, without food or drink; and when they came to, they professed to have seen heaven and hell, to have seen God, angels, the devil and the damned; they would prophesy, and, under the pretense of Divine inspiration, predict the time of the end of the world, and the ushering in of the great millennium.

This was the most troublesome delusion of all; it made such an appeal to the ignorance, superstition, and credulity of the people, even saint as well as sinner. I watched this matter with a vigilant eye. If I opposed it, I would have to meet the clamor of the multitude; and if any one opposed it, these very visionists would single him out, and denounce the dreadful judgments of God against him. They would even set the very day that God was to burn the world, . . . They would prophesy, that if any one did oppose them, God would send fire down from heaven and consume him, like the blasphemous Shakers. They would proclaim that they could heal all manner of diseases, and raise the dead, . . . They professed to have converse with spirits of the dead in heaven and hell, like the modern spirit rappers. Such a state of things I never saw before, and I hope in God I shall never see again.

I pondered well the whole matter in view of my responsibilities, searched the Bible for the true fulfillment of promise and prophecy, prayed to God for light and Divine aid, and proclaimed open war against these delusions. In the midst of them along came the Shakers, and Mr. Rankin, one of the Presbyterian revival preachers, joined them; Mr. G. Wall, a visionary local preacher among the Methodists, joined them; all the country was in commotion.

I made public appointments and drew multitudes together, and openly showed from the Scriptures that these delusions were false. Some of these visionary men and women prophesied that God would kill me. The Shakers soon pretended to seal my damnation. But nothing daunted, for I knew Him in whom I had believed, I threw my appointments in the midst of them, and proclaimed to listening thousands the more sure word of prophecy. This mode of attack threw a damper on these visionary, self-deluded, false prophets, sobered some, reclaimed others, and stayed the fearful tide of delusion that was sweeping over the country.

/ / /

JOHN ROSS

# 20 The Trail of Tears

*John Ross, of mixed Cherokee and white ancestry, was exactly the phenomenon that led Georgians and their great ally, Andrew Jackson, to insist on the removal of the so-called "civilized tribes." Ross epitomized the "civilized," literate, prosperous, politically astute native American who successfully competed with whites. He had fought as an officer under Jackson against the Creek Indians at Horseshoe Bend. In the years after the War of 1812, he became a leader of the Cherokee nation as well as the successful owner of a 300-acre plantation run with the labor of more than twenty slaves. As leader of the fight against the removal, Ross was the chief author of the nation's* Memorial and Petition *against Jackson's policy and took the bitter responsibility for managing his people's journey west (in which his wife, Quatie, was one of the many casualties) after all his efforts to prevent it had failed.*

*Ross never ceased his service to the Cherokee, remaining as principal chief of the nation in Indian territory until his death in 1866. He also developed a new cotton plantation in the West, again using numerous slaves.*

## TO THE SENATE AND HOUSE OF REPRESENTATIVES

Washington City February 22ed 1837

The memorial and petition of the undersigned, a delegation appointed by the Cherokee nation in full council respectfully showeth:

That the Cherokee Nation deeply sensible of the evils under which they are now laboring and the still more frightful miseries which they have too much reason to apprehend, have in the most formal and solemn manner known to them, assembled in General Council to deliberate upon their existing relations with the Government of the United States, and to lay their case with respectful deference before your honorable bodies.

Invested with full powers to conclude an arrangement upon all the matters which interest them we have arrived at the seat of Government, and, in accordance with our usual forms of proceeding have notified the Honorable the Secretary of War [Benjamin F. Butler] that we had reached this place and, through him, solicited an interview with the Executive [Andrew Jackson]. This request has not yet been granted, nor has it to this day received an official answer, but we have reason to apprehend from circumstances which have reached us that we shall be denied this application, and are thus compelled in the discharge of our duty to our constituents, to submit to your Honorable bodies the memorial of which we are the bearers.

On former occasions we have in much detail laid before you the prominent facts of our case. We have reminded you of our long and intimate connexion with the United States, of the scenes of peril and difficulty which we have shared in common; of the friendship which had so long been generously proffered and affectionately and gratefully accepted; of the aids which were supplied us in promoting our advancement in the arts of civilized life, of the political principles which we had imbibed, of the religious faith we have been taught.

We have called your attention to the progress which under your auspices we have made, of the improvements which have marked our social and individual states; our lands brought into cultivation, our natural resources developed, our farms, workshops and factories, approximating in character and value to those of our brethren whose example we had diligently imitated.

A smooth and beautiful prospect of future advancement was opened before us. Our people had abandoned the pursuits, the habits and the tastes of the savage, and had put on the vestments of civilization, of intelligence and of a pure religion. The progress we had made furnished us with the most assured hopes of continued improvement, and we indulged in the anticipation that the time was not far distant when we should be recognised, on the footing of equality by the brethren from whom we had received all which we were now taught to prize.

This promise of golden sunshine is now overspread. Clouds and darkness have obscured its brilliancy. The winds are beginning to mutter their awful forebodings, the tempest is gathering thick and heavy over our heads, and threatens to burst upon us with terrific energy and overwhelming ruin.

In this season of calamity, where can we turn with hope or confidence? On all former occasions of peril or of doubt the Government of the United States spread over us its broad and paternal shield. It invited us to seek an asylum and a protection under its mighty arm. It assisted us with its encouragement and advice, it soothed us with its consoling assurances, it inspired us with hope and gave us a feeling of confidence and security.

But alas! this our long-cherished friend seems now to be alienated from us: this our father has raised his arm to inflict the hostile blow; this strength so long our protection is now exerted against us, and on the wide scene of existence no human aid is left us. Unless you avert your arm we are destroyed. Unless your feelings of affection and compassion are once more awakened towards your destitute and despairing children our annihilation is complete.

It is a natural inquiry among all who commiserate our situation what are the causes which have led to this disastrous revolution, to this entire change of relations? By what agency have such results been accomplished?

We have asked, and we reiterate the question how have we offended? Show us in what manner we have, however unwittingly, inflicted upon you a wrong, you shall yourselves be the judges of the extent and manner of compensation. Show us the offence which has awakened your feelings of justice against us and we will submit to that measure of punishment which you shall tell us we have merited. We cannot bring to our recollections anything we have done or anything we have omitted calculated to awaken your resentment against us.

But we are told a treaty has been made and all that is required at our hands is to comply with its stipulations. Will the faithful historian, who shall hereafter record our lamentable fate, say—the Cherokee Nation executed a treaty by which they freely and absolutely ceded the country in which they were born and educated, the property they had been industriously accumulating and improving, and, abandoning the high road to which they had been advancing from savagism had precipitated themselves into worse than their pristine degradation, will not the reader of such a narrative require the most ample proof before he will credit such a story? Will he not inquire where was the kind and parental guardian who had heretofore aided the weak, assisted the forlorn, instructed the ignorant and elevated the depressed? Where was the Government of the United States with its vigilant care over the Indian when such a bargain was made? How will he be surprised at hearing that the United States was a party to the transaction—that the authority of that Government, and the representatives of that people, which had for years been employed in leading the Cherokees from ignorance to light, from barbarism to civilization, from paganism to christianity, who had taught them new habits and new hopes was the very party which was about to appropriate to itself the fruits of the Indian's industry, the birth places of his children and the graves of his ancestors.

If such a recital could command credence must it not be on the ground that experience had shown the utter failure of all the efforts and the disappointment of all the hopes of the philanthropist and the Christian? That the natives of this favored spot of God's creation were incapable of improvement and unsusceptible of education and that they in wilful blindness, spurning the blessings which had been proffered and urged upon them would pertinaciously prefer the degradation from which it had been attempted to lead them and the barbarism from which it had been sought to elevate them?

How will his astonishment be augmented when he learns that the Cherokee people almost to a man denied the existence and the obligation of the alleged compact—that they proclaimed it to have been based in fraud and concocted in perfidy—that no authority was ever given to those who undertook in their names and on their behalf to negotiate it; that it was repudiated with unexampled unanimity when it was brought to their knowledge; that they denied that it conferred any rights or imposed any obligations.

Yet such must be the story which the faithful historian must record. In the name of the whole Cherokee people we protest against this unhallowed and unauthorized and unacknowledged compact. We deny its binding force. We recognise none of its stipulations. If contrary to every principle of justice it is to be enforced upon us, we shall at least be free from the disgrace of self humiliation. We hold the solemn disavowal of its provisions by eighteen thousand of our people.

We, the regularly commissioned delegation of the Cherokee Nation in the face of Heaven and appealing to the Searcher of all hearts for the truth of our statements ask you to listen to our remonstrances. We implore you to examine into the truth of our allegations. We refer you to your own records, to your own agents, to men deservedly enjoying your esteem and confidence as our witnesses, and we proffer ourselves ready if you will direct the inquiry to establish the truth of what we aver. If we fail to substantiate our statements overwhelm us with ignominy and disgrace. Cast us off from you forever. If however on the other hand every allegation we make shall be sustained by the most convincing and abundant proof, need we make further or stronger appeals than the simple facts of the case will themselves furnish, to secure your friendship, your sympathy and your justice.

We will not and we cannot believe after the long connexion that has subsisted between us, after all that has been done and all that has been promised that our whole nation will be forcibly ejected from their native land and from their social hearths without the pretence of crime, without charge, without evidence, without trial: that we shall be exiled from all that we hold dear and venerable and sacred, and driven into a remote, a strange and a sterile region, without even the imputation of guilt. We will not believe that this will be done by our ancient allies, our friends, our brethren. Yet between this and the abrogation to the pretended treaty there is no medium. Such an instrument so obtained, so contaminated cannot cover the real nature of the acts which it is invoked to sanction. If power is to be exerted let it come unveiled. We shall but submit and die.

/ / /

*Jno Ross*

## *TO WINFIELD SCOTT**

Sir — Cherokee Agency East October 6th 1838

I had the honor to receive your communication of the 3rd inst. on the subject of my requisition of the 2ed and the state of the emigration generally. In reply, I beg leave to say, that although those detachments, only, which are in the greatest state of forwardness, are formally announced in my estimates and requisition; it ought to be borne in mind that, our efforts are directed, to carrying on the emigration with so much dispatch that, simultaneous preparations must be going on for the whole number of detachments by land, and even for the final clearing out of the sick, the infirm, the aged &c by water, who are unable to bear the fatigues of the journey by land. And that these preparations, may be made, with the least possible delay, I deemed it indispensable to have the necessary funds in readiness.

With regard to the number in some of the detachments, I would respectfully observe that the number one thousand, was understood by the Cherokees to be merely a common measure, assumed as the basis of the pecuniary calculations; and not as a precise, stipulated number which must absolutely be filled by each detachment; yet, their intention was, that each detachment should approximate that number as nearly as might be convenient. And it was expected that some would exceed and some come short of it.

In regard to Capt. [Hair] Conrad's detachment, I am sorry to say that it has been greatly diminished by causes beyond human control. That detachment was not, at first, expected to be large, and the amount of sickness with which it has been visited has greatly reduced its numbers, and even deprived it of the original conductor. I am happy to find, however, that a considerable number who have recovered are now on their way to join their friends in that detachment.

Mr. [George] Hick's detachment was expected to number one thousand or more, but the same afflictive causes have operated extensively among them also, and a considerable number were unavoidably left behind. In addition to this it may not be improper to say that Mr. Hicks and some of the other conductors have had to contend with extraneous, counteracting influences which were used to frustrate their arrangements in particular, and to embarrass and retard the progress of the general arrangements, between yourself and the authorities of the nation. And here, Sir, permit me to say, that having secured your confidence in our good faith and integrity, on which we place the highest estimate; we should be extremely sorry that you should find the authority or the moral influence of the Nation inadequate to the prompt and

*Major General Scott was in overall charge of the Cherokee removal.

faithful, discharge of its duties. I trust there does exist, in the Nation, a sufficient amount of energy, moral and official, for the performance of all its engagements. And here it may be proper to call your attention to the fact that certain individual Cherokees namely [John A.] Bell, [William] Boling & their associates under the assumed protection of the United States prompted and sustained, as I am assured, by individuals in official stations, of whose conduct I have more than once verbally complained; have been practising a course of interference, tending to retard the progress and disturb the arrangements of the detachments preparing for the road. We have refrained from exercising, the National Authority over those persons, from the feeling of uncertainty, whether, they were to be considered under the jurisdiction of the United States or that of the Cherokee Nation. If they are under the control of the Nation it would be desirable to have the fact known; but if they are under the control of the U. States we would respectfully call upon you to apply the corrective. In this connexion, it may not be out of place to add, that the continuing to issue rations, by the Govt. Agents at places from which the detachments have removed or after the regular organization of the detachments preparatory to their journey, as well as issuing, at the Agency, to little secluded parties, some of them many miles distant; is calculated to produce delay, in their being embodied with the detachments to which they properly belong, and more especially so, when this practice is connected with a systematic propagation of falsehoods and misrepresentations by the individuals alluded to and their emissaries.

The counteracting of these malign influences by prudent and gentle means, has, it is true, occasioned a little undesirable delay; but I have the pleasure to say, that our movements are now in a state of activity, which I trust will preclude all cause of complaint, with the assurance that our best efforts will be exerted to carry out our arrangements, with all reasonable dispatch. I remain with high respect, Sir, your obt. Servt.

*Jno Ross*

## *TO MATTHEW ARBUCKLE**

Sir Illinois [Cherokee Nation] Apl 23rd 1839

From the many complaints which are daily made to me by Cherokees who have been recently removed into this country, of their sufferings, from the want of being properly subsisted with provisions, I am constrained to address you this hasty letter. It is reported that, apart

*Brigadier General Arbuckle was area commander in the Indian Territory.

from the scantiness of the ration allowed under the contract made on the part of the United States Government with [James] Glasgow & [James] Harrison, many inconveniences have been experienced by the Cherokee people, from the irregularity of proceedings on the part of those employed for carrying out the contract.

It has also been stated that the contractors were only required to furnish "one pound of fresh beef, three half pints of corn & four qts. of salt to every 100 lbs. of beef—or, if they (the contractors) choose they might furnish in lieu of the beef, ¾ lb. salt pork or bacon provided the Indians will receive it." The beef being poor & not considered wholesome this season of the year, the Cherokees have generally objected to and refused receiving it and have insisted on being furnished with Salt Pork or Bacon in lieu of the beef, but it seems that the contractors do not choose and have refused to comply with the demand; saying that they were only bound to furnish Beef rations. Yet they would commute the ration by paying in money one dollar pr. month for the same. Thus the Cherokees are placed in a situation by compulsion to accept of either the beef or the money offered or to go unsupplied altogether. Here I must beg leave to remark, that previous to the removal of the Cherokees from the East to the West, the subject of providing subsistence for them after their arrival in this country was fully discussed with Major Genl. [Winfield] Scott who communicated with the War Deptmt. in reference to it. And we were afterwards informed by that distinguished officer that the Hon. Secry. of War [Joel R. Poinsett] had decided that the Cherokees should at least for a time be subsisted with provisions in kind, until they could provide for themselves, and then such an arrangement as would be most satisfactory to them should be made with them through Capt. Collins. Now Sir, it is evident from the exorbitant prices of meat and bread stuffs in this country that the Cherokees who have thus been forced to receive commutation in money from the contractors at the rate stated will soon be found in a starving condition—instead of being provided with subsistence as was anticipated and promised them. If the articles of agreement entered into with the contractors are to be construed so as to leave it wholly optional with them whether to furnish Salt Pork or Bacon in lieu of Beef, then it is obvious that there were no practical advantage for the interest of the Cherokees to have inserted any clause in that instrument in regard to Salt Pork or Bacon—for its effect has only been and will continue to be to mislead the mind of the people. And how it can be reconciled with the obligations imposed by the contract for the contractors to adopt the mode of commuting the subsistence rations they have engaged to furnish the Cherokees with and that too by a rate fixed by themselves, is a mystery which the Cherokees cannot understand—for it is not pretended that such a right or discretion has ever been given to them by the contract with the agents or the U.S. Govt. for subsisting the Cherokees. Nor can the sacred principle of justice sanction such a course under existing circumstances. Confiding however in the fair intentions of the Government towards them on this subject, the Cherokees still believe that the Hon. Secry. of War will when deemed expedient commute their rations at a rate at least equal to any sum fully ample to purchase provisions with for their comfortable subsistence—and that no sum less will be offered than what others would engage to supply the same for. I beg leave herewith to lay before you copies of sundry letters which I have just received from several leading men on behalf of the Cherokees on this very unpleasant subject. And in conclusion will further remark, that the health and existence of the whole Cherokee people who have recently been removed to this distant country demands a speedy remedy for the inconveniences and evils complained of, & unless a change of the quantity and the kind of rations as well as of the mode of issuing the same, be made from that which has heretofore been granted and observed, the Cherokees must inevitably suffer. Therefore to avoid hunger & starvation they are reduced to the necessity of calling upon you and other officers as the proper representatives of the U.S. Govt. in this matter, to take immediate steps as will ensure the immediate subsistence of the Cherokees who have recently been removed here, with ample and wholesome provisions, until such other arrangements, as may be most satisfactory to them, can be made for subsisting themselves &c. When every thing in reference to the late removal of the Cherokee nation from the East to the West is considered, and seen that it has been consummated through the military authority of the U.S. Govt. I trust you will pardon me for addressing this communication to you, especially when you are assured that the Cherokee people have been taught to expect that justice and protection would be extended to them through the Commanding General in this Hemisphere.

/ / /

*Jno Ross*

*JOHN DOYLE*

# 21 A Young Irishman Comes to America, 1818

*John Doyle adapted rapidly to life in the United States. He moved readily from city to city and from one occupation to another in search of opportunity, adjusting smoothly to American economic life. Doyle also had advantages over many other immigrants: he was literate in English, was evidently familiar with city life, and was not part of the massive and desperate Irish migration during the years of the great potato famine in the early 1840s. His wife, Fanny, answered his plea to join him a year after he had arrived.*

We were safely landed in Philadelphia on the 7th of October [1818] and I had not so much as would pay my passage in a boat to take me ashore. My distress and confusion for the want of three or four pence was very great, and such was the jealousy and miserableness of the passengers that there was not one who would lend another even that sum. I, however, contrived to get over, and God is my witness that at that moment, I would as soon the ground would open and swallow me up. It was not long till I made out my father, whom I instantly knew, and no one could describe our feelings when I made myself known to him, and received his embraces, after an absence of seventeen years.

The old man was quite distracted about me. He done nothing that entire day but bring me about to his friends. Their manner of receiving me was quite amusing; one would say you are welcome, sir, from the old country; another, you are welcome to this free country—you are welcome to this land of liberty. Pray sir, are you not happy to have escaped from the tyranny of the old country? When you would deny the tyranny and give the preference to home, they would look amazed and say, "What sir, would you not rather live in a free country than in slavery?" In short they imagine here that we can not act or speak in Ireland but as the authorities please. Their ignorance and presumption are disgusting, their manners worse. As to politeness and good nature, they are totally unknown and though they all pretend to be well acquainted with the affairs of Europe they are entirely ignorant of all transactions there, or at the best know them imperfectly. If my father's love could do me any good I did not want for it, for it amounted to jealousy.

The morning after landing I went to work to the printing and to my great surprise I found that my hand was very little out. There is an immensity of printing done in America, still it is not as good as other businesses, and I think a journeyman printer's wages might be averaged at 7½ dollars a week all the year round. In New York it may not be so much as they are often out of work. The bookbinding may be put upon a footing with the printing; they execute work here remarkably well. I worked in Philadelphia for four and one-half weeks and saved £6, that is counting four dollars to the pound....

I wrote to poor Lewis [his brother] who gave me the most pressing invitation to come to New York where I now am, and where I every day experience from them some fresh kindness. My father put every obstacle he could in my way to prevent my going to New York but when he found that all he could do would not change my mind and that his entreaties to stay with him were in vain, he parted with me drowned in tears to such a pitch that he was unable to speak and since my arrival here he is every week writing to me to go back. I found the printing and bookbinding overpowered with hands in New York. I remained idle for twelve days in consequence; when finding there was many out of employment like myself I determined to turn myself to something else, seeing that there was nothing to be got from idleness. The trifle that I had saved was going from me fast. I drove about accordingly and was engaged by a bookseller to hawk maps for him at 7 dollars a week. This I done much to his satisfaction but when the town was well supplied he discharged me and instead of paying me my entire bill he stopped 9 dollars for maps which he said I made him no return for. I had to look for justice but was defeated for want of a person to prove my account. I lost the 9 dollars which I reckon to be 45 shillings. However, I got such an insight into the manners and customs of the natives whilst going among them with the maps as served me extremely. I now had about 60 dollars of my own saved, above every expense. These I laid out in the purchase of pictures on New Year's Day, which I sell ever since. I am doing astonishingly well, thanks be to God and was able on the 26th of this month to make a deposit of 100 dollars in the bank of the United States.

Thus you see, my dearest Fanny, God has at length done something for us; every penny of it is my own hard earnings and I am now convinced that it is only by deserving his blessing that we can hope or expect to merit His favors; *apropos,* I must inform you that I made a solemn promise to God while at sea that if it was His goodness to spare my life till I get ashore, I would make a hearty confession of my sins, which I thank Him for having granted me time and grace to perform, and this I mention, my love, because I know that it will be a source of pleasure to you; though living happy in the midst of my brother's family whom you know that I always loved and being as yet very successful in dealing in the pictures and indeed I may say in everything I have taken in hand since I came to America, I feel, particularly in the evenings, when I return home, a lonesomeness and lowness of spirits which oppress me almost to fainting. Oh my dearest Fanny if I could but convince you now that I am so many thousand miles from you of how insipid and distressing society and particularly women is to me, you would pity me of all creatures and fly to fill up that vacancy in my mind and spirits which my absence from you occasions....

As yet it's only natural I should feel lonesome in this country, ninety-nine out of every hundred who come to it are at first disappointed. They need never expect to realize the high expectations they have of it. Still it's a fine country and a much better place for a poor man than Ireland. It's a money-making country too, and much as they grumble at first after a while they never think of leaving it, though they could get a passage home every day for a trifle if they wished it. I have seen a great many of the Kilkenny people here, and they are all in good health except James Maxwell with whom the climate does not seem to agree. It gives me great courage to find that I have now more to the good and made more of my short time than most of them who are here two or three years. The fact is some of them earn a good deal, but they indulge too much in drink.

A man who can make a living at home has no business to come to the United States.... One thing I think is certain that if the emigrants knew before hand what they have to suffer for about the first six months after leaving home in every respect they would never come here. However, an enterprising man, desirous of advancing himself in the world will despise everything for coming to this free country, where a man is allowed to thrive and flourish, without having a penny taken out of his pocket by government; no visits from tax gatherers, constables or soldiers, every one at liberty to act and speak as he likes, provided it does not hurt another, to slander and damn government, abuse public men in their office to their faces, wear your hat in court and smoke a cigar while speaking to the judge as familiarly as if he was a common mechanic, hundreds go unpunished for crimes for which they would surely be hung in Ireland; in fact, they are so tender of life in this country that a person should have a very great interest to get himself hanged for anything!

*JAMES FENIMORE COOPER*

# 22 *Shooting Pigeons*

*James Fenimore Cooper (1789–1851), born in upstate New York, was a prolific writer. His most significant works are the* Leather-stocking Tales, *a series of five novels about life on the American frontier. The series takes its name from its hero, a woodsman who is variously called Natty Bumppo, Deerslayer, Hawkeye, Pathfinder, Leather-stocking, and the "trapper."*

*This excerpt, set in the 1780s, is taken from* The Pioneers *(1823), the first novel in the series to be published. Here Cooper describes a pigeon hunt. The passage furnishes one of the earliest lessons in environmentalism to be found in American literature. It is remarkable that one of the most popular writers of the era perceived the limits of the seemingly inexhaustible American landscape in an era of reckless exploitation of natural resources.*

If the heavens were alive with pigeons, the whole village seemed equally in motion, with men, women, and children. Every species of fire-arms, from the French ducking-gun with a barrel near six feet in length, to the common horseman's pistol, was to be seen in the hands of the men and boys; while bows and arrows, some made of the simple stick of a walnut sapling, and others in a rude imitation of the ancient cross-bows, were carried by many of the latter.

The houses and the signs of life apparent in the village, drove the alarmed birds from the direct line of their flight, toward the mountains, along the sides and near the bases of which they were glancing in dense masses, equally wonderful by the rapidity of their motion, and their incredible numbers.

We have already said, that across the inclined plane which fell from the steep ascent of the mountain to the banks of the Susquehanna, ran the highway, on either side of which a clearing of many acres had been made at a very early day. Over those clearings, and up the eastern mountain, and along the dangerous path that was cut into its side, the different individuals posted themselves, and in a few moments that attack commenced.

Among the sportsmen was the tall, gaunt form of Leather-stocking, walking over the field, with his rifle hanging on his arm, his dogs at his heels; the latter now scenting the dead or wounded birds, that were beginning to tumble from the flocks, and then crouching under the legs of their master, as if they participated in his feelings at this wasteful and unsportsmanlike execution.

The reports of the fire-arms became rapid, whole volleys rising from the plain, as flocks of more than ordinary numbers darted over the opening, shadowing the field like a cloud; and then the light smoke of a single piece would issue from among the leafless bushes on the mountain, as death was hurled on the retreat of the affrighted birds, who were rising from a volley, in a vain effort to escape. Arrows, and missiles of every kind, were in the midst of the flocks; and so numerous were the birds, and so low did they take their flight, that even long poles, in the hands of those on the sides of the mountain, were used to strike them to the earth.

During all this time, Mr. Jones, who disdained the humble and ordinary means of destruction used by his companions, was busily occupied, aided by Benjamin, in making arrangements for an assault of more than ordinarily fatal character. Among the relics of the old military excursions, that occasionally are discovered throughout the different districts of the western part of New-York, there had been found in Templeton, at its settlement, a small swivel, which would carry a ball of a pound weight. It was thought to have been deserted by a war-party of the whites, in one of their inroads into the Indian settlements, when, perhaps, convenience or their necessity induced them to leave such an incumbrance behind them in the woods. This miniature cannon had been released from the rust, and being mounted on little wheels, was now in a state for actual service. For several years it was the sole organ for extraordinary rejoicings used in those mountains. On the mornings of the Fourths of July, it would be heard ringing among the hills; and even Captain Hollister, who was the highest authority in that part of the country on all such occasions, affirmed that, considering its dimensions, it was no despicable gun for a salute. It was somewhat the worse for the service it had performed, it is true, there being but a trifling difference in size between the touch-hole and the muzzle. Still, the grand conceptions of Richard had suggested the importance of such an instrument in hurling death at his nimble enemies. The swivel was dragged by a horse into a part of the open space that the Sheriff thought most eligible for planting a battery of the kind, and Mr. Pump proceeded to load it. Several handfuls of duck-shot were placed on top of the powder, and the major-domo announced that his piece was ready for service.

The sight of such an implement collected all the idle spectators to the spot, who, being mostly boys, filled the air with cries of exultation and delight. The gun was pointed high, and Richard, holding a coal of fire in a pair of tongs, patiently took his seat on a stump, awaiting the appearance of a flock worthy of his notice.

So prodigious was the number of the birds, that the scattering fire of the guns, with the hurling of missiles, and the cries of the boys, had no other effect than to break off small flocks from the immense masses that continued to dart along the valley, as if the whole of the feathered tribe were pouring through that one pass. None pretended to collect the game, which lay scattered over the fields in such profusion as to cover the very ground with the fluttering victims.

Leather-stocking was a silent, but uneasy spectator of all these proceedings, but was able to keep his sentiments to himself until he saw the introduction of the swivel into the sports.

"This comes of settling a country!" he said—"here have I known the pigeons to fly for forty long years, and, till you made your clearings, there was nobody to skear or to hurt them. I loved to see them come into the woods, for they were company to a body; hurting nothing; being, as it was, as harmless as a garter-snake. But now it gives me sore thoughts when I hear the frighty things whizzing through the air, for I know it's only a motion to bring out all the brats in the village. Well! the Lord won't see the waste of his creatures for nothing, and right will be done to the pigeons, as well as others, by-and-by.—There's Mr. Oliver, as bad as the rest of them, firing into the flocks, as if he was shooting down nothing but Mingo warriors."

Among the sportsmen was Billy Kirby, who, armed with an old musket, was loading and without even looking into the air, was firing and shouting as his victims fell even on his own person. He heard the speech of Natty, and took upon himself to reply—

"What! old Leather-stocking," he cried, "grumbling at the loss of a few pigeons! If you had to sow your wheat twice, and three times, as I have done, you wouldn't be so massyfully feeling'd toward the devils. Hurrah, boys! scatter the feathers. This is better than shooting at a turkey's head and neck, old fellow."

"It's better for you, maybe, Billy Kirby," replied the indignant old hunter, "and all them that don't know how to put a ball down a rifle barrel, or how to bring it up again with a true aim; but it's wicked to be shooting into flocks in this wasty manner; and none do it, who know how to knock over a single bird. If a body has a craving for pigeon's flesh, why, it's made the same as all other creatures, for man's eating; but not to kill twenty and eat one. When I want such a thing I go into the woods till I find one to my liking, and then I shoot him off the branches, without touching the feather of another, though there might be a hundred on the same tree. You couldn't do such a thing, Billy Kirby—you couldn't do it, if you tried."

The fire from the distant part of the field had driven a single pigeon below the flock to which it belonged, and, frightened with the constant reports of the muskets, it was approaching the spot where the disputants stood, darting first from one side and then to the other, cutting the air with the swiftness of lightning, and making a noise with its wings not unlike the rushing of a bullet. Unfortunately for the woodchopper, notwithstanding his vaunt, he did not see this bird until it was too late to fire as it approached, and he pulled his trigger at the unlucky moment when it was darting immediately over his head. The bird continued its course with the usual velocity.

Natty [Leather-stocking] lowered the rifle from his arm when the challenge was made, and waiting a moment, until the terrified victim had got in a line with his eye, and had dropped near the bank of the lake, he raised it again with uncommon rapidity, and fired. It might have been chance, or it might have been skill, that produced the result; it was probably a union of both; but the pigeon whirled over in the air, and fell into the lake, with a broken wing. At the sound of his rifle, both his dogs started from his feet, and in a few minutes the "slut" brought out the bird, still alive.

The wonderful exploit of Leather-stocking was noised through the field with great rapidity, and the sportsmen gathered in, to learn the truth of the report.

"What!" said young Edwards, "have you really killed a pigeon on the wing, Natty, with a single ball?"

"Haven't I killed loons before now, lad, that dive at the flash?" returned the hunter. "It's much better to kill only such as you want, without wasting your powder and lead, than to be firing into God's creatures in this wicked manner. But I came out for a bird, and you know the reason why I like small game, Mr. Oliver, and now I have got one I will go home, for I don't relish to see these wasty ways that you are all practysing as if the least thing wasn't made for use, and not to destroy."

"Thou sayest well, Leather-stocking," cried Marmaduke, "and I begin to think it time to put an end to this work of destruction."

"Put an ind, Judge, to your clearings. An't the woods his work as well as the pigeons? Use, but don't waste. Wasn't the woods made for the beasts and birds to harbor in? and when man wanted their flesh, their skins, or their feathers, there's the place to seek them. But I'll go to the hut with my own game, for I wouldn't touch one of the harmless things that cover the ground here, looking up with their eyes on me, as if they only wanted tongues to say their thoughts."

With this sentiment in his mouth, Leather-stocking threw his rifle over his arm, and followed by his dogs, stepped across the clearing with great caution, taking care not to tread on one of the wounded birds in his path. He soon entered the bushes on the margin of the lake, and was hid from view.

Whatever impression the morality of Natty made on the Judge, it was utterly lost on Richard. He availed himself of the gathering of the sportsmen, to lay a plan for one "fell swoop" of destruction. The musket men were drawn up in battle array, in a line extending on each side of his artillery, with orders to await the signal of firing from himself.

"Stand by, my lads," said Benjamin, who acted as an aide-de-camp on this occasion; "stand by, my hearties, and when Squire Dickens heaves out the signal to begin firing, d'ye see, you may open upon them in a broadside. Take care and fire low, boys, and you'll be sure to hull the flock."

"Fire low!" shouted Kirby—"hear the old fool! If we fire low, we may hit the stumps, but not ruffle a pigeon."

"How should you know, you lubber?" cried Benjamin, with a very unbecoming heat for an officer on the eve of battle—"how should you know, you grampus? Haven't I sailed aboard of the Boadishy for five years? and wasn't it a standing order to fire low, and to hull your enemy? Keep silence at your guns, boys, and mind the order that is passed."

The loud laughs of the musket men were silenced by the more authoritative voice of Richard, who called for attention and obedience to his signals.

Some millions of pigeons were supposed to have already passed, that morning, over the valley of Templeton; but nothing like the flock that was now approaching had been seen before. It extended from mountain to mountain in one solid blue mass, and the eye looked in vain, over the southern hills, to find its termination. The front of this living column was distinctly marked by a line but very slightly indented, so regular and even was the flight. Even Marmaduke forgot the morality of Leather-stocking as it approached, and, in common with the rest, brought his musket to a poise.

"Fire!" cried the Sheriff, clapping a coal to the priming of the cannon. As half of Benjamin's charge escaped through the touch-hole, the whole volley of the musketry preceded the report of the swivel. On receiving this united discharge of small-arms, the front of the flock darted upward, while, at the same instant, myriads of those in the rear rushed with amazing rapidity into their places, so that when the column of white smoke gushed from the mouth of the little cannon, an accumulated mass of objects was gliding over its point of direction. The roar of the gun echoed along the mountains, and died away to the north, like distant thunder, while the whole flock of alarmed birds seemed, for a moment, thrown into one disorderly and agitated mass. The air was filled with their irregular flight, layer rising about layer, far above the tops of the highest pines, none daring to advance beyond the dangerous pass; when, suddenly, some of the leaders of the feathered tribe shot across the valley, taking their flight directly over the village, and hundreds of thousands in their rear followed the example, deserting the eastern side of the plain to their persecutors and the slain.

"Victory!" shouted Richard, "victory! we have driven the enemy from the field."

"Not so, Dickens," said Marmaduke: "the field is covered with them; and, like the Leather-stocking, I see nothing but eyes, in every direction, as the innocent sufferers turn their heads in terror. Full one-half of those that have fallen are yet alive; and I think it is time to end the sport, if sport it be."

"Sport!" cried the Sheriff; "it is princely sport! There are some thousands of the blue-coated boys on the ground, so that every old woman in the village may have a pot-pie for the asking."

"Well, we have happily frightened the birds from this side of the valley," said Marmaduke, "and the carnage must of necessity end, for the present.—Boys, I will give you six-pence a hundred for the pigeons' heads only; so go to work and bring them into the village."

This expedient produced the desired effect, for every urchin on the ground went industriously to work to wring the necks of the wounded birds. Judge Temple retired toward his dwelling with that kind of feeling that many a man has experienced before him, who discovers, after the excitement of the moment has passed, that he has purchased pleasure at the price of misery to others. Horses were loaded with the dead; and, after this first burst of sporting, the shooting of pigeons became a business, with a few idlers, for the remainder of the season. Richard, however, boasted for many a year, of his shot with the "cricket;" and Benjamin gravely asserted, that he thought they killed nearly as many pigeons on that day, as there were Frenchmen destroyed on the memorable occasion [in 1782] of [British Admiral] Rodney's victory.

*RAMON MARTINEZ CARO*

# 23 *Santa Anna Loses Texas*

*The base of the giant obelisk that marks the battlefield at San Jacinto is inscribed:*

> *Measured by its results, San Jacinto was one of the decisive battles of the world. The freedom of Texas from Mexico won here led to annexation and to the Mexican War, resulting in the acquisition by the United States of the states of Texas, New Mexico, Arizona, Nevada, California, Utah, and parts of Colorado, Wyoming, Kansas, and Oklahoma. Almost one-third of the present area of the American nation, nearly a million square miles, changed sovereignty.*

*The following memoir by the secretary to Mexican dictator and general Antonio Lopez de Santa Anna suggests why Sam Houston's inexperienced and undermanned army so quickly triumphed over Mexican forces. Ramon Caro's use of the footnote, while not to be recommended to the average student of history, raises that scholarly aid almost to an art form. It is hard to miss the import of Caro's graphic presentation of the dissension among Mexican leaders and the overconfidence and braggadocio of Santa Anna. Caro's critique of Santa Anna's military skills differs only by the force of its sarcasm from what historians have generally concluded about Texas's favorite villain.*

His Excellency says in his report, a most original document, that when the enemy discovered our troops, it began firing upon them from a redoubt it had built for its protection; that he raised a trench and, placing two six-pounders in position, kept a constant fire in reply without suffering any losses;[1] that he immediately reconnoitered the bank of the river both to the right and to the left for a distance of two leagues in search of a crossing to surprise the enemy that night; that his efforts were fruitless[2] because the river is both deep and very wide; and that

1. Perhaps His Excellency does not consider the death of the two soldiers and a mule driver a loss.

2. All the officers and men present at the time, some of whom are in this capital now, may declare to what efforts His Excellency refers, and whether he again mounted a horse or moved from his tent until the time for our departure, after we arrived before San Felipe.

its waters were high and not even a small canoe could be found. He further states that the rivers of that country present great difficulties to an expeditionary army[3] because they are large and subject to floods in the spring as a result of the melting of the snow in the mountains[4] and the frequent rains which themselves cause numerous delays in the operations.

His Excellency continues: "On the 8th I ordered the construction of two barges (flatboats), for which it was necessary to bring the lumber from the distant houses. After the work was begun, it was seen that it would require ten or twelve days for their construction because of the lack of carpenters, and that it would take three or more days to place them where they were to be used. I considered such a delay an irreparable waste of time.[5]

"General Filisola had not arrived at the Colorado, and General Gaona, who should have joined our force long since, *did not even say when he would be able to join us.* The conditions faced by the leader of the enemy were no longer unknown to me. Intimidated as he was by the successive triumphs of our army; overcome by the rapidity of our marches over a country which offers so many natural obstacles, some of them almost insurmountable to the enemy,[6] and suffering from want and desertion which impelled him to look for his salvation in the retreat he was undertaking, there was nothing more advisable than to pursue him and give him battle before he could improve his condition.

"We were unable to cross the Brazos at San Felipe.[7] In view of these circumstances, I decided to reconnoiter the right bank of the river for ten or twelve leagues, taking for granted that this flank was covered

3. Why was the necessary equipment for crossing these rivers not taken by the army? His Excellency may claim that he did not know the country, but why did he not consult with those who did? Most of the difficulties encountered were well known beforehand.

4. When His Excellency speaks of melting snows in the mountains, has he forgotten that he was speaking of the immense plains of Texas? He alone has ever seen mountains in the deserts of Texas.

5. Two American carpenters who had joined our forces, aided by two other men, finished one of the said barges in a day and a half. In three days, therefore, they could have finished the two. How does His Excellency figure out it would take ten or twelve days?

6. "Obstacles that were almost insurmountable to the enemy" says the general, to the enemy who was acquainted with the country, who had at their disposal steamboats, barges, canoes, etc. Maybe they were no obstacles to us who lacked all these facilities.

7. I do not see why. After the two barges were completed, a matter of three days, would the enemy, intimidated by our triumphs, terror stricken, suffering from desertion and want, and in addition, immensely inferior to our force in number, have prevented us from crossing? Our force consisted of more than 2,000 men.

by the division of General Urrea, who, as I have stated before, was on his way to Brazoria. On the 9th, I left San Felipe for this purpose with 500 grenadiers and riflemen and fifty mounted men,[8] leaving General Ramírez y Sesma with the rest of his division to be reenforced at any moment by that of General Gaona.[9] Three days later, after painful marches and countermarches, during one of which I walked for five leagues, I took possession of Thompson's Crossing in spite of the efforts of a small detachment of the enemy that tried to defend it but succeeded only in wounding one grenadier and our bugler. As a result of this unexpected operation, I also succeeded in capturing a fine flatboat and two canoes from the enemy.[10] The staff, the officers, and the troops conducted themselves with bravery and courage in this engagement.

"Through some of the colonists taken, among them a *Mexican*[11] I discovered that the heads of the Texan government, Don Lorenzo de Zavala, and the other leaders of the revolution were at Harrisburg, twelve leagues distant on the right bank of Buffalo Bayou; and that

8. Why reconnoiter the right bank when it was known that the only enemy that existed was on the left? Why not reconnoiter the left bank where the enemy was? With forces vastly superior to those of the enemy, now intimidated, and with fortune still smiling upon us, as His Excellency claims, why were we not led directly to the enemy in order to destroy it? The route along the right bank was better suited to the future designs of His Excellency, who already saw himself arriving in Harrisburg, proceeding on to New Washington, thence to Nacogdoches, and as far as the Sabine, returning along the coast to Cópano, and embarking there for Matamoros. (Orders had already been issued to General Vital Fernández at Matamoros to dispatch the Mexican war schooner *El Bravo* to El Cópano to await there orders from His Excellency.) From there he was to go on to Tampico, continuing by land to San Luis Potosí, where he would join the *travelers* and descend upon the capital of the republic to be received with triumphs, ovations, offers of the presidency, etc. This was the true motive for his decision.

9. His Excellency has already stated that General Gaona had not even communicated to him when he was likely to join him. As a matter of fact, Gaona was, at this time, lost in the desert beyond Bastrop and could not tell when he would arrive.

10. It is worth while noticing that this brilliant measure was not decided upon prior to our departure from San Felipe, but that it was the result of an unforeseen coincidence. Soon after we left San Felipe four Americans on horseback were sighted and we left our road to follow them, but not succeeding in overtaking them, we returned to our former route. Colonel Treviño, who had gone ahead of us, found a negro and his wife in one of the houses and took them to His Excellency to whom they declared that they had come from Thompson's Crossing where there were a few Americans. His Excellency offered the mulatto 100 *pesos* to return to Thompson's to tell the Americans he had seen us but that we had taken a different route. The mulatto fulfilled his mission, going to Thompson's immediately and returning at once to serve as guide. It was thus that we captured the crossing, but the mulatto never received the 100 *pesos*.

11. I did not know that a Mexican could be a colonist in his own country.

their arrest was certain if our troops marched upon them without loss of time. More important than the news was the rapidity of our march, which, if successful, would completely disconcert the rebellion.[12] Without confiding in any one I decided to take advantage of the opportunity. I crossed with the grenadiers.[13]

"To intercept Houston's march and to destroy with one stroke the armed forces and the hopes of the revolutionists was too important a blow to allow the opportunity to escape.[14]

"In the early morning of the 19th I sent Captain Marcos Barragán with some dragoons to the crossing at Lynchburg, three leagues distant from New Washington, to keep a lookout and to give me timely notice of the arrival of Houston.[15] At eight o'clock, the morning of the 20th, Capt. Barragán came to me and told me that Houston was approaching Lynchburg. All the members of the division heard of the approach of the enemy with joy, and, in the highest spirits, continued the march already started towards that place.[16]

"When I arrived, Houston had taken possession of the woods on the banks of Buffalo Bayou, whose waters join the San Jacinto at that point and flow into those of Galveston. His position would force him to fight or take to the water. The enthusiasm of my troops was such that I immediately engaged him in battle;[17] but, although our fire was

12. There is no doubt that the idea was brilliant, preferring to disconcert the rebellion rather than stamp it out as he could have done by attacking it at San Felipe as indicated. But let us consider for a moment the state and the ramifications of the revolution at this time. The revolutionists had been destroyed at San Patricio, la Bahía, and Béxar, and there was no other force left in the field except Houston's, cut off at Groce's Crossing. I do not know why His Excellency preferred to take possession of four or six men who made up the cabinet in order to execute them to falling upon Houston and destroying him. He, being a military man, may know the reason.

13. It is a well-known fact in the army that immediately after our arrival at Thompson's the troops were ordered to cross to the opposite side at once in a canoe, this operation having taken place, therefore, before learning the important news to which His Excellency refers.

14. Why was the enemy allowed to escape at San Felipe? At that time we had over 2,000 men, as it has been stated, and the enemy was intimidated and terror-stricken. Why the desire of giving it battle now with the hope of destroying it when we had only 700 men? The facts cannot be reconciled. I suspected as much all the time.

15. It is true that Capt. Barragán went to Lynchburg Crossing with some dragoons on the 19th, but not to observe the arrival of Houston. He was to prepare the barges that were to be used by our troops in crossing the river at that point.

16. It is true that we were already on our way to that point but for the purpose of crossing the river at Lynchburg in order to continue to Anahuac, as previously arranged. It is to be noted that His Excellency ordered both Harrisburg and New Washington burned before we left. He did likewise with several houses along our route.

17. If the situation of the enemy was so desperate, why didn't His Excellency press the engagement to a decisive termination?

returned, I was unable to draw him from the woods. I wanted to draw him out to a place that suited me better.[18] I retired about one thousand *varas* and camped on a hill that gave me an advantageous position, with water on the rear, heavy woods to our right as far as the banks of the San Jacinto, open plains to the left, and a clear front.[19] While taking our position, the cannonade was kept up by the enemy and Capt. Fernando Urriza was wounded. About one hundred men sallied forth from the woods and daringly threw themselves upon my escort placed on our left.[20]

"At nine o'clock on the morning of the 21st, in full view of the enemy, General Cós arrived with 400 men[21] from the battalions of Aldama, Guerrero, Toluca, and Guadalajara. He left one hundred men under the command of Colonel Mariano García to bring up the baggage that was detained at a bad crossing near Harrisburg. These men never joined us. I immediately saw that my order with respect to the 500 *chosen* infantry had been disregarded, for the greater part of the reenforcement was made up of recruits that had been distributed among our troops at San Luis Potosí and Saltillo.[22] In view of the circumstances that made me superior to the enemy, this serious disobedience instantly caused me the greatest displeasure, realizing that the reenforcement so anxiously awaited and

18. If the position did not suit His Excellency, could the enemy have been in such a distressing situation as to be forced to fight or take to the water? The enemy could not have exercised such poor judgment as to choose the worst location to encamp, having reached the ground long before our forces.

19. We shall later see whether the open plains helped us to prevent our being completely surprised, and that at four in the afternoon.

20. From the report the reader is given the impression that this engagement took place contemporaneously with the cannonade. It did not occur until about five in the afternoon, more or less.

21. Later on we shall see what His Excellency says the enemy thought of this reenforcement of 400 men.

22. Regarding these 500 *picked* men of which His Excellency speaks so much, let us see what General Filisola says in his official communication to the government, of May 14th of last year, inserted in his *Representación* made to the government about the Texas campaign, the 19th of August of the same year. He says: "His Excellency crossed to the left bank of the Brazos at Old Fort, on the 15th of the said month, and immediately marched upon Harrisburg with the Matamoros battalion, the chosen companies of Guerrero, *primero activo de México*, and Toluca, a six-pounder, and sixty picked dragoons. He left me instructions to send General Cós with 500 men and two pieces of artillery to Velasco. On the 17th I received orders from His Excellency reducing the number of troops to be taken by General Cós to 200 men, and on the 18th I received new orders instructing me to send General Cós to him with 500 infantry and 500 cases of rifle ammunition. This order was complied with on that day, the force being made up from the battalions of Guerrero, Aldama, and Guadalajara." There is nothing here to indicate that he asked for *picked* troops, and, I place more confidence in the testimony and known probity of Filisola.

with which I expected to inflict a decisive blow to the enemy was insufficient.[23]

"Fatigued as a result of having spent the morning on horseback, and not having slept the night before, I lay down under the shade of some trees while the troops ate their rations. I sent for General Manuel Fernández Castrillón, who was acting as major general, and I ordered him to keep a close watch and to advise me of the slightest movement of the enemy.[24] I also asked him to wake me up as soon as the troops had eaten, for it was necessary to take decisive action as soon as possible.[25]

"As fatigue and long vigils provoke heavy slumber, I was sleeping soundly[26] when the din and fire of battle awoke me. I immediately became aware that we were being attacked and that great disorder prevailed. The enemy had surprised our advance posts. . . .[27]

23. Three is the charm. This may be the reason for the three attempts made by His Excellency to strike the decisive blow. In San Felipe he tried it by going in search of the enemy on the right bank of the river, when he knew it was on the left bank at Groce's Crossing. At Harrisburg he marched to arrest the members of the cabinet of Texas to shoot them, but they, being aware of the fate that awaited them, fled. The last attempt was at San Jacinto, fateful and tragic day whose effects we have seen. Some fatalists may still exclaim that it was fate! There is no fate. All these evils and disasters have had their origin in the lack of foresight and mismanagement of the campaign from the beginning. The Prince of the Peace has truthfully said in his memoirs recently published "The greatest evils often have their origin in a careless slip or an oversight at the beginning of our undertakings. To this we give the name of fatality." Would that his undertakings had ended there! It would not have been so bad. His weakness and fear later sacrificed the most sacred interests of our country, making her drink the cup of bitterness to its very dregs in the dismemberment of her territory.

24. Fortunately, dead men tell no tales. It is for this reason that the conduct of this officer is attacked here and later on, without regard for the fact that he fell in the glorious defence of his country.

25. According to the orders issued, the attack was not to have taken place until early the next day. What decisive action was to take place when the troops finished their meal? If General Castrillón and many brave companions fell, death sealing their lips, fortunately some have miraculously survived them to enlighten the nation as to the facts and to honor the memory of the brave men who fell in her defence.

26. It is well that His Excellency admits it. If a general-in-chief, who has been confronted by the enemy for only twenty-four hours, an enemy who on the day before makes a false attack to feel our strength, is forced to lie down and rest from the hardships of one night's vigil, what can be expected from the unfortunate soldiers, really fatigued by the many hardships of the campaign? Can they be blamed if they too, were sleeping at the time of the attack? When the head sleeps, the rest of the body is not awake.

27. The horrible memory of that moment makes the pen drop from my hand for a few minutes. Imagine our being surprised at four in the afternoon, in the middle of an open plain, with nothing to obstruct the view of the enemy from our front! They succeeded in advancing to within 200 yards from our trenches without being

"Although the evil was done, I thought for a moment that it might be repaired. I ordered the permanent battalion of Aldama to reenforce that of Matamoros which was sustaining the line of battle; and hurriedly organized an attack column under orders of Col. Manuel Céspedes, composed of the permanent battalion of Guerrero and detachments from Toluca and Guadalajara, which, simultaneously with the column of Col. Luelmo, marched forward to check the principal advance of the enemy.[28] My efforts were all in vain. The front line was abandoned by the two battalions that were holding it, notwithstanding the continuous fire of our artillery commanded by the brave Lieut. Arenal. The two newly organized columns were dispersed, Col. Céspedes[29] being wounded and Capt. Luelmo killed. General Castrillón who ran from side to side to restore order among our ranks, fell mortally wounded.[30] The recruits bunched themselves[31] and confused the tried soldiers, and neither the first nor the second made any use of their weapons. In the meantime the enemy, taking advantage of the opportunity, carried their charge forward rapidly, and shouting madly,[32] secured a victory in a few minutes which they did not dream was possible.[33]

"All hope lost, with everyone escaping as best he could, my despair was as great as the danger I was in. A servant of my aide-de-camp, Juan Bringas, with noble kindness offered me the horse of his master, and

discovered, and from there they spread death and terror among our ranks. This is unpardonable. Our country, our honor, humanity, the shades of the bleeding victims sacrificed by that criminal negligence call for vengeance. The shadows of those who fell, so cowardly murdered, at Refugio, Goliad, and the Alamo had called for vengeance for some time. Divine Providence, tired of so many injustices, may at last avenge them all.

28. The principal movement of the enemy was the complete surprise which it was able to carry out. At that time, His Excellency was sleeping soundly. The rest of the engagement developed with lightning rapidity, so that by the time he reached our front line it had already been defeated and completely routed. When did he organize the two columns, then? Colonel Céspedes is here now and can testify as to the truth.

29. He was wounded in our trenches so seriously that he is still suffering from the effects of his wound.

30. His daring and loyalty in trying to overcome the confusion, which has no parallel or equal, cost him his life, but he died while carrying out his duty.

31. Those who were recruits and those who were tried veterans all were completely confused by the suddenness of the unexpected surprise.

32. Their war cry was "Remember the Alamo."

33. I do not see why, when their scouts had made certain of the absolute disregard that reigned in our camp, succeeding in burning the bridge on our rear at three, thus cutting off our retreat. Observers placed on the top of trees near us had watched our camp and given an account of our lack of precautions. Why then, should they not have imagined a victory over an enemy that had given itself up to sleep without even posting advance guards?

earnestly pleaded that I save myself. I looked about for my escort and was told by two dragoons who were hurriedly saddling their horses[34] that their companions and officers had fled. I remembered that General Filisola was at Thompson's Crossing, sixteen leagues distant, and, without hesitation, I tried to make my way to that place through the enemy's ranks.[35] They pursued me and overtook me[36] a league and a half from the battlefield, at a large creek where the bridge had been burnt. I turned my horse loose and with difficulty took refuge in a grove of small pines. The coming of night permitted me to evade their vigilance. The hope of rejoining the army and of vindicating its honor gave me strength to cross the creek with the water above my waist, and

34. It is too much to admit that even the cavalry had unsaddled their horses and turned them loose to graze, while the enemy was in sight.

35. God forbid that His Excellency should have made his way through the enemy. I was a short distance away—not exactly among the enemy—when I saw him coming already in flight and I followed him immediately. Thank God we were not among the last who fled, for of those very few survived to tell the tale. We continued at full speed until we reached the bridge on the Brazos, eight miles away, but only to find it burned. We retraced our steps a short distance and entered a small thicket, where he dismounted and left me. I followed a path with Lieut. Col. José Maríra Castillo Iberri, Capt. Marcos Barragán, and some others whose names I do not recall. They all succeeded in crossing a creek, but I was prevented from following them by the approach of the enemy who was already entering the woods. I turned back and hid among some thick brush. There I remained all night in constant danger of death, for to make things worse it was a full moon night. After daybreak, totally exhausted, I gave myself up to two of the enemy who were passing nearby. Fortunately, one of them was French and when I addressed him in his language he prevented his companion from firing his gun, which he was making ready. Would that I had not had this good luck, for had I been shot I would have been spared the many sufferings and agonies which I endured during the five and a half months I was a prisoner. What is still more, I would have been spared the sad and cruel disappointment with which His Excellency repaid me for my well-known good services as his secretary, a fact known to all the army, forgetting my noble conduct while a prisoner with him. I shall refer to this further on.

They took me to Houston, whom I found suffering from a wound in his foot. Hardly had I disclosed my identity as the secretary to His Excellency when this very fact provoked such indignation among his followers (mostly adventurers) that had I not been sitting by the side of Houston, more than a hundred bullets would have made me their mark. The mere name of His Excellency or anything closely connected with him provoked the greatest indignation.

Houston addressed several questions to me to ascertain the whereabouts of His Excellency, to all of which I truthfully replied that I did not know where he was. After he spoke to his followers, calming them, he sent me with one of his aides to the place where the other officers who had been taken prisoner were being kept.

36. Had they done so, His Excellency would have never written the report which I am now refuting. We were too far ahead for them to overtake us. On the other

I continued on my route afoot. In an abandoned house I found some clothes which I exchanged for my wet ones. At eleven o'clock on the 22nd, I was overtaken again by my pursuers[37] just as I was crossing a plain, and thus I fell into their hands. Not recognizing me because of my clothes, they asked me if I had seen General Santa Anna.[38] I replied that he was ahead of me and this happy thought saved me from being assassinated on the spot as I found out later."[39]

hand, the enemy was not pursuing definite individuals, for they knew nobody, much less, His Excellency, who wore no military insignia.

37. Not his pursuers, but the pursuers of all of us. His Excellency insists in believing that they were pursuing him only.

38. I cannot understand how a person who is known, as he claims he was, could disguise himself by merely changing his clothes. (That is all the disguise he had.) How did he alter his face? I would like him to answer that.

39. A very happy and opportune thought. Had I been in the place of His Excellency, I would have replied in the affirmative. Did he deny his identity only when he was arrested? Let it be, lest it be said that the desire to incriminate guides my pen.

*EDWARD GOULD BUFFUM*

# 24 *Six Months in the Gold Mines*

*Edward Gould Buffum was an army lieutenant in California during the Mexican War when news of the gold strikes first spread. As soon as he mustered out in September 1848, Buffum headed for the gold fields. His* Six Months in the Gold Mines, *hurriedly published in 1850 "in consequence of the public interest in all that pertains to California," is one of the most important accounts of the California gold rush. Many ambitious easterners, relying on his detailed accounts of mining procedures, used the book as a combined atlas and instruction manual as they headed west in search of riches. Buffum's vivid and exciting account of life on the mining frontier still attracts students of the American West.*

Next morning early, in better spirits than we had enjoyed for a week previously, we started for Yuba River [north of Sacramento]. About a mile from the camping-place we struck into the mountains, the same range at whose base we had been before travelling, and which are a portion of the Sierra Nevada. The hills here were steep and rugged, but covered with a magnificent growth of oak and red-wood. As we reached the summit of a lofty hill, the Yuba River broke upon our view, winding like a silver thread beneath us, its banks dotted with white tents, and fringed with trees and shrubbery.

We had at last reached the "mines," although a very different portion of them than that for which we started. We turned out our tired horses, and immediately set forth on an exploring expedition. As my clothing was all dirty and wet, I concluded to indulge in the luxury of a new shirt, and going down to the river found a shrewd Yankee in a tent surrounded by a party of naked Indians, and exposing for sale jerked beef at a dollar a pound, flour at a dollar and a half do., and for a coarse striped shirt which I picked up with the intention of purchasing, he coolly asked me the moderate price of sixteen dollars! I looked at my dirty shirt, then at the clean new one I held in my hand, and finally at my little gold bag, not yet replenished by digging, and concluded to postpone my purchase until I had struck my pick and crowbar into the bowels of the earth, and extracted therefrom at least a sufficiency to purchase a shirt. The diggings on Yuba River had at that time been discovered only about three months, and were confined entirely to the "bars," as they are called, extending nearly a mile each way from where the road strikes the river, on both its banks. The principal diggings were then called the "upper" and the "lower diggings," each about half a mile above and below the road. We started for the upper diggings to "see the elephant," and winding through the hills, for it was impossible to travel all the way on the river's bank, struck the principal bar then wrought on the river. This has since been called Foster's Bar, after an American who was then keeping a store there, and who had a claim on a large portion of the bar.

Upon reaching the bar, a curious scene presented itself. About one hundred men, in miner's costume, were at work, performing the various portions of the labour necessary in digging the earth and working a rocking machine. The apparatus then used upon the Yuba River, and which has always been the favourite assistant of the gold-digger, was the common rocker or cradle, constructed in the simplest manner. It consists of nothing more than a wooden box or hollowed log, two sides and one end of which are closed, while the other end is left open. At the end which is closed and called the "mouth" of the machine, a sieve, usually made of a plate of sheet iron, or a piece of raw hide, perforated with holes about half an inch in diameter, is rested upon the sides. A number of " bars" or "rifflers," which are little pieces of board from one to two inches in height, are nailed to the bottom, and extend laterally across it. Of these, there are three or four in the machine, and one at the "tail," as it is called, i. e. the end where the dirt is washed out. This, with a pair of rockers like those of a child's cradle, and a handle to rock it with, complete the description of the machine, which being placed with the rockers upon two logs, and the "mouth" elevated at a slight angle above the tail, is ready for operation. Modified and improved as this may be, and as in fact it already has been, so long as manual labour is employed for washing gold, the "cradle" is the best agent to use for that purpose.

The manner of procuring and washing the golden earth was this. The loose stones and surface earth being removed from any portion of the bar, a hole from four to six feet square was opened, and the dirt extracted therefrom was thrown upon a raw hide placed at the side of the machine. One man shovelled the dirt into the sieve, another dipped up water and threw it on, and a third rocked the "cradle." The earth, thrown upon the sieve, is washed through with the water, while the stones and gravel are retained and thrown off. The continued motion of the machine, and the constant stream of water pouring through it, washes the earth over the various bars or rifflers to the "tail," where it runs out, while the gold, being of greater specific gravity, sinks to the bottom, and is prevented from escaping by the rifflers. When a certain amount of earth has been thus washed (usually about sixty pans full are called " a washing"), the gold, mixed with a heavy black sand, which is always found mingled with gold in California, is taken out and washed in a tin pan, until nearly all the sand is washed away. It is then put into a cup or pan, and when the day's labour is over is dried before the fire, and the sand remaining carefully blown out. This is a simple explanation of the process of gold-washing in the placers of California. At present, however, instead of dipping and pouring on water by hand, it is usually led on by a hose or forced by a pump, thereby giving a better and more constant stream, and saving the labour of one man. The excavation is continued until the solid rock is struck, or the water rushing in renders it impossible to obtain any more earth, when a new place is opened. We found the gold on the Yuba in exceedingly fine particles, and it has always been considered of a very superior quality. We inquired of the washers as to their success, and they, seeing we were "green horns," and thinking we might possibly interfere with them, gave us either evasive answers, or in some cases told us direct lies. We understood from them that they were making about twenty dollars per day, while I afterwards learned, from the most positive testimony of two men who were at work there at the time, that one hundred dollars a man was not below the average estimate of a day's labour.

On this visit to Foster's Bar I made my first essay in gold-digging. I scraped up with my hand my tin cup full of earth, and washed it in the river. How eagerly I strained my eyes as the earth was washing out, and the bottom of the cup was coming in view! and how delighted, when, on reaching the bottom, I discerned about twenty little golden particles sparkling in the sun's rays, and worth probably about fifty cents. I wrapped them carefully in a piece of paper, and preserved them for a long time,—but, like much more gold in larger quantities, which it has since been my lot to possess, it has escaped my grasp, and where it now is Heaven only knows.

The labour on Yuba River appeared very severe, the excavations being sometimes made to a depth of twelve feet before the soil containing the gold, which was a gravelly clay, was reached. We had not brought our tools with us, intending, if our expedition in the mountains had succeeded, that one of our party should return for our remaining stock of provisions and tools. We had no facilities for constructing a machine, and no money to buy one (two hundred dollars being the price for which a mere hollowed pine log was offered us), and besides, all the bars upon which men were then engaged in labour were "claimed," a claim at that time being considered good when the claimant had cleared off the top soil from any portion of the bar. We returned to our camp, and talked over our prospects, in a quandary what to do. Little did we then dream that, in less than six months, the Yuba River, then only explored some three miles above where we were, would be successfully wrought for forty miles above us, and that thousands would find their fortunes upon it.

We concluded to return to the *Embarcadero*, and take a new start. Accordingly, next morning we packed up and set off, leaving at work upon the river about two hundred men. Having retraced our steps, we arrived at Sutter's Fort in safety on the evening of November 30th, just in time to find the member of our party whom we had left behind, packing all our remaining provisions and tools into a cart, ready to start for the "dry diggings" on the following morning.

The history of John A. Sutter, and his remarkable settlement on the banks of the Sacramento, has been one of interest since California first began to attract attention. Captain Sutter is by birth a Swiss, and was formerly an officer in the French army. He emigrated to the United States, became a naturalized citizen, and resided in Missouri several years. In the year 1839 he emigrated to the then wilderness of California, where he obtained a large grant of land, to the extent of about eleven leagues, bordering on the Sacramento River, and made a settlement directly in the heart of an Indian country, among tribes of hostile savages. For a long time he suffered continual attacks and depredations from the Indians, but finally succeeded, by kind treatment and good offices, in reducing them to subjection, and persuading them to come into his settlement, which he called New Helvetia. With their labour he built a large fort of *adobes* or sunburnt bricks, brought a party of his Indians under military discipline, and established a regular garrison. His wheat-fields were very extensive, and his cattle soon numbered five thousand, the whole labour being performed by Indians. These he paid with a species of money made of tin, which was stamped with dots, indicating the number of days' labour for which each one was given; and they were returned to him in exchange for cotton cloth, at a dollar a yard, and trinkets and sweetmeats at corresponding prices. The discovery of the gold mines of California has, however, added more to Sutter's fame than did his bold settlement in the wilderness. This has introduced him to the world almost as a man of gold, and connected his name for ever with the most prized metal upon earth. He is quite "a gentleman of the old school," his manners being very cordial and prepossessing. . . .

With all our worldly gear packed in an ox-wagon, we left Sutter's Fort on the morning of the 1st of December, and travelling about seven miles on the road, encamped in a beautiful grove of evergreen oak, to give the cattle an opportunity to lay in a sufficient supply of grass and acorns, preparatory to a long march. As we were to remain here during the day, we improved the opportunity by taking our dirty clothing, of which by that time we had accumulated a considerable quantity, down to the banks of the American Fork, distant about one mile from camp, for the purpose of washing. While we were employed in this laborious but useful occupation, Higgins called my attention to the salmon which were working up the river over a little rapid opposite us. Some sport suggested itself; and more anxious for this than labour, we dropped our half-washed shirts, and started back to camp for our rifles, which we soon procured, and brought down to the river. In making their way over the bar, the backs of the salmon were exposed some two inches above water; and the instant one appeared, a well-directed rifle-ball perforated his spine. The result was, that before dark Higgins and myself carried into camp thirty-five splendid salmon, procured by this novel mode of sport. We luxuriated on them, and gave what we could not eat for supper and breakfast to some lazy Indians, who had been employed the whole day in spearing some half dozen each. There is every probability that the salmon fishery will yet prove a highly lucrative business in California.

Next morning we packed up and made a fresh start. That night we encamped at the "Green Springs," about twenty-five miles distant from Sutter's Fort. These springs are directly upon the road, and bubble up from a muddy black loam, while around them is the greenest verdure,—the surrounding plain being dotted with beautiful groves and magnificent flowers. Their waters are delicious.

As the ox-team was a slow traveller, and quarters were to be looked for in our new winter home, on the next morning Higgins and myself were appointed a deputation to mount two horses we had brought with us and proceed post-haste to the "dry diggings." We started at 10 A.M., and travelled through some beautiful valleys and over lofty hills. As we reached the summit of a high ridge, we paused by common consent to gaze upon the landscape and breathe the delicious air. The broad and fertile valleys of the Sacramento and San Joaquin lay stretched at our feet like a highly coloured map. The noble rivers which lend their names to these rich valleys were plainly visible, winding like silver threads through dark lines of timber fringing their banks; now plunging amid dense forests, and now coming in view sparkling and bright as the riches they contain; the intermediate plains, here parched and browned with the sun's fierce rays; there brilliant with all the hues of the rainbow, and dotted with the autumnal flowers and open groves of evergreen oak. Herds of elk, black-tailed deer, and antelope browsed near the mountain sides, on the summit of which the eagle builds his eyry. The surrounding atmosphere, fragrant with delightful odours, was so pure and transparent as to render objects visible at a great distance, and so elastic and bracing as to create a perceptible effect on our feelings. Far in the distance the massive peak of Shaste reared its snow-capped head, from amid a dense forest, fourteen thousand feet into the sky. We arrived at what was then called Weaver's Creek, about dusk....

The "dry diggings" of Weaver's Creek being a fair specimen of dry diggings in all parts of the mining region, a description of them will give the reader a general idea of the various diggings of the same kind in California. They are called "dry" in contradistinction to the "wet" diggings, or those lying directly on the banks of streams, and where all the gold is procured by washing. As I before said, the stream coursed between lofty tree-clad hills, broken on both sides of the river into little ravines or gorges. In these ravines most of the gold was found. The loose stones and top earth being thrown off, the gravelly clay that followed it was usually laid aside for washing, and the digging continued until the bottom rock of the ravine was reached, commonly at a depth of from one to six feet. The surface of this rock was carefully cleared off, and usually found to contain little crevices and holes, the latter in miner's parlance called "pockets," and in which the gold was found concealed, sparkling like the treasures in the cave of Monte Cristo. A careful examination of the rock being made, and every little crevice and pocket being searched with a sharp pointed-knife, gold in greater or less quantities invariably made its appearance. I shall never forget the delight with which I first struck and worked out a crevice. It was the second day after our installation in our little log hut; the first having been employed in what is called "prospecting," or searching for the most favourable place at which to commence operations. I had slung pick, shovel, and bar upon my shoulder, and trudged merrily away to a ravine about a mile from our house. Pick, shovel, and bar did their duty, and I soon had a large rock in view. Getting down into the excavation I had made, and seating myself upon the rock, I commenced a careful search for a crevice, and at last found one extending longitudinally along the rock. It appeared to be filled with a hard, bluish clay and gravel, which I took out with my knife, and there at the bottom, strewn along the whole length of the rock, was bright, yellow gold, in little pieces about the size and shape of a grain of barley. Eureka! Oh how my heart beat! I sat still and looked at it some minutes before I touched it, greedily drinking in the pleasure of gazing upon gold that was in my very grasp, and feeling a sort of independent bravado in allowing it to remain there. When my eyes were sufficiently feasted, I scooped it out with the point of my knife and an iron spoon, and placing it in my pan, ran home with it very much delighted. I weighed it, and found that my first day's labour in the mines had made me thirty-one dollars richer than I was in the morning.

The gold, which, by some great volcanic eruption, has been scattered upon the soil over an extensive territory, by the continual rains of the winter season has been sunk into the hills, until it has reached either a hard clay which it cannot penetrate, or a rock on which it rests. The gold in the hills, by the continual rains, has been washing lower and lower, until it has reached the ravines. It has washed down the ravines until it has there reached the rock, and thence, it has washed along the bed of the ravines until it has found some little crevice in which it rests, where the water can carry it no farther. Here it gathers, and thus are formed the "pockets" and "nests" of gold, one of which presents such a glowing golden sight to the eye of the miner, and such a field for his imagination to revel in. How often, when I have struck one of these, have I fondly wished that it might reach to the centre of the earth, and be filled as it was at its mouth with pure, bright, yellow gold.

Our party's first day's labour produced one hundred and fifty dollars, I having been the most successful of all. But we were satisfied, although our experience had not fulfilled the golden stories we had heard previous to our reaching the *placers*. Finding the average amount of gold dug on Weaver's Creek at that time to be about an ounce per day to a man, we were content so long as we could keep pace with our neighbours. There is a spirit of emulation among miners which prevents them from being ever satisfied with success whilst others around them are more successful. We continued our labours for a week, and found, at the end of that time, our whole party had dug out more than a thousand dollars; and after paying for our house, and settling between ourselves our little private expenses, we were again on a clear track, unencumbered by debt, and in the heart of a region where treasures of unknown wealth were lying hidden in the earth on which we daily trod.

About this time, the most extravagant reports reached us from the Middle Fork, distant in a northerly direction about thirty miles from Weaver's Creek. Parties who had been there described the river as being lined with gold of the finest quality. One and two hundred dollars was not considered a great day's labour, and now was the time to take advantage of it, while in its pristine richness. The news was too blooming for me to withstand. I threw down my pickaxe, and leaving a half-wrought crevice for some other digger to work out, I packed up and held myself in readiness to proceed by the earliest opportunity, and with the first party ready to go for the Middle Fork. . . .

Passing to the northward of the Dry Diggings, we encamped at dusk in a little oak grove about three miles from Sutter's Mill, killed a deer, ate a hearty supper, spread our blankets on the ground, and slept quietly and peacefully beneath a star-studded and cloudless heaven. Next morning we went into Culoma, the Indian name for the territory around Sutter's Mill, and here we were to purchase our provisions previous to going to the river. Three stores only, at that time, disputed the trade at what is now the great centre of the northern mining region; and where now are busy streets, and long rows of tents and houses, was a beautiful hollow, which, in our romantic version, we named as we were entering it, "The Devil's Punch-Bowl." Surrounded on all sides by lofty mountains, its ingress and egress guarded by an ascent and descent through narrow passes, it seemed like a huge bowl which some lofty spirit might seize, and placing it to his lips, quaff the waters of the golden stream that circled through it. Here it was that gold was first discovered in California; this was the locality where was commenced a new era, and where a new page was opened in the history of mankind.

/ / /

The city of Sacramento had assumed a very different aspect at the time I reached it on my return from the northern mines, from that which it exhibited when I previously left it. Where the old store-ship used to be, on the banks of the Sacramento, tall-masted ships were moored, and the extensive plain on which I pitched my tent was dotted with houses. Around the fort itself, which is nearly two miles from the bank of the river, houses had begun to spring up. Building-lots which, four months previously, had sold at from fifty to two hundred dollars, were now held by their owners at from one to three thousand. I looked on with astonishment at the remarkable progress, and then little thought that the ensuing six months would develope a growth, both in size and prices, which would entirely outstrip what I then witnessed.

Getting on board a launch, I spent a weary five days in sailing down the Sacramento, and arrived at San Francisco in the early part of May. What a change had occurred in six months! San Francisco, when I saw it before, was almost entirely deserted, everybody having gone to the mines. Now it was being daily recruited by the arrival of travellers across the plains, by vessels around Cape Horn, by Sandwich Islanders, Chinese, French, English, and Mexicans. The age of speculation had commenced. The building-lots which, when I landed in San Francisco, were granted by the alcaldes for the sum of fifteen dollars, and in the autumn before were worth but five hundred, had now risen in value to from three to five thousand. Hundreds and thousands of men with capital were arriving, who readily seized upon the opportunities for speculating. Houses were going up on the vacant lots, and the town beginning to assume an air of business. Goods of all kinds had fallen in price, owing to the arrival of fleets of loaded ships from all parts of the world, and in some cases from wilful neglect on the part of consignees. Large hotels had been erected, and life began to be rendered comfortable. Gambling in all its forms was carried on to an enormous extent, and money, as before, was almost as plentiful as the sea-sands.

HARRIET HANSON ROBINSON

# 25 The Lowell Textile Workers

*As a young girl in the 1830s, Harriet Hanson Robinson worked in the new textile mills in Lowell, Massachusetts. More than sixty years later, in 1898, Robinson published a book,* Loom and Spindle, *that tells of her experiences.*

*When the mills first opened, the owners adopted a paternal attitude to encourage respectable girls to work in the factories. Reasonable wages and working conditions combined with carefully chaperoned boarding houses and the encouragement of literary journals to create a genteel atmosphere. But as Robinson makes clear, within a few years the pressure of business competition led to changes. Deeply troubled by the harsh conditions under which many young women labored, Robinson herself later became active in the women's suffrage movement. She lived into the early twentieth century.*

## CHAPTER II. CHILD-LIFE IN THE LOWELL COTTON-MILLS

In 1831, under the shadow of a great sorrow, which had made her four children fatherless,—the oldest but seven years of age,—my mother was left to struggle alone; and, although she tried to earn bread enough to fill our hungry mouths, she could not do it, even with the help of kind friends. And so it happened that one of her more wealthy neighbors, who had looked with longing eyes on the one little daughter of the family, offered to adopt me. But my mother, who had had a hard experience in her youth in living amongst strangers, said, "No; while I have one meal of victuals a day, I will not part with my children." I always remembered this speech because of the word "victuals," and I wondered for a long time what this good old Bible word meant.

/ / /

That was a hard, cold winter; and for warmth's sake my mother and her four children all slept in one bed, two at the foot and three at the head,—but her richer neighbor could not get the little daughter; and, contrary to all the modern notions about hygiene, we were a healthful and a robust brood.

/ / /

Shortly after this my mother's widowed sister, Mrs. Angeline Cudworth, who kept a factory boarding-house in Lowell, advised her to come to that city.

/ / /

I had been to school constantly until I was about ten years of age, when my mother, feeling obliged to have help in her work besides what I could give, and also needing the money which I could earn, allowed me, at my urgent request (for I wanted to earn *money* like the other little girls), to go to work in the mill. I worked first in the spinning-room as a "doffer." The doffers were the very youngest girls, whose work was to doff, or take off, the full bobbins, and replace them with the empty ones.

/ / /

Some of us learned to embroider in crewels, and I still have a lamb worked on cloth, a relic of those early days, when I was first taught to improve my time in the good old New England fashion. When not doffing, we were often allowed to go home, for a time, and thus we were able to help our mothers in their housework. We were paid two dollars a week; and how proud I was when my turn came to stand up on the bobbin-box, and write my name in the paymaster's book, and how indignant I was when he asked me if I could "write." "Of course I can," said I, and he smiled as he looked down on me.

The working-hours of all the girls extended from five o'clock in the morning until seven in the evening, with one-half hour for breakfast and for dinner. Even the doffers were forced to be on duty nearly fourteen hours a day, and this was the greatest hardship in the lives of these children. For it was not until 1842 that the hours of labor for children under twelve years of age were limited to ten per day; but the "ten-hour law" itself was not passed until long after some of these little doffers were old enough to appear before the legislative committee on the subject, and plead, by their presence, for a reduction of the hours of labor.

I do not recall any particular hardship connected with this life, except getting up so early in the morning, and to this habit, I never was, and never shall be, reconciled, for it has taken nearly a lifetime for me to make up the sleep lost at that early age. But in every other respect it was a pleasant life. We were not hurried any more than was for our good, and no more work was required of us than we were able easily to do.

Most of us children lived at home, and we were well fed, drinking both tea and coffee, and eating substantial meals (besides luncheons) three times a day. We had very happy hours with the older girls, many of whom treated us like babies, or talked in a motherly way, and so had a good influence over us. And in the long winter evenings, when we could not run home between the doffings, we gathered in groups and told each other stories, and sung the old-time songs our mothers had sung, such as "Barbara Allen," "Lord Lovell," " Captain Kid," "Hull's Victory," and sometimes a hymn.

Among the ghost stories I remember some that would delight the hearts of the "Society for Psychical Research." The more imaginative ones told of what they had read in fairy books, or related tales of old castles and distressed maidens; and the scene of their adventures was sometimes laid among the foundation stones of the new mill, just building.

And we told each other of our little hopes and desires, and what we meant to do when we grew up. For we had our aspirations; and one of us, who danced the "shawl dance," as she called it, in the spinning-room alley, for the amusement of her admiring companions, discussed seriously with another little girl the scheme of their running away together, and joining the circus.

/ / /

I cannot tell how it happened that some of us knew about the English factory children, who, it was said, were treated so badly, and were even whipped by their cruel overseers. But we did know of it, and used to sing, to a doleful little tune, some verses called, "The Factory Girl's Last Day." I do not remember it well enough to quote it as written, but have refreshed my memory by reading it lately in Robert Dale Owen's writings:—

*"The Factory Girl's Last Day."*

"'Twas on a winter morning,
The weather wet and wild,
Two hours before the dawning
The father roused his child,
Her daily morsel bringing,
The darksome room he paced,
And cried, 'The bell is ringing—
My hapless darling, haste!

The overlooker met her
As to her frame she crept;
And with this thong he beat her,
And cursed her when she wept.

It seemed as she grew weaker,
  The threads the oftener broke,
The rapid wheels ran quicker,
  And heavier fell the stroke."

The song goes on to tell the sad story of her death while her "pitying comrades" were carrying her home to die, and ends:—

"That night a chariot passed her,
  While on the ground she lay;
The daughters of her master,
  An evening visit pay.
Their tender hearts were sighing,
  As negroes' wrongs were told,
While the white slave was dying
  Who gained her father's gold."

In contrast with this sad picture, we thought of ourselves as well off, in our cosey corner of the mill, enjoying ourselves in our own way, with our good mothers and our warm suppers awaiting us when the going-out bell should ring.

/ / /

## *CHAPTER IV. THE CHARACTERISTICS OF THE EARLY FACTORY GIRLS.*

When I look back into the factory life of fifty or sixty years ago, I do not see what is called "a class" of young men and women going to and from their daily work, like so many ants that cannot be distinguished one from another; I see them as individuals, with personalities of their own. This one has about her the atmosphere of her early home. That one is impelled by a strong and noble purpose. The other,—what she is, has been an influence for good to me and to all womankind.

Yet they were a class of factory operatives, and were spoken of (as the same class is spoken of now) as a set of persons who earned their daily bread, whose condition was fixed, and who must continue to spin and to weave to the end of their natural existence. Nothing but this was expected of them, and they were not supposed to be capable of social or mental improvement. That they could be educated and developed into something more than mere work-people, was an idea that had not yet entered the public mind. So little does one class of persons really know about the thoughts and aspirations of another! It was the good fortune of these early mill-girls to teach the people of that time that this sort of labor is not degrading; that the operative is not only "capable of virtue," but also capable of self-cultivation.

At the time the Lowell cotton-mills were started, the factory girl was the lowest among women. In England, and in France particularly, great injustice had been done to her real character; she was represented as subjected to influences that could not fail to destroy her purity and self-respect. In the eyes of her overseer she was but a brute, a slave, to be beaten, pinched, and pushed about. It was to overcome this prejudice that such high wages had been offered to women that they might be induced to become mill-girls, in spite of the opprobrium that still clung to this "degrading occupation." At first only a few came; for, though tempted by the high wages to be regularly paid in "cash," there were many who still preferred to go on working at some more *genteel* employment at seventy-five cents a week and their board.

But in a short time the prejudice against factory labor wore away, and the Lowell mills became filled with blooming and energetic New England women.

/ / /

In 1831 Lowell was little more than a factory village. Several corporations were started, and the cotton-mills belonging to them were building. Help was in great demand; and stories were told all over the country of the new factory town, and the high wages that were offered to all classes of work-people,—stories that reached the ears of mechanics' and farmers' sons, and gave new life to lonely and dependent women in distant towns and farmhouses. Into this Yankee El Dorado, these needy people began to pour by the various modes of travel known to those slow old days. The stage-coach and the canal-boat came every day, always filled with new recruits for this army of useful people. The mechanic and machinist came, each with his home-made chest of tools, and often-times his wife and little ones. The widow came with her little flock and her scanty housekeeping goods to open a boarding-house or variety store, and so provided a home for her fatherless children. Many farmers' daughters came to earn money to complete their wedding outfit, or buy the bride's share of housekeeping articles.

Women with past histories came, to hide their griefs and their identity, and to earn an honest living in the "sweat of their brow." Single young men came, full of hope and life, to get money for an education, or to lift the mortgage from the home-farm. Troops of young girls came by stages and baggage-wagons, men often being employed to go to other States and to Canada, to collect them at so much a head, and deliver them at the factories.

/ / /

[The] country girls had queer names, which added to the singularity of their appearance. Samantha, Triphena, Plumy, Kezia, Aseneth, Elgardy, Leafy, Ruhamah, Lovey, Almaretta, Sarepta, and Florilla were among them.

Their dialect was also very peculiar. On the broken English and Scotch of their ancestors was ingrafted the nasal Yankee twang; so that many of them, when they had just come *daown,* spoke a language almost unintelligible. But the severe discipline and ridicule which met them was as good as a school education, and they were soon taught the "city way of speaking."

Their dress was also peculiar, and was of the plainest of homespun, cut in such an old-fashioned style that each young girl looked as if she had borrowed her grandmother's gown. Their only head-covering was a shawl, which was pinned under the chin; but after the first payday, a "shaker" (or "scooter") sunbonnet usually replaced this primitive head-gear of their rural life.

But the early factory girls were not all country girls. There were others also, who had been taught that "work is no disgrace." There were some who came to Lowell solely on account of the social or literary advantages to be found there. They lived in secluded parts of New England, where books were scarce, and there was no cultivated society. They had comfortable homes, and did not perhaps need the *money* they would earn; but they longed to see this new "City of Spindles," . . .

The laws relating to women were such, that a husband could claim his wife wherever he found her, and also the children she was trying to shield from his influence; and I have seen more than one poor woman skulk behind her loom or her frame when visitors were approaching the end of the aisle where she worked. Some of these were known under assumed names, to prevent their husbands from trusteeing their wages. It was a very common thing for a male person of a certain kind to do this, thus depriving his wife of *all* her wages, perhaps, month after month. The wages of minor children could be trusteed, unless the children (being fourteen years of age) were given their time. Women's wages were also trusteed for the debts of their husbands, and children's for the debts of their parents.

/ / /

It must be remembered that at this date woman had no property rights. A widow could be left without her share of her husband's (or the family) property, a legal "incumbrance" to his estate. A father could make his will without reference to his daughter's share of the inheritance. He usually left her a home on the farm as long as she remained single. A woman was not supposed to be capable of spending her own or of using other people's money. In Massachusetts, before 1840, a woman could not legally be treasurer of her own sewing-society, unless some man were responsible for her.

The law took no cognizance of woman as a money-spender. She was a ward, an appendage, a relict. Thus it happened, that if a woman did not choose to marry, or, when left a widow, to re-marry, she had no choice but to enter one of the few employments open to her, or to become a burden on the charity of some relative.

In almost every New England home could be found one or more of these women, sometimes welcome, more often unwelcome, and leading joyless, and in many instances unsatisfactory, lives. The cotton-factory was a great opening to these lonely and dependent women. From a condition approaching pauperism they were at once placed above want; they could earn money, and spend it as they pleased; and could gratify their tastes and desires without restraint, and without rendering an account to anybody . . . .

Among the older women who sought this new employment were very many lonely and dependent ones, such as used to be mentioned in old wills as "incumbrances" and "relicts," and to whom a chance of earning money was indeed a new revelation. How well I remember some of these solitary ones! As a child of eleven years, I often made fun of them—for children do not see the pathetic side of human life—and imitated their limp carriage and inelastic gait. I can see them now, even after sixty years, just as they looked,—depressed, modest, mincing, hardly daring to look one in the face, so shy and sylvan had been their lives. But after the first pay-day came, and they felt the jingle of silver in their pockets, and had begun to feel its mercurial influence, their bowed heads were lifted, their necks seemed braced with steel, they looked you in the face, sang blithely among their looms or frames, and walked with elastic step to and from their work. And when Sunday came, homespun was no longer their only wear; and how sedately gay in their new attire they walked to church, and how proudly they dropped their silver fourpences into the contribution-box! It seemed as if a great hope impelled them,—the harbinger of the new era that was about to dawn for them and for all women-kind.

/ / /

## *CHAPTER V. CHARACTERISTICS (CONTINUED).*

One of the first strikes of cotton-factory operatives that ever took place in this country was that in Lowell, in October, 1836. When it was announced that the wages were to be cut down, great indignation was felt, and it was decided to strike, *en masse*. This was done. The mills were shut down, and the girls went in procession from their several corporations to the "grove" on Chapel Hill, and listened to "incendiary" speeches from early labor reformers.

One of the girls stood on a pump, and gave vent to the feelings of her companions in a neat speech, declaring that it was their duty to resist all attempts at cutting down the wages. This was the first time a woman had spoken in public in Lowell, and the event caused surprise and consternation among her audience.

Cutting down the wages was not their only grievance, nor the only cause of this strike. Hitherto the corporations had paid twenty-five cents a week towards the board of each operative, and now it was their purpose to have the girls pay the sum; and this, in addition to the cut in wages, would make a difference of at least one dollar a week. It was estimated that as many as twelve or fifteen hundred girls turned out, and walked in procession through the streets. They had neither flags nor music, but sang songs, a favorite (but rather inappropriate) one being a parody on "I won't be a nun."

"Oh! isn't it a pity, such a pretty girl as I—
Should be sent to the factory to pine away and die?
Oh! I cannot be a slave,
I will not be a slave,
For I'm so fond of liberty
That I cannot be a slave."

My own recollection of this first strike (or "turn out" as it was called) is very vivid. I worked in a lower room, where I had heard the proposed strike fully, if not vehemently, discussed; I had been an ardent listener to what was said against this attempt at "oppression" on the part of the corporation, and naturally I took sides with the strikers. When the day came on which the girls were to turn out, those in the upper rooms started first, and so many of them left that our mill was at once shut down. Then, when the girls in my room stood irresolute, uncertain what to do, asking each other, "Would you?" or "Shall we turn out?" and not one of them having the courage to lead off, I, who began to think they would not go out, after all their talk, became impatient, and started on ahead, saying, with childish bravado, "I don't care what you do, *I* am going to turn out, whether any one else does or not"; and I marched out, and was followed by the others.[1]

As I looked back at the long line that followed me, I was more proud than I have ever been since at any success I may have achieved, and more proud than I shall ever be again until my own beloved State gives to its women citizens the right of suffrage.

The agent of the corporation where I then worked took some small revenges on the supposed ringleaders; on the principle of sending the

1. I was then eleven years and eight months old. H.H.R.

weaker to the wall, my mother was turned away from her boarding-house, that functionary saying, "Mrs. Hanson, you could not prevent the older girls from turning out, but your daughter is a child, and *her* you could control."

It is hardly necessary to say that so far as results were concerned this strike did no good. The dissatisfaction of the operatives subsided, or burned itself out, and though the authorities did not accede to their demands, the majority returned to their work, and the corporation went on cutting down the wages.

And after a time, as the wages became more and more reduced, the best portion of the girls left and went to their homes, or to the other employments that were fast opening to women, until there were very few of the old guard left; and thus the *status* of the factory population of New England gradually became what we know it to be to-day.

/ / /

*PRISCILLA MERRIMAN EVANS*

# 26 Pulling a Handcart to the Mormon Zion

*The men and women who settled the Far West often endured extraordinary physical hardships and dangers to reach their destinations. The Mormon pioneers who walked from Iowa City, Iowa, to Salt Lake City, Utah, pulling handcarts made of hickory behind them, were driven by both economic and religious motives. The handcart immigrants were poor: if they could have afforded to migrate any other way they would have. They spoke one or more of a variety of languages—German, Welsh, Danish, Swedish—as well as English. And they did not all have so successful a journey as the pregnant Mrs. Evans. With her one-legged husband, she walked the 1000 miles in five months, arriving in Salt Lake City in October 1856, comfortably ahead of the winter weather. In two parties later that year, hundreds died in winter blizzards.*

*Nine more handcart companies reached the Mormon Zion in the five years after the Evanses' journey. All received rich welcomes with prayers and hymns. Priscilla Merriman Evans concluded her narrative by saying that she always "thanked the Lord for a contented mind, a home and something to eat."*

I, Priscilla Merriman Evans, born May 4, 1835 at Mounton New Marbeth, Pembrokeshire, Wales, am the daughter of Joseph and Ann James Merriman. About 1839, father moved his family from Mounton up to Tenby, about ten miles distant. Our family consisted of father, mother, Sarah, aged six, and myself, aged four. Tenby was a beautiful place, as are all those Celtic Islands, with remains of old castles, vine-and moss-covered walls, gone to ruin since the time of the Conqueror. . . .

When we were settled in our new home, we girls were sent to school, as children were put in school very young. There was a path leading up Castle Hill to the school, and another leading around the beautiful old moss-covered Castle down to the seashore, where the children played in the sand and gathered shells at intermission. The children also loved to wander around in the many rooms of the Castle, but shunned the lower regions, or basement rooms, for they had heard weird stories of dungeons and dark places, where in early times, people were shut up and kept until they died.

Besides reading, writing, spelling, and arithmetic, we were taught sewing and sampler making. The sampler work was done in cross stitch, worked in bright colors, on canvas made for that purpose. . . . We were also taught the Bible. I was greatly interested in school, but was taken out at eleven years of age, owing to the illness in our family. I was a natural student, and greatly desired to continue my studies, but mother's health was very poor, so I was taken out to help with the work. My sister, Sarah, continued school, as she did not like housework and wished to learn a trade. She went to Mrs. Hentin and learned the millinery trade. Mother's health continued [to be] poor, and she died at the birth of her eighth child, Emma, when I was sixteen. I had many duties for a girl so young, caring for my sisters and brothers. While Sarah was learning millinery, she would sometimes wake me in the night to try on a hat—one she was practicing on. She learned the millinery business and then went up to London, opened a shop of her own and was very successful. She married a gentleman . . . who was devoted to her, and followed her to London. She died at the birth of her fourth child.

[When] Mother died on the eighth of November 1851 . . . the responsibility of the family rested on my young shoulders. . . . After the death of my mother we were very lonely, and one evening I accompanied my father to the house of a friend. When we reached there, we learned that they were holding a cottage meeting. Two Mormon Elders were the speakers, and I was very much interested in the principles they advocated. I could see that my father was very worried, and would have taken me away, had he known how. When he became aware that I believed in the Gospel as taught by the Elders, I asked him if he had ever heard of the restored Gospel. He replied, "Oh, yes, I have heard of Old Joe Smith, and his Golden Bible." When my father argued against the principles taught by the Elders, I said, "If the Bible is true, then Mormonism is true."

My father was very much opposed to my joining the Church . . . as he thought the Saints were too slow to associate with. . . . But I had found the truth and was baptized into the Church of Jesus Christ of Latter-day Saints in Tenby, February 26, 1852. My sister Sarah took turns with me going out every Sunday. She would go where she pleased on Sunday, while I would walk seven miles to Stepaside and attend the Mormon meeting. My father was very much displeased with me going out every Sunday. He forbade me to read the Church literature, and threatened to burn all I brought home. At the time I had a Book of Mormon borrowed from a friend, and when Father found out I had it, he began looking for it. It was in plain sight, among other books in the book case. I saw him handling it with the other books, and I sent up a silent prayer that he might not notice it, which he did not, although it was before him in plain sight. I do not think my father was as bitter against the principles of the Gospel as he seemed to be, for many times when the Elders were persecuted, he defended them, and gave them food and shelter. But he could not bear the idea of my joining them and leaving home.

About this time, Thomas D. Evans, a young Mormon Elder, was sent up from Merthyr Tydfil, Wales, as a missionary to Pembrokeshire. He was a fine speaker, and had a fine tenor voice, and I used to like to go around with the missionaries and help with the singing. Elder Evans and I seemed to be congenial from our first meeting, and we were soon engaged. He was traveling and preaching the restored Gospel without purse or script. Perhaps his mission will be better understood if I give a little account: [his father had died] and left his mother a widow with eight children, Thomas D. being four years old and the youngest. He was placed in a large forge of two-thousand men at the age of seven years to learn the profession of Iron Roller. At nine years of age, he had the misfortune to lose his left leg at the knee. He went through the courses and graduated as an Iron Roller. When I think of [when they met in 1852] it seems that we had put the world aside, and were not thinking of our worldly pleasures, and what our next dress would be. We had no dancing in those days, but we were happy in the enjoyment of the spirit of the Gospel. . . .

I was familiar with the Bible doctrine, and when I heard the Elders explain it, it seemed as though I had always known it, and it sounded like music in my ears. We had the spirit of gathering and were busy making preparations to emigrate.

About that time the Principle of Plurality of Wives was preached to the world, and it caused quite a commotion in our branch. One of the girls came to me with tears in her eyes and said, "Is it true that Brigham Young has nine wives? I can't stand that, Oh, I can't stand it!" I asked her how long it had been since I had heard her testify that she knew the Church was true, and I said if it was then, it is true now. I told her I did not see anything for her to cry about. After I talked to her awhile, she dried her eyes and completed her arrangements to get married and emigrate. She came with us. My promised husband and I went to Merthyr to visit his Mother, brothers, sisters, and friends, preparatory to emigrating. His family did all in their power to persuade him to remain with them. They were all well off, and his brothers said they would send him to school, support his wife, and pay all of his expenses but all to no avail. He bade them all goodbye, and returned to Tenby.

I think I would have had a harder time getting away, had it not been that my father was going to be married again, and I do not suppose the lady cared to have in the home, the grown daughter who had taken the place of the mother for so many years.

Elder Thomas D. Evans, my promised husband, and I walked the ten miles from Tenby to Pembroke, where we got our license and were married, and walked back to Tenby. We were married on the third of April, 1856. On our return from Pembroke we found a few of our friends awaiting us with supper ready. We visited our friends and relatives and made our preparations to emigrate to Zion. We took a tug from Pembroke to Liverpool, where we set sail on the 17th of April, 1856, on the sailing vessel S.S. Curling. Captain Curling said he would prefer to take a load of Saints than others, as he always felt safe with Saints on board. We learned that the next trip across the water that he was loaded with gentiles and his vessel sank with all on board. We were on the sea five weeks; we lived on the ship's rations. I was sick all the way. [Priscilla was then pregnant with their first child.]

We landed in Boston on May 23rd, then travelled in cattle cars . . . to Iowa City. We remained in Iowa City three weeks, waiting for our carts to be made. We were offered many inducements to stay there. My husband was offered ten dollars a day to work at his trade of Iron Roller, but money was no inducement to us, for we were anxious to get to Zion. We learned afterwards that many who stayed there apostatized or died of cholera.

When the carts were ready we started on a three-hundred-mile walk to Winterquarters on the Missouri River. There were a great many who made fun of us as we walked, pulling our carts, but the weather was fine and the roads were excellent and although I was sick and we were tired out at night, we still thought, "This is a glorious way to come to Zion."

We began our journey of one thousand miles on foot with a handcart for each family, some families consisting of man and wife, and some had quite large families. There were five mule teams to haul the tents and surplus flour. Each handcart had one hundred pounds of flour, that was to be divided and [more got] from the wagons as required. At first we had a little coffee and bacon, but that was soon gone and we had no use for any cooking utensils but a frying pan. The flour was self-raising and we took water and baked a little cake; that was all we had to eat.

After months of travelling we were put on half rations and at one time, before help came, we were out of flour for two days. We washed out the flour sacks to make a little gravy.

Our company was three-hundred Welsh Saints. There were about a dozen in our tent, six of whom could not speak the Welsh language, myself among the number. Don't you think I had a pleasant journey traveling for months with three-hundred people of whose language I could not understand a word? My husband could talk Welsh, so he could join in their festivities when he felt like it. [Priscilla spoke no Welsh because English was the language she learned at home and Welsh was not taught in school.]

There were in our tent my husband with one leg, two blind men . . . a man with one arm, and a widow with five children. The widow, her children, and myself were the only ones who could not talk Welsh.

My husband was commissary for our tent, and he cut his own rations short many times to help little children who had to walk and did not have enough to eat to keep up their strength.

The tent was our covering, and the overcoat spread on the bare ground with the shawl over us was our bed. My feather bed, and bedding, pillows, all our good clothing, my husband's church books, which he had collected through six years of missionary work, with some genealogy he had collected, all had to be left in a storehouse. We were promised that they would come to us with the next emigration in the spring, but we never did receive them. It was reported that the storehouse burned down, so that was a dreadful loss to us.

Edward Bunker was the Captain of our Company. His orders of the day were, "If any are sick among you, and are not able to walk, you must help them along, or pull them on your carts." No one rode in the wagons. Strong men would help the weaker ones, until they themselves were worn out, and some died from the struggle and want of food, and were buried along the wayside. It was heart rending for parents to move on and leave their loved ones to such a fate, as they were so helpless, and had no material for coffins. Children and young folks, too, had to move on and leave father or mother or both.

Sometimes a bunch of buffaloes would come and the carts would stop until they passed. Had we been prepared with guns and ammunition, like people who came in wagons, we might have had meat, and would not have come to near starving. President Young ordered extra cattle sent along to be killed to help the sick and weak, but they were never used for that purpose. One incident happened which came near being serious. Some Indians came to our camp and my husband told an Indian who admired me that he could have me for a pony. He was always getting off jokes. He thought no more about it, but in a day or two, here came the Indian with the pony, and wanted his pretty little squaw. It was no joke with him. I never was so frightened in all my life. There was no place to hide, and we did not know what to do. The Captain was called, and they had some difficulty in settling with the Indian without trouble.

In crossing rivers, the weak women and the children were carried over the deep places, and they waded the others. We were much more fortunate than those who came later, as they had snow and freezing weather. Many lost limbs, and many froze to death. President Young advised them to start earlier, but they got started too late. My husband, in walking from twenty to twenty-five miles per day [had pain] where the knee rested on the pad: the friction caused it to gather and break and was most painful. But he had to endure it, or remain behind, as he was never asked to ride in a wagon.

One incident shows how we were fixed for grease. My husband and John Thayne, a butcher, in some way killed an old lame buffalo.

They sat up all night and boiled it to get some grease to grease the carts, but he was so old and poor, there was not a drop of grease in him. We had no grease for the squeaking carts or to make gravy for the children and old people.

We reached Salt Lake City on October 2, 1856, tired, weary, with bleeding feet, our clothing worn out and so weak we were nearly starved, but thankful to our Heavenly Father for bringing us to Zion. William R. Jones met us on the Public Square in Salt Lake City and brought us to his home in Spanish Fork. I think we were over three days coming from Salt Lake City to Spanish Fork by ox team, but what a change to ride in a wagon after walking 1330 miles from Iowa City to Salt Lake City!

We stayed in the home of an ex-bishop, Stephen Markham. His home was a dugout. It was a very large room built half underground. His family consisted of three wives, and seven children. . . . There was a large fireplace in one end with bars, hooks, frying pans, and bake ovens, where they did the cooking for the large family, and boiled, fried, baked, and heated their water for washing.

There was a long table in one corner, and pole bedsteads fastened to the walls in the three other corners. They were laced back and forth with rawhide cut in strips, and made a nice springy bed. There were three trundle beds, made like shallow boxes, with wooden wheels, which rolled under the mother's bed in the daytime to utilize space. There was a dirt roof, and the dirt floor was kept hard and smooth by sprinkling and sweeping. The bed ticks were filled with straw raised in Palmyra before the famine. [Palmyra, on the river between Spanish Fork and Utah Lake, suffered the famine to which Priscilla Evans alludes shortly before the Evanses' arrival. Fifty families moved to Spanish Fork and lived in the dugouts she describes.]

Aunt Mary [Markham] put her two children . . . in the foot of her bed and gave us the trundle bed. . . . How delightful to sleep on a bed again, after sleeping on the ground for so many months with our clothes on. We had not slept in a bed since we left the ship *Sam Curling*.

On the 31st of December, 1856, our first daughter was born. . . . My baby's wardrobe was rather meager: I made one night gown from her father's white shirt, another out of a factory lining of an oilcloth sack. Mrs. Markham gave me a square of homemade linsey for a shoulder blanket, and a neighbor gave me some old underwear, that I worked up into little things. They told me I could have an old pair of jean pants left at the adobe yard. I washed them and made them into petticoats. I walked down to the Indian farm and traded a gold pen for four yards of calico that made her two dresses.

One day my husband went down in the field to cut some willows to burn. The ax slipped and cut his good knee cap. It was with difficulty that he crawled to the house. He was very weak from the loss of blood.

My baby was but a few days old, and the three of us had to occupy the trundle bed for awhile.

Wood and timber were about thirty miles up in the canyon, and when the men went after timber to burn, they went in crowds, armed, for they never knew when they would be attacked by Indians. Adobe houses were cheaper than log or frame, as timber was so far away. Many of the people who had lived in the dugouts after coming from Palmyra got into houses before the next winter. They exchanged work with each other, and in that way got along fine. Mr. Markham had an upright saw, run by water. The next spring they got timber from the canyon, and my husband helped Mr. Markham put up a three-roomed house and worked at farming.

He worked for William Markham a year, for which he received two acres of land. I helped in the house, for which, besides the land, we got our board and keep. The next Spring we went to work for ourselves. We saved our two acres of wheat, and made adobes for a two-roomed house, and paid a man in adobes for laying it up. It had a dirt roof. He got timber from Mr. Markham to finish the doors, windows, floors, shelves, and to make furniture. My husband made me a good big bedstead and laced it with rawhides. There were benches and the frames of chairs with the rawhide seat, with the hair left on; a table, shelves in the wall on either side of the fireplace, which was fitted with iron bars and hooks to hang kettles on to boil, frying pans and bake oven. A tick for a bed had to be pieced out of all kinds of scraps, as there were no stores, and everything was on a trade basis.

If one neighbor had something they could get along without, they would exchange it for something they could use. We were lucky to get factory, or sheeting to put up to the windows instead of glass. We raised a good crop of wheat that fall, for which we traded one bushel for two bushels of potatoes. We also exchanged for molasses and vegetables. We had no tea, coffee, meat, or grease of any kind for seasoning. No sugar, milk, or butter. In 1855–1856 the grasshoppers and crickets took the crops and the cattle nearly all died. They were dragged down in the field west [and left to die].

Before my second baby, Jennie, was born, I heard that a neighbor was going to kill a beef. I asked her to save me enough tallow for one candle. But the beef was like the buffalo we killed crossing the plains—there was no tallow in it.

By this time we had two children, with no soap to wash our clothes. Grease of all kinds was out of the question, so I took an ax and gunny sack and went into the field where the dead cattle had been dragged, and I broke up all the bones I could carry home. I boiled them in saleratus and lime, and it made a little jelly-like soap. The saleratus was gathered on top of the ground.

My husband had never driven a team before he came to Utah. He had traveled and preached for the six years previous to coming to Utah, and he knew nothing about any kind of work but his profession of Iron Roller. His hands were soft and white, but he soon wore blisters . . . in learning to make adobes, digging ditches, making roads, driving oxen, and doing what was required of pioneers in a new country.

The large bedstead [was good to have] for when my third child was born, two had to go to the foot of the bed, but it did not work. Jennie had to go to the foot alone. Caliline Louisa . . . was the third child, and although Emma was the oldest and just a baby herself, she could not be tempted to go to the foot of the bed, but was determined to sleep on her father's bosom, which she had done since the birth of Jennie. We went down to the marshy land and gathered a load of cattails, which I stripped and made me a good bed and pillows. They were as soft as feathers.

Our first fence around our lot was made of willows. Slender stakes were put in a certain distance apart, and the willows woven in back and forth. There was a board gate with rawhide hinges and flat rocks were laid on the walks, as we were located down under a long hill, and when it rained, it was very muddy. There were many mud walls in the early days of Spanish Fork, as the material in them cost nothing. The mud was mixed stiff enough with straw in it so it would not run, and a layer was put on, until high enough. Rock fences were also used, and were very durable.

There were no stores. Sometimes someone would come around with their basket of needles, pins, buttons, thread, and notions, but I had no money to buy with. Men who had no teams worked two days for the use of a team one day. Shovels were so scarce that when men were working in the roads and ditches, they had to take turns using the shovels.

My husband worked at Camp Floyd and got money enough to get him a good yoke of oxen. One day, while working in the canyon, a man above him . . . let a log roll down and broke the leg of one of the oxen. That was a calamity.

I traded for a hen . . . and got a setting of eggs somewhere else, and I have never been without chickens in all of my married life since. I could not get a thread to sew, so I raveled a strip of hickory shirting for dark sewing thread and factory for white, when I could get it. When we could get grease for light, we put a button in a rag, and braided the top, setting the button in the grease, after dipping the braided part in the grease.

On the 4th of August, 1861, our fourth child and first son, David T., was born. . . . In that year my husband's mother and step-father came [from Wales]. They drove their own team across the plains, two oxen, two cows, and they brought many useful things for their comfort. His parents lived with us, making eight in the family. Our rooms were small, and as grandma had left a good home and plenty, she became quite dissatisfied with our crowded condition.

We bought a lot on Main Street, and my husband gave his parents our first little home with five acres of land. They had a good ox team, two cows, a new wagon, and they soon got pigs, chickens and a few sheep. It wasn't long before they were well off. We moved up near our lot into a one-roomed adobe house with a garrett, so to be near while my husband was building our new house. While living in that one room, the Indians were quite bad, and he was broken of his rest by standing guard nights and working in the day time.

It was indeed comfortable to be in a good house with a shingled roof and good floors. He set out an orchard of all kinds of fruit; also currents and gooseberries, planted lucern . . . in a patch by itself for cows and pigs. We had a nice garden spot, and we soon had butter, milk, eggs, and meat. We raised our bread, potatoes, and vegetables. While our fruit trees were growing is when the saleratus helped. When I had the babies all about the same size, I could not get out to gather saleratus as others did; so we went with team and wagon, pans, buckets, old brooms, and sacks down on the alkali land, between Spanish Fork and Springville. The smallest children were put under the wagon on a quilt, and the rest of us swept and filled the sacks, and the happiest time was when we were headed for home. The canyon wind seemed always to blow and our faces, hands and eyes were sore for some time after. We took our saleratus over to Provo, where they had some kind of refining machinery where it was made into soda for bread. It was also used extensively in soap making. We got our pay in merchandise.

Another source of income before our fruit trees began to bear was the wild ground cherries. They grew on a vine or bush about six inches high, were bright yellow when ripe, were full of soft seed and about the size of a cherry. They made fine pies and all we had to spare sold readily at a good price when dried.

Most people who had land kept a few sheep which furnished them meat, light and clothing. We had no sheep, but I, and my oldest daughter, learned to spin and we did spinning on shares to get our yarn for stockings and socks, which we knitted for the family. Before this time my sister, Sarah, had sent me a black silk dress pattern, with other things, which I sold [and] I bought a cow and a pair of blankets. Before the building of the Provo factory, the people had wool-picking bees. The wool was greased and the trash picked out of it; then it was carded into rolls. We made our own cloth, which was mostly gray in color, for dresses, by mixing the black and white wool. If a light gray was wanted, more white than black was put in, and dark was added if a darker gray was wanted. The dresses for grown people were three widths, and for younger women two widths, one yard wide. There was a row of bright colors—red, blue, green—about half way up the skirt, which was hemmed and pleated onto a plain waist with coat sleeves. When our dresses wore thin in front, they could be turned back to front and upside down, and have a new lease on life. With madder, Indigo, logwood, copperas, and other roots, I have colored beautiful fast colors. We were kept busy in those days carding, spinning, knitting, and doing all of our own sewing by hand.

After getting settled in our new home, my husband went over to Camp Floyd, where he worked quite a bit. He found a friend who was selling out prior to leaving for California. He bought quite a number of articles, which greatly helped us. One thing was a door knob and lock. He also bought me a stepstove. Stoves were very scarce at that time in Spanish Fork. I had never cooked on a stove in my life, and I burned my first batch of bread. Where I came from people mixed their dough and had it baked in the public oven, and at home we had a grate with an oven at the side. When the soldier camp broke up, they left many useful things which helped the people.

On the 9th of July, 1863, our second son, J.J. Evans, was born. He was the first child born in our new home. After our fruit trees began to bear, we invited in our neighbor's young folks and had cutting bees. The peaches were spread on a scaffolding to dry, then sold at a good price. We kept some for our own use. On July 16, 1865, our daughter Sarah Amelia was born. . . . On May 4, 1867 Charles Abram was born. Thomas Isaac was born on May 8, 1869, and died when six months old. My husband farmed down on the river bottom, and between times he freighted produce to Salt Lake City, as he had come to Camp Floyd before the soldiers left, and brought some merchandise for the people. . . . My husband had poor luck farming. His farm was in the low land, near the river where the sugar factory now stands. Sometimes it would be high water, sometimes grasshoppers or crickets would take his crop; so he got discouraged with farming, sold his farm and put up a store. We had just got well started in the business and had got a bill of goods, when in the spring of 1875 my husband was called on another mission to England.

Before starting on his mission he sold his team and all available property, also mortgaged our home, for although he was called to travel without purse or scrip, he had to raise enough money to pay his passage and his expenses to his field of labor in Europe. He had too tender a heart for a merchant; he simply could not say no when people came to him with pitiful stories of sickness and privation. He would give them credit, and the consequence was that when he was suddenly called on a mission, the goods were gone and there were hundreds of dollars coming to us from the people, some of which we never got. Everything was left in my hands.

On the 24th of October 1875, after my husband's departure, our daughter Ada was born . . . I nursed her, along with my little granddaughter Maud, as twins, kept all the books and accounts . . . and was sustained as President and Secretary of the Relief Society Teachers, which office I held through many re-organizations.

During my husband's absence, we had considerable sickness. My little daughter, Mary, came near dying with scarlet fever. To help out, our eldest daughter, Emma, got a position as clerk in the Co-op store. I appreciated that action of the Board very much, as before that time they had not been employing lady clerks and she was the first girl to work in the store. . . .

My husband had a bottle green suit while on his mission. He had gotten so tired of seeing all gray suits that he asked me if I thought I could make him a bottle green suit. He bought the wool, and I had it carded into rolls, then I was particular to spin it very even. I scoured the yarn white, then with Indigo, yellow flowers and a liquid made from rabbit brush, the color was set. The yarn had to stay in this mixture for some time, and when it came out it was a pretty dark, bottle green. I took the yarn down to one of Pres. Hansen's wives who wove it into cloth. I ripped up an old suit for a pattern and made his suit all by hand, backstitching every stitch, until it was smooth on the right side as machine work. We did all of our sewing by hand. I took a large dinner plate and cut from the cloth the crown of a cap, lined it and put a band on it. He got a patent-leather visor in Salt Lake and when it was all finished, it was surely swell for those days, and would not look out of place in this day of caps.

In 1877, my twelfth child was born . . . I have had seven daughters and five sons. . . .

My husband's health was not good after his return from his mission. He had pneumonia twice. We sold our home on Main Street, paid off the mortgage and put up a little house on the five acres of land we had given his parents. They had left it to us when they died. We have some of our children as near neighbors and are quite comfortable in our new home.

# *Questions for Part III*

1 Describe Lewis and Clark's role as representatives of the United States government to the native Americans. How effective do you think their diplomacy was? How would you describe their attitude toward native Americans?

2 Cartwright describes the religious "camp-meeting" very vividly. Do we have anything like that today? What are the "jerks"?

3 What does the experience of John Ross and the Cherokee nation tell you about the values of white Americans in Jacksonian America? Why do you think the Cherokee were removed despite having adopted values and ways of living similar to those of other Americans?

4 What do you think were the requirements for successful adaptation to American life for immigrants like John Doyle?

5 In the excerpt by Cooper, what is Leather-stocking's viewpoint? How is it "modern"? What is Billy Kirby's? Who do you think is speaking for Cooper? Why do you think so?

6 Compare Caro's account of the fall of the Alamo to the one in your textbook. Do you think Caro's version does justice to both sides?

7 Imagine that you were in the eastern United States reading Buffum's contemporary account of the gold rush. What advice would you give someone considering whether or not to head west in search of gold in California?

8 Describe the changes at Lowell, related by Robinson, as they affected the workers. How did the workers attempt to fight back? Were they successful?

9 Comment on the way Evans tells her story and what her attitude seems to have been. Do you agree with her?

# PART IV | REFORM, SLAVERY, CIVIL WAR, AND RECONSTRUCTION

*Movement from the nationalism of the earlier nineteenth century to antebellum sectionalism dominated the thirty years leading to the Civil War. Both Northerners and Southerners resolutely proceeded westward, but the rapidly growing Southwest, including Alabama, Mississippi, and Louisiana, developed an economy and a society different from those of the new Northwest, which included Ohio, Illinois, and Wisconsin. One region was plantation, the other farm; one slave labor, the other free; one produced agrarian aristocrats, the other cities, entrepreneurs, and lawyers; one grew conservative and fearful of change while the other spawned liberal religions and reforms. Beneath it all was a basic—and national—antipathy to the black race that made Southerners fearful of the abolition of slavery and Northerners committed to halting its expansion into their own society.*

*The readings in this section reflect in one way or another the crises the nation faced. Slaves—both men and women—describe their experiences of the "peculiar institution." Henry Merrell's memoir illustrates the effect of slavery on efforts to industrialize the South. Harriet Tubman's life reveals the heroism required for African Americans to resist slavery directly. Timothy Shay Arthur and Sojourner Truth both provide insight into the reform ferment of the northern states before the Civil War.*

*The armed conflicts in Kansas in the late 1850s were a prelude to the war itself, and John Brown's role there was a shocking rehearsal for his daring exploits a few years later at Harper's Ferry. The impact of this terrible war is apparent both in Clara Barton's picture of the battlefield and in the accounts of the devastation wrought by William T. Sherman's march through Georgia.*

*We see the first painful and difficult reactions to the close of the Civil War as African-American Southerners react to Reconstruction and the first efforts are made to educate the ex-slaves. The revolution in race relations carried with it striking changes in the most important forms of property and economic relations: ownership of the land and the crops planted on it. By the 1880s, sharecropping had emerged as a replacement for slavery and the hierarchical relations that were a part of slavery. Victory for the Union did not end the crisis over the place of African-American men and women in American life. The Thirteenth, Fourteenth, and Fifteenth Amendments to the Constitution initiated a revolution that, more than a century later, remains incomplete.*

*TIMOTHY SHAY ARTHUR*

# 27 *Ten Nights in a Bar Room*

*Of all the reform movements of the antebellum period, the crusade against alcohol probably attracted the largest group of active supporters. Timothy Shay Arthur's* Ten Nights in a Bar Room and What I Saw There, *published in 1854, was the most popular of all the attacks on the tavern and was a best seller second only to* Uncle Tom's Cabin *during the 1850s. Like Mrs. Stowe's antislavery novel,* Ten Nights *also became a widely performed stage melodrama. It continues to be performed in the present, although now largely for its quaint moralism.*

*Yet the book itself is—like* Uncle Tom's Cabin*—a far more shrewd work than we generally remember. The "Sickle and Sheaf" is not a city dive but a respectable roadhouse. The novel is not an evangelical tract about liquor stealing souls, but an often subtle account of the presence of a tavern corrupting the Republican virtue of the town of Cedarville. And the plot does not turn on ethnic stereotypes: Simon Slade is a hard-working miller improving himself and Cedarville by opening a well-appointed tavern on the Post Road; his patrons are the solid, presumably Protestant, citizens and even the gentry of the town. Only the results of Slade's well-meant enterprise are lurid and melodramatic.*

The state of affairs in Cedarville, it was plain, from the partial glimpses I had received, was rather desperate. Desperate, I mean, as regarded the various parties brought before my observation. An eating cancer was on the community, and so far as the eye could mark its destructive progress, the ravages were fearful. That its roots were striking deep, and penetrating, concealed from view, in many unsuspected directions, there could be no doubt. What appeared on the surface was but a milder form of the disease, compared with its hidden, more vital, and more dangerous advances.

I could not but feel a strong interest in some of these parties. The case of young Hammond had from the first awakened concern; and now a new element was added in the unlooked-for appearance of his mother on the stage, in a state that seemed one of partial derangement. The gentleman at whose office I met Mr. Harrison on the day before—the reader will remember Mr. H. as having come to the "Sickle and Sheaf" in search of his sons—was thoroughly conversant with the affairs of the village, and I called upon him early in the day in order to make some inquiries about Mrs. Hammond. My first question, as to whether he knew the lady, was answered by the remark—

"Oh, yes. She is one of my earliest friends."

The allusion to her did not seem to awaken agreeable states of mind. A slight shade obscured his face, and I noticed that he sighed involuntarily.

"Is Willy her only child?"

"Her only living child. She had four; another son and two daughters; but she lost all but Willy when they were quite young. And," he added, after a pause—"it would have been better for her, and for Willy too, if he had gone to the better land with them."

"His course of life must be to her a terrible affliction," said I.

"It is destroying her reason," he replied, with emphasis. "He was her idol. No mother ever loved a son with more self-devotion than Mrs. Hammond loved her beautiful, fine-spirited, intelligent, affectionate boy. To say that she was proud of him, is but a tame expression. Intense love—almost idolatry—was the strong passion of her heart. How tender, how watchful was her love! Except when at school, he was scarcely ever separated from her. In order to keep him by her side, she gave up her thoughts to the suggestion and maturing of plans for keeping his mind active and interested in her society—and her success was perfect. Up to the age of sixteen or seventeen, I do not think he had a desire for other companionship than that of his mother. But this, you know, could not last. The boy's maturing thought must go beyond the home and social circle. The great world, that he was soon to enter, was before him; and through loopholes that opened here and there he obtained partial glimpses of what was beyond. To step forth into this world where he was soon to be a busy actor and worker, and to step forth alone, next came in the natural order of progress. How his mother trembled with anxiety as she saw him leave her side. Of the dangers that would surround his path, she knew too well; and these were magnified by her fears—at least so I often said to her. Alas! how far the sad reality has outrun her most fearful anticipations.

"When Willy was eighteen—he was then reading law—I think I never saw a young man of fairer promise. As I have often heard it remarked of him, he did not appear to have a single fault. But he had a dangerous gift—rare conversational powers, united with great urbanity of manner. Every one who made his acquaintance became charmed with his society; and he soon found himself surrounded by a circle of young men, some of whom were not the best companions he might have chosen. Still, his own pure instincts and honorable principles were his safeguard; and I never have believed that any social allurements would have drawn him away from the right path if this accursed tavern had not been opened by Slade."

"There was a tavern here before the 'Sickle and Sheaf' was opened," said I.

"Oh, yes. But it was badly kept, and the bar-room visitors were of the lowest class. No respectable young man in Cedarville would have been seen there. It offered no temptations to one moving in Willy's circle. But the opening of the 'Sickle and Sheaf' formed a new era. Judge Hammond—himself not the purest man in the world, I'm afraid—gave his countenance to the establishment, and talked of Simon Slade as an enterprising man who ought to be encouraged. Judge Lyman and other men of position in Cedarville followed his bad example and the bar-room of the 'Sickle and Sheaf' was at once voted respectable. At all times of the day and evening you could see the flower of our young men going in and out, sitting in front of the bar-room, or talking hand and glove with the landlord, who, from a worthy miller, regarded as well enough in his place, was suddenly elevated into a man of importance, whom the best in the village were delighted to honor.

"In the beginning Willy went with the tide, and in an incredibly short period was acquiring a fondness for drink that startled and alarmed his friends. In going in through Slade's open door he entered the downward way, and has been moving onward with fleet footsteps ever since. The fiery poison inflamed his mind at the same time that it dimmed his noble perceptions. Fondness for mere pleasure followed, and this led him into various sensual indulgences and exciting modes of passing the time. Every one liked him—he was so free, so companionable, and so generous—and almost every one encouraged, rather than repressed, his dangerous proclivities. Even his father for a time treated the matter lightly, as only the first flush of young life. 'I commenced sowing my wild oats at quite as early an age,' I have heard him say. 'He'll cool off, and do well enough. Never fear.' But his mother was in a state of painful alarm from the beginning. Her truer instincts, made doubly acute by her yearning love, perceived the imminent danger; and in all possible ways did she seek to lure him from the path in which he was moving at so rapid a pace. Willy was always very much attached to his mother, and her influence over him was strong; but in this case he regarded her fears as chimerical. The way in which he walked was to him so pleasant, and the companions of his journey so delightful, that he could not believe in the prophesied evil; and when his mother talked to him in her warning voice, and with a sad countenance, he smiled at her concern and made light of her fears.

"And so it went on, month after month, and year after year, until the young man's sad declensions were the town talk. In order to throw his mind into a new channel—to awaken, if possible, a new and better interest in life—his father ventured upon the doubtful experiment we spoke of yesterday: that of placing capital in his hands, and making him an equal partner in the business of distilling and cotton-spinning.

The disastrous—I might say disgraceful result—you know. The young man squandered his own capital, and heavily embarrassed his father.

"The effect of all this upon Mrs. Hammond has been painful in the extreme. We can only dimly imagine the terrible suffering through which she has passed. Her present aberration was first visible after a long period of sleeplessness, occasioned by distress of mind. During the whole of two weeks, I am told, she did not close her eyes; the most of that time walking the floor of her chamber and weeping. Powerful anodynes, frequently repeated, at length brought relief. But when she awoke from a prolonged period of unconsciousness, the brightness of her reason was gone. Since then she has never been clearly conscious of what was passing around her; and well for her, I have sometimes thought it was, for even obscurity of intellect is a blessing in her case. Ah me! I always get the heartache when I think of her."

"Did not this event startle the young man from his fatal dream, if I may so call his mad infatuation?" I asked.

"No. He loved his mother, and was deeply afflicted by the calamity; but it seemed as if he could not stop. Some terrible necessity appeared to be impelling him onward. If he formed good resolutions—and I doubt not that he did—they were blown away like threads of gossamer the moment he came within the sphere of old associations. His way to the mill was by the 'Sickle and Sheaf;' and it was not easy for him to pass there without being drawn into the bar, either by his own desire for drink, or through the invitation of some pleasant companion who was lounging in front of the tavern."

/ / /

The man was strongly excited.

"Thus it is," he continued; "and we who see the whole extent, origin, and downward rushing force of a widely sweeping desolation, lift our voices of warning almost in vain. Men who have everything at stake—sons to be corrupted and daughters to become the wives of young men exposed to corrupting influences—stand aloof, questioning and doubting as to the expediency of protecting the innocent from the wolfish designs of bad men, who, to compass their own selfish ends, would destroy them body and soul. We are called fanatics, ultraists, designing, and all that, because we ask our law-makers to stay the fiery ruin. Oh, no! we must not touch the traffic. All the dearest and best interests of society may suffer, but the rum-seller must be protected. He must be allowed to get gain, if the jails and poorhouses are filled and the graveyards made fat with the bodies of young men stricken down in the flower of their years, and of wives and mothers who have died of broken hearts. Reform, we are told, must commence at home. We must rear temperate children, and then we shall have temperate men. That when there are none to desire liquor, the rum-seller's traffic will cease. And all the while society's true benefactors are engaged in doing this, the weak, the unsuspecting, and the erring must be left an easy prey, even if the work requires for its accomplishment a hundred years. Sir! a human soul destroyed through the rum-seller's infernal agency is a sacrifice priceless in value. No considerations of worldly gain can, for an instant, be placed in comparison therewith. And yet souls are destroyed by thousands every year; and they will fall by tens of thousands ere society awakens from its fatal indifference and lays its strong hand of power on the corrupt men who are scattering disease, ruin and death broadcast over the land!

"I always get warm on this subject," he added, repressing his enthusiasm. "And who that observes and reflects can help growing excited? The evil is appalling, and the indifference of the community one of the strangest facts of the day."

While he was yet speaking, the elder Mr. Hammond came in. He looked wretched. The redness and humidity of his eyes showed want of sleep, and the relaxed muscles of his face exhaustion from weariness and suffering. He drew the person with whom I had been talking aside, and continued in earnest conversation with him for many minutes—often gesticulating violently. I could see his face, though I heard nothing of what he said. The play of his features was painful to look upon, for every changing muscle showed a new phase of mental suffering.

"Try and see him, will you not?" he said, as he turned, at length, to leave the office.

"I will go there immediately," was answered.

"Bring him home, if possible."

"My very best efforts shall be made."

Judge Hammond bowed, and went out hurriedly.

"Do you know the number of the room occupied by the man Green?" asked the gentleman as soon as his visitor had retired.

"Yes. It is No. 11."

"Willy has not been home since last night. His father, at this late day, suspects Green to be a gambler. The truth flashed upon him only yesterday; and this, added to his other sources of trouble, is driving him, so he says, almost mad. As a friend, he wishes me to go to the "Sickle and Sheaf' and try and find Willy. Have you seen anything of him this morning?"

I answered in the negative.

"Nor of Green?"

"No."

"Was Slade about when you left the tavern?"

"I saw nothing of him."

"What Judge Hammond fears may be all too true—that in the present condition of Willy's affairs, which have reached the point of disaster, his tempter means to secure the largest possible share of property yet in his power to pledge or transfer; to squeeze from his victim the last drop of blood that remains, and then fling him ruthlessly from his hands."

"The young man must have been rendered almost desperate, or he would never have returned as he did last night. Did you mention this to his father?"

"No. It would have distressed him the more without effecting any good. He is wretched enough. But time passes, and none is to be lost now. Will you go with me?"

I walked to the tavern with him, and we went into the bar together. Two or three men were at the counter, drinking.

"Is Mr. Green about this morning?" was asked by the person who had come in search of young Hammond.

"Haven't seen anything of him."

"Is he in his room?"

"I don't know."

"Will you ascertain for me?"

"Certainly. Frank,"—and he spoke to the landlord's son, who was lounging on a settee,—"I wish you would see if Mr. Green is in his room."

"Go and see yourself. I'm not your waiter," was growled back, in an ill-natured voice.

"In a moment I'll ascertain for you," said Matthew, politely.

After waiting on some new customers, who were just entering, Matthew went upstairs to obtain the desired information. As he left the bar-room, Frank got up and went behind the counter, where he mixed himself a glass of liquor, and drank it off, evidently with real enjoyment.

"Rather a dangerous business for one so young as you are," remarked the gentleman with whom I had come, as Frank stepped out of the bar and passed near where we were standing. The only answer to this was an ill-natured frown, and an expression of face which said, almost as plainly as words, "It's none of your business."

"Not there," said Matthew, now coming in.

"Are you certain?"

"Yes, sir."

But there was a certain involuntary hesitation in the barkeeper's manner which led to a suspicion that his answer was not in accordance with the truth. We walked out together, conferring on the subject, and both concluded that his word was not to be relied upon.

"What is to be done?" was asked.

"Go to Green's room," I replied, "and knock at the door. If he is there, he may answer, not suspecting your errand."

"Show me the room."

I went with him, and pointed out No. 11. He knocked lightly, but there came no sound from within. He repeated the knock; all was silent.

Again and again he knocked, but there came back only a hollow reverberation.

"There's no one there," said he, returning to where I stood, and we walked downstairs together. On the landing, as we reached the lower passage, we met Mrs. Slade. I had not, during this visit at Cedarville, stood face to face with her before. Oh! what a wreck she presented, with her pale, shrunken countenance, hollow, lustreless eyes, and bent, feeble body. I almost shuddered as I looked at her. What a haunting and sternly rebuking spectre she must have moved, daily, before the eyes of her husband.

"Have you noticed Mr. Green about, this morning?" I asked.

"He hasn't come down from his room yet," she replied.

"Are you certain?" said my companion. "I knocked several times at the door just now, but received no answer."

"What do you want with him?" asked Mrs. Slade, fixing her eyes upon us.

"We are in search of Willy Hammond, and it has been suggested that he is with Green."

"Knock twice lightly, and then three times more firmly," said Mrs. Slade; and as she spoke she glided past us with a noiseless tread.

"Shall we go up together?"

I did not object, for, although I had no delegated right of intrusion, my feelings were so much excited in the case that I went forward, scarcely reflecting on the propriety of so doing.

The signal knock found instant answer. The door was softly opened, and the unshaven face of Simon Slade presented itself.

"Mr. Jacobs!" he said, with surprise in his tones. "Do you wish to see me?"

"No, sir; I wish to see Mr. Green," and with a quick, firm pressure against the door, he pushed it wide open. The same party was there that I had seen on the night before,—Green, young Hammond, Judge Lyman, and Slade. On the table at which the three former were sitting were cards, slips of paper, an inkstand and pens, and a pile of banknotes. On a side-table, or, rather, butler's tray, were bottles, decanters and glasses.

"Judge Lyman! Is it possible?" exclaimed Mr. Jacobs, the name of my companion; "I did not expect to find you here."

Green instantly swept his hands over the table to secure the money and bills it contained; but, ere he had accomplished his purpose young Hammond grappled three or four narrow strips of paper and hastily tore them into shreds.

"You're a cheating scoundrel!" cried Green, fiercely, thrusting his hand into his bosom as if to draw from thence a weapon; but the words were scarcely uttered ere Hammond sprung upon him with the fierceness of a tiger, bearing him down upon the floor. Both hands were already about the gambler's neck, and, ere the bewildered spectators could interfere, and drag him off, Green was purple in the face, and nearly strangled.

"Call me a cheating scoundrel!" said Hammond, foaming at the mouth as he spoke. "Me! whom you have followed like a thirsty bloodhound. Me! whom you have robbed, and cheated, and debased from the beginning! Oh! for a pistol to rid the earth of the blackest-hearted villain that walks its surface. Let me go, gentlemen! I have nothing left in the world to care for,—there is no consequence I fear. Let me do society one good service before I die!"

And with one vigorous effort he swept himself clear of the hands that were pinioning him, and sprung again upon the gambler with the fierce energy of a savage beast. By this time Green had got his knife free from its sheath, and, as Hammond was closing upon him in his blind rage, plunged it into his side. Quick almost as lightning the knife was withdrawn, and two more stabs inflicted ere we could seize and disarm the murderer. As we did so, Willy Hammond fell over with a deep groan, the blood flowing from his side.

In the terror and excitement that followed Green rushed from the room. The doctor, who was instantly summoned, after carefully examining the wound and the condition of the unhappy young man, gave it as his opinion that he was fatally injured.

Oh! the anguish of the father, who had quickly heard of the dreadful occurrence, when this announcement was made. I never saw such fearful agony in any human countenance. The calmest of all the anxious group was Willy himself. On his father's face his eyes were fixed as if by a kind of fascination.

"Are you in much pain, my poor boy?" sobbed the old man, stooping over him, until his long white hair mingled with the damp locks of the sufferer.

"Not much, father," was the whispered reply. "Don't speak of this to mother yet. I'm afraid it will kill her."

What could the father answer? Nothing! And he was silent.

*CHARLES BALL ET AL.*

# 28 | *Life under the Lash*

*The authors of the more than one hundred extant book-length accounts of slavery were by no means typical ex-slaves. Most of them succeeded in gaining their freedom by escape or purchase, which was not the lot of their less fortunate brothers and sisters. Most were highly literate. Some had help in writing their accounts from abolitionists and other ghost writers and editors. Nevertheless, historians in recent decades have discovered how generally accurate—in fact how indispensable—their narratives are for any serious understanding of the institution of American slavery.*

*The sampling of the literature presented here provides insight into the work regimen of a plantation, living conditions of slaves, the agonizing limits slavery set on parental authority, and the slaves' struggle to keep control of their religious life.*

## CHARLES BALL

### *The Work Regimen of a Tobacco Plantation**

In Maryland and Virginia, although the slaves are treated with so much rigour, and oftimes with so much cruelty, I have seen instances of the greatest tenderness of feeling on the part of their owners. I, myself, had three masters in Maryland, and I cannot say now, even after having resided so many years in a state where slavery is not tolerated, that either of them (except the last, who sold me to the Georgians, and was an unfeeling man,) used me worse than they had a moral right to do, regarding me merely as an article of property, and not entitled to any rights as a man, political or civil. My mistresses, in Maryland, were all good women; and the mistress of my wife, in whose kitchen I spent my Sundays and many of my nights, for several years, was a lady of most benevolent and kindly feelings. She was a true friend to me, and I shall always venerate her memory. . . .

If the proprietors of the soil in Maryland and Virginia, were skillful cultivators—had their lands in good condition—and kept no more slaves on each estate, than would be sufficient to work the soil in a proper manner, and kept up the repairs of the place—the condition of

*Ball had been a slave in Maryland, South Carolina, and Georgia.

the coloured people would not be, by any means, a comparatively unhappy one. I am convinced, that in nine cases in ten, the hardships and suffering of the coloured population of lower Virginia, are attributable to the poverty and distress of its owners. In many instances, an estate scarcely yields enough to feed and clothe the slaves in a comfortable manner, without allowing anything for the support of the master and family; but it is obvious, that the family must first be supported, and the slaves must be content with the surplus—and this, on a poor, old, worn out tobacco plantation, is often very small, and wholly inadequate to the comfortable sustenance of the hands, as they are called. There, in many places, nothing is allowed to the poor Negro, but his peck of corn per week, without the sauce of a salt herring, or even a little salt itself. . . .

The general features of slavery are the same everywhere; but the utmost rigour of the system, is only to be met with, on the cotton plantations of Carolina and Georgia, or in the rice fields which skirt the deep swamps and morasses of the southern rivers. In the tobacco fields of Maryland and Virginia, great cruelties are practiced—not so frequently by the owners, as by the overseers of the slaves; but yet, the tasks are not so excessive as in the cotton region, nor is the press of labour so incessant throughout the year. It is true, that from the period when the tobacco plants are set in the field, there is no resting time until it is housed; but it is planted out about the first of May, and must be cut and taken out of the field before the frost comes. After it is hung and dried, the labor of stripping and preparing it for the hogshead in leaf, or of manufacturing it into twist, is comparatively a work of leisure and ease. Besides, on almost every plantation the hands are able to complete the work of preparing the tobacco by January, and sometimes earlier; so that the winter months, form some sort of respite from the toils of the year. The people are obliged, it is true, to occupy themselves in cutting wood for the house, making rails and repairing fences, and in clearing new land, to raise the tobacco plants for the next year; but as there is usually time enough, and to spare, for the completion of all this work, before the season arrives for setting the plants in the field; the men are seldom flogged much, unless they are very lazy or negligent, and the women are allowed to remain in the house, in the very cold, snowy, or rainy weather. . . .

In Maryland I never knew a mistress or a young mistress, who would not listen to the complaints of the slaves. It is true, we were always obliged to approach the door of the mansion, with our hats in our hands, and the most subdued and beseeching language in our mouths—but, in return, we generally received words of kindness, and very often a redress of our grievances; though I have known very great ladies, who would never grant any request from the plantation hands, but always referred them and their petitions to their master, under a pretence, that they could not meddle with things that did not belong to the house.

The mistresses of the great families, generally gave mild language to the slaves; though they sometimes sent for the overseer and had them severely flogged; but I have never heard any mistress, in either Maryland or Virginia, indulge in the low, vulgar and profane vituperations, of which I was myself the object, in Georgia, for many years, whenever I came into the presence of my mistress. Flogging—though often severe and excruciating in Maryland, is not practiced with the order, regularity and system, to which it is often reduced in the South. On the Potomac, if a slave gives offence, he is generally chastised on the spot, in the field where he is at work, as the overseer always carried a whip—sometimes a twisted cow-hide, sometimes a kind of horse-whip, and very often a simple hickory switch or gad, cut in the adjoining woods. For stealing meat, or other provisions, or for any of the higher offences, the slaves are stripped, tied up by the hands—sometimes by the thumbs—and whipped at the quarter—but many times, on a large tobacco plantation, there is not more than one of these regular whippings in a week—though on others, where the master happens to be a bad man, or a drunkard—the back of the unhappy Maryland slaves, is seamed with scars from his neck to his hips.

## *JOSIAH HENSON**

### *"We Lodged in Log Huts"*

My earliest employments were, to carry buckets of water to the men at work, and to hold a horse-plough, used for weeding between the rows of corn. As I grew older and taller, I was entrusted with the care of master's saddle-horse. Then a hoe was put into my hands, and I was soon required to do the day's work of a man; and it was not long before I could do it, at least as well as my associates in misery.

A description of the everyday life of a slave on a Southern plantation illustrates the character and habits of the slave and the slaveholder, created and perpetuated by their relative position. The principal food of those upon my master's plantation consisted of corn-meal and salt herrings; to which was added in summer a little buttermilk, and the few vegetables which each might raise for himself and his family, on the little piece of ground which was assigned to him for the purpose, called a truck-patch.

In ordinary times we had two regular meals in a day: breakfast at twelve o'clock, after laboring from daylight, and supper when the work of the remainder of the day was over. In harvest season we had three. Our dress was of tow-cloth; for the children, nothing but a shirt; for the

*Henson had been a slave in Maryland before he escaped.

older ones a pair of pantaloons or a gown in addition, according to the sex. Besides these, in the winter a round jacket or overcoat, a wool-hat once in two or three years, for the males, and a pair of coarse shoes once a year.

We lodged in log huts, and on the bare ground. Wooden floors were an unknown luxury. In a single room were huddled, like cattle, ten or a dozen persons, men, women, and children. All ideas of refinement and decency were, of course, out of the question. We had neither bedsteads, nor furniture of any description. Our beds were collections of straw and old rags, thrown down in the corners and boxed in with boards; a single blanket the only covering. Our favourite way of sleeping, however, was on a plank, our heads raised on an old jacket and our feet toasting before the smouldering fire. The wind whistled and the rain and snow blew in through the cracks, and the damp earth soaked in the moisture till the floor was miry as a pig-sty. Such were our houses. In these wretched hovels were we penned at night, and fed by day; here were the children born and the sick—neglected.

## *FRANCIS HENDERSON**

### *Living Conditions on the Plantation*

Our houses were but log huts—the tops partly open—ground floor—rain would come through. My aunt was quite an old woman, and had been sick several years; in rains I have seen her moving from one part of the house to the other, and rolling her bedclothes about to try to keep dry—everything would be dirty and muddy. I lived in the house with my aunt. My bed and bedstead consisted of a board wide enough to sleep on—one end on a stool, the other placed near the fire. My pillow consisted of my jacket—my covering was whatever I could get. My bedtick was the board itself. And this was the way the single men slept—but we were comfortable in this way of sleeping, being used to it. I only remember having but one blanket from my owners up to the age of nineteen, when I ran away.

Our allowance was given weekly—a peck of sifted corn meal, a dozen and a half herrings, two and a half pounds of pork. Some of the boys would eat this up in three days—then they had to steal, or they could not perform their daily tasks. They would visit the hog-pen, sheep-pen, and granaries. I do not remember one slave but who stole some things—they were driven to it as a matter of necessity. I myself did this—many a time have I, with others, run among the stumps in chase of a sheep, that we might have something to eat.... In regard to cooking, sometimes many have to cook at one fire, and before

*Henderson escaped from slavery at the age of nineteen.

all could get to the fire to bake hoe cakes, the overseer's horn would sound: then they must go at any rate. Many a time I have gone along eating a piece of bread and meat, or herring broiled on the coals—I never sat down at a table to eat except at harvest time, all the time I was a slave. In harvest time, the cooking is done at the great house, as the hands they have are wanted in the field. This was more like people, and we liked it, for we sat down then at meals. In the summer we had one pair of linen trousers given us—nothing else; every fall, one pair of woolen pantaloons, one woolen jacket, and two cotton shirts.

My master had four sons in his family. They all left except one, who remained to be a driver. He would often come to the field and accuse the slave of having taken so and so. If we denied it, he would whip the grown-up ones to make them own it. Many a time, when we didn't know he was anywhere around, he would be in the woods watching us—first thing we would know, he would be sitting on the fence looking down upon us, and if any had been idle, the young master would visit him with blows. I have known him to kick my aunt, an old woman who had raised and nursed him, and I have seen him punish my sisters awfully with hickories from the woods.

The slaves are watched by the patrols, who ride about to try to catch them off the quarters, especially at the house of a free person of color. I have known the slaves to stretch clothes lines across the street, high enough to let the horse pass, but not the rider; then the boys would run, and the patrols in full chase would be thrown off by running against the lines. The patrols are poor white men, who live by plundering and stealing, getting rewards for runaways, and setting up little shops on the public roads. They will take whatever the slaves steal, paying in money, whiskey, or whatever the slaves want. They take pigs, sheep, wheat, corn—anything that's raised they encourage the slaves to steal: these they take to market next day. It's all speculation—all a matter of self-interest, and when the slaves run away, these same traders catch them if they can, to get the reward. If the slave threatens to expose his traffic, he does not care—for the slave's word is good for nothing—it would not be taken.

## *JACOB STROYER*

### *Parents and Children*

Gilbert was a cruel [slave] boy. He used to strip his fellow Negroes while in the woods, and whip them two or three times a week, so that their backs were all scarred, and threatened them with severer punishments if they told; this state of things had been going on for quite a while. As I was a favorite with Gilbert, I always managed to escape a whipping, with the promise of keeping the secret of the punishment of the rest. . . . But finally, one day, Gilbert said to me, "Jake," as he used to call me, "you am a good boy, but I'm gwine to wip you some to-day, as I wip dem toder boys." Of course I was required to strip off my only garment, which was an Osnaburg linen shirt, worn by both sexes of the Negro children in the summer. As I stood trembling before my merciless superior, who had a switch in his hand, thousands of thoughts went through my little mind as to how to get rid of the whipping. I finally fell upon a plan which I hoped would save me from a punishment that was near at hand. . . . I commenced reluctantly to take off my shirt, at the same time pleading with Gilbert, who paid no attention to my prayer. . . . Having satisfied myself that no mercy was to be found with Gilbert, I drew my shirt off and threw it over his head, and bounded forward on a run in the direction of the sound of the [nearby] carpenters. By the time he got from the entanglement of my garment, I had quite a little start of him. . . . As I got near to the carpenters, one of them ran and met me, into whose arms I jumped. The man into whose arms I ran was Uncle Benjamin, my mother's uncle. . . . I told him that Gilbert had been in the habit of stripping the boys and whipping them two or three times a week, when we went into the woods, and threatened them with greater punishment if they told. . . . Gilbert was brought to trial, severely whipped, and they made him beg all the children to pardon him for his treatment to them.

[My] father . . . used to take care of horses and mules. I was around with him in the barn yard when but a very small boy; of course that gave me an early relish for the occupation of hostler, and I soon made known my preference to Col. Singleton, who was a sportsman, and an owner of fine horses. And, although I was too small to work, the Colonel granted my request; hence I was allowed to be numbered among those who took care of the fine horses and learned to ride. But I soon found that my new occupation demanded a little more than I cared for. It was not long after I had entered my new work before they put me upon the back of a horse which threw me to the ground almost as soon as I had reached his back. It hurt me a little, but that was not the worst of it, for when I got up there was a man standing near with a switch in hand, and he immediately began to beat me. Although I was a very bad boy, this was the first time I had been whipped by anyone except father and mother, so I cried out in a tone of voice as if I would say, this is the first and last whipping you will give me when father gets hold of you.

When I had got away from him I ran to father with all my might, but soon found my expectation blasted, as father very coolly said to me, "Go back to your work and be a good boy, for I cannot do anything for you." But that did not satisfy me, so on I went to mother with my complaint and she came out to the man who had whipped me; he was a groom, a white man master had hired to train the horses. Mother and he began to talk, then he took a whip and started for her, and she ran from him, talking all the time. I ran back and forth between mother and him until he stopped beating her. After the fight between the groom and mother, he took me back to the stable yard and gave me a severe flogging. And, although mother failed to help me at first, still I had faith that when he had taken me back to the stable yard, and commenced whipping me, she would come and stop him, but I looked in vain, for she did not come.

Then the idea first came to me that I, with my dear father and mother and the rest of my fellow Negroes, were doomed to cruel treatment through life, and was defenseless. But when I found that father and mother could not save me from punishment, as they themselves had to submit to the same treatment, I concluded to appeal to the sympathy of the groom, who seemed to have full control over me; but my pitiful cries never touched his sympathy. . . .

One day, about two weeks after Boney Young [the white man who trained horses for Col. Singleton] and mother had the conflict, he called me to him. . . . When I got to him he said, "Go and bring me the switch, sir." I answered, "yes, sir," and off I went and brought him one . . . [and] . . . he gave me a first-class flogging. . . .

When I went home to father and mother, I said to them, "Mr. Young is whipping me too much now, I shall not stand it, I shall fight him." Father said to me, "You must not do that, because if you do he will say that your mother and I advised you to do it, and it will make it hard for your mother and me, as well as for yourself. You must do as I told you, my son: do your work the best you can, and do not say anything." I said to father, "But I don't know what I have done that he should whip me; he does not tell me what wrong I have done, he simply calls me to him and whips me when he gets ready." Father said, "I can do nothing more than to pray to the Lord to hasten the time when these things shall be done away; that is all I can do. . . . "

## *PETER RANDOLPH**

### *Religion of the Slaves*

Many say the Negroes receive religious education—that Sabbath worship is instituted for them as for others, and were it not for slavery, they would die in their sins—that really, the institution of slavery is a benevolent missionary enterprise. Yes, they are preached to, and I will give my readers some faint glimpses of these preachers, and their doctrines and practices.

In Prince George County there were two meeting-houses intended for public worship. Both were occupied by the Baptist denomination. These houses were built by William and George Harrison, brothers . . .

*Randolph, a slave in Virginia, received his freedom following his owner's death.

that their slaves might go there on the Sabbath and receive instruction, such as slave-holding ministers would give. The prominent preaching to the slaves was, "'Servants, obey your masters'. Do not steal or lie, for this is very wrong. Such conduct is sinning against the Holy Ghost, and is base ingratitude to your kind masters, who feed, clothe and protect you. . . ." I should think, when making such statements, the slaveholders would feel the rebuke of the Apostle and fall down and be carried out from the face of day, as were Ananias and Sapphira, when they betrayed the trust committed to them, or refused to bear true testimony in regard to that trust.

There was another church, about fourteen miles from the one just mentioned. It was called "Brandon's church," and there the white Baptists worshiped. . . .

There was one Brother Shell who used to preach. One Sabbath, while exhorting the poor, impenitent, hard-hearted, ungrateful slaves, so much beloved by their masters, to repentance and prayerfulness, while entreating them to lead good lives, that they might escape the wrath (of the lash) to come, some of his crocodile tears overflowed his cheek. . . . But, my readers, Monday morning, Brother Shell was afflicted with his old malady, hardness of heart, so that he was obliged to catch one of the sisters by the throat, and give her a terrible flogging.

The like of this is the preaching, and these are the men that spread the Gospel among the slaves. Ah! such a Gospel had better be buried in oblivion, for it makes more heathens than Christians. Such preachers ought to be forbidden by the laws of the land ever to mock again at the blessed religion of Jesus, which was sent as a light to the world. . . .

Not being allowed to hold meetings on the plantation, the slaves assemble in the swamps, out of reach of the patrols. They have an understanding among themselves as to the time and place of getting together. This is often done by the first one arriving breaking boughs from the trees, and bending them in the direction of the selected spot. Arrangements are then made for conducting the exercises. They first ask each other how they feel, the state of their minds, etc. The male members then select a certain space, in separate groups, for their division of the meeting. Preaching in order, by the brethren; then praying and singing all round, until they generally feel quite happy. The speaker usually commences by calling himself unworthy, and talks very slowly, until, feeling the spirit, he grows excited, and in a short time, there fall to the ground twenty or thirty men and women under its influence. Enlightened people call it excitement; but I wish the same was felt by everybody, so far as they are sincere.

The slave forgets all his sufferings, except to remind others of the trials during the past week, exclaiming: "Thank God, I shall not live here always!" Then they pass from one to another, shaking hands, and bidding each other farewell, promising, should they meet no more on earth, to strive and meet in heaven, where all is joy, happiness and liberty. As they separate, they sing a parting hymn of praise.

Sometimes the slaves meet in an old log-cabin, when they find it necessary to keep a watch. If discovered, they escape, if possible; but those who are caught often get whipped. Some are willing to be punished thus for Jesus' sake. Most of the songs used in worship are composed by the slaves themselves, and describe their own sufferings. Thus:

"Oh, that I had a bosom friend,
  To tell my secrets to,
One always to depend upon
  In everything I do!"
"How do I wander, up and down!
  I seem a stranger, quite undone;
None to lend an ear to my complaint,
  No one to cheer me, though I faint."

Some of the slaves sing—

"No more rain, no more snow,
No more cowskin on my back!"

Then they change it by singing—

"Glory be to God that rules on high."

In some places, if the slaves are caught praying to God, they are whipped more than if they had committed a great crime. The slaveholders will allow the slaves to dance, but do not want them to pray to God. Sometimes, when a slave, on being whipped, calls upon God, he is forbidden to do so, under threat of having his throat cut, or brains blown out. Oh, reader! this seems very hard—that slaves cannot call on their Maker, when the case most needs it. Sometimes the poor slave takes courage to ask his master to let him pray, and is driven away, with the answer, that if discovered praying, his back will pay the bill.

HENRY MERRELL

# 29 Creating Industry in the Antebellum South

*In March 1981, the historian James L. Skinner III discovered in the top drawer of an old chest in a house in Roswell, Arkansas, an old record book that began, "My name is Henry Merrell. No middle name. Never had one. Have always got on without one." After ten years of research into the life of Henry Merrell, in 1991* The Autobiography of Henry Merrell, Industrial Missionary to the South *was published.*

*The story was worth the long wait. Merrell, an engineer born in 1816 in Utica, New York, found his way to Georgia in 1839, then to Arkansas in 1856, spending most of his life and energies developing industries, principally textile mills, in the inhospitable atmosphere of the slave South. There Merrell discovered some of the more subtle effects of slavery: the beliefs that hard labor is for slaves; that a gentleman does not roll up his sleeves; and that planters do not invest in industry—they buy land or slaves or many good carriages and horses. Merrell spent his entire adult life in the South and even served the Confederate government, but was essentially a frustrated and very premature representative of an attitude that bloomed long after his prime: the idea of an industrialized "New South."*

With a stout heart, and the best of resolutions, I parted from my mother, and Sisters, and brother Sam, and "all inquiring friends," bending my steps Southward, while my school-mates generally sought to establish their fortunes in the West. Not many young men in those days were content to plod through life in the places where they were born and raised. Some to mend their fortunes, some for a better position in society, & a few for health, emigrated. It was said to be the Genius of the American people. Whatever the causes, I am sure that the few who remained behind and took up affairs where their fathers laid them down, enjoyed the more innocent lives, and longer lives, & had more comfort if not more wealth in the long run.

I was to proceed to Paterson, N. Jersey, and for a while look after the building of machinery for the new Factory in Georgia. There I learned a great deal more about my business, than I was able to impart, for Mr. Rogers (Rogers, Ketchum & Grosvenor) was a great mechanic. True to my own maxims, I attended strictly to business. So much so indeed that I made no acquaintance outside the shop. My landlady notified me that a certain young lady(?) wished me to know that she was in love with me. I had just curiosity enough to take one good look at her in the street in order to see what sort of a somebody it might be, & she was indeed good looking enough, with jewelry in her ears and all that; but positively upon my honor I never spoke to her. I wondered a little if she saw "anything green about me," & that was all the thought I bestowed upon her. Had I been idle, it might have been otherwise, which shows advantage of active employment, "Satan finds some mischief still for idle hands to do."

When the machinery was safe on board the good ship "Milledgeville" bound from N. York to the port of Savannah, I went on board, the only passenger. In those days there were no sea-going steamers. The experiment had been tried in the coasting trade; but the art of building suitable craft had not yet arrived at sufficient perfection, and the losses of the steamers "Home" & the "Pulaski," on the Southern coast, had caused a strong prejudice against any more experiments in that line on this side of the ocean. And nothing further was attempted until after the success of the British ship the "Great Western," had demonstrated the practicability of sea-going steamers. After that, ocean navigations by steam increased and multiplied rapidly enough, but no coasting steamer gained the confidence of the Southern folk until the appearance in those waters of the "Southerner," Capt. Berry, & even then it was as much confidence in the man as in the ship.

The traveling public of Georgia and Carolina, after the heart-rending tragedies of the "Pulaski" and the "Home," was very sore on that subject. Scarcely an extensive family among them that had not lost some friend or kin by those events, and their minds were greatly embittered towards those Northern ship-owners who offered inducements for them to risk all they held dear on board half-built steamers that were already or would have been condemned in their own waters. However, in the course of ten or fifteen years afterwards, all that was reconciled, and finally a noble line of steamers plied from New York to Philadelphia and Baltimore to the ports of Charleston and Savannah, and there was no longer any question as to their sea going qualities.

I was ten days at sea on board the "Milledgeville," & arrived at Savannah early in May. This was my first sea voyage. I have been [on] many voyages since, but never across the ocean; and let me say once for all that I am not fond of the Sea, because I suffer a great deal from sea-sickness. But for that, sea-going would be my delight, and I apprehend that sea-sickness is a wise provision to prevent everybody going to sea. As it is, few go upon salt water unless they have business there.

The scenery below Savannah on the river, with rice plantations on either hand, as seen from the City, is said to resemble no little the banks of the river Nile as seen from the City of Cairo.

/ / /

Arrived at Roswell in Cobb County in the month of May 1839. . . . Of this manufacturing town I was not the founder; that honor was due to old Mr. Roswell King the father of Barrington King. I was not the responsible agent; that office belonged to Barrington King Esq. who filled it with great firmness, & probably retains it for life. I finally arrived at the dignity of assistant Agent, & so shared in that responsibility, but my part in the building up of that place was limited to the Engineering & Mechanical departments & the organizing & discipline of the hands: no light undertaking, I now think, for a very young man, considering the rough population that I had to deal with, & the remoteness of the place from mechanical facilities. But I had a strong will then, & I must say of Mr. King that he never weakened my hands, but "backed" me at every emergency.

/ / /

There were two sources from which to draw this future supply of Southern manufacturers and mechanics. *First,* the sons of gentlemen rich & poor, & *Second* the factory boys themselves as they grew up under my own eye and developed the qualifications of which I was in quest. I might have added a *Third* class: to wit the Negroes themselves, but at that time prejudices barred my way in that direction, & I will not say whether they were my own prejudices or those of others; perhaps we shared them all around.

*First* then, the sons of gentlemen rich and poor, educated and ignorant. For them to labor was disreputable. That was the miserable *Esprit de corps* of their class. I have been told by young gentlemen from the low country of Georgia that, until they saw me, they had never seen a white man do a hand's turn of work. Even the overseers and Negro drivers rode on horseback, & were exempt from labor. To such my practical answer was to take off my coat, roll up my sleeves, & go at doing something useful, although I had no occasion to do so. The duties of my post did not require it. When I saw young gentlemen escorting young ladies down the hill to visit the works, I would off jacket in like manner, to show my contempt for their one maxim & standard of gentility. That was before I married. After that event, my wife rather exacted from me more dignity, & I had no right to go counter to all her Southern prejudices.

But bravely as I played the blunt mechanic, when I was a young fellow, it was sometimes a bitter pill to feel that I was looked upon with contempt by young gentlemen & ladies to whom I was conscious of being quite equal in point of birth, education and refinement. I did it, however, from a sense of duty. I did it to vindicate the fashion of my native town, where every young man of every station is forced by public opinion to "hang out his shingle"—*i.e.,* to have some visible means of livelihood in case of future reverses of fortune. I was too proud to sink the shop in order to go into polite society. I was resolved that Southern society should receive me on equal terms as a scientific mechanic, or not at all. And if not at all, so much the better for me; it would leave me the more leisure to improve my mind.

Moreover, I considered that I had "a calling to fulfill" & that was, as I have before stated, to promote a system of Southern Manufactures, which I hoped would, in the course of time, reconcile Southern with Northern interests, & neutralize the efforts of mad and ultra politicians on both sides to use the general government as a tool to legislate for a class, or for a section against the interests of the whole, and I thought if I could induce the sons of gentlemen to accept my views of the dignity of labor, so much the better for them; if not, I must bring forward the low class of white people & make men of them.

/ / /

The state of health, & the want of Society at the Long Shoals Factory caused me to yield to my own wife's wish to live in the town of Greensboro, sixteen miles distant. This move was just as it should be in respect to my family, but the worst thing possible for the Factory. A Cotton Factory, of all things, is the worst to be managed by an absentee. When I located my home in Greensboro, I should have resigned my Agency of the Factory. From that time things gradually ran down on my hands. I saw it year after year growing worse and worse. My anxieties increased to irritability. My frequent rides to and from the works in all kinds of weather impaired my health and spirits. I became indifferent to society, & made no friends. All this time the grinding effects of the Tariff of 1846 began to be felt by the Manufacturers of Georgia, as it had been already felt by those at the North. Profits reached the lowest living point & below. Imported goods did not exactly take the place of ours, but they did take the place of Northern manufactures, driving their looms and spindles into direct competition with us.

And it finally became manifest that we had too many factories in the State of Georgia for the trade of our own Country, & too many for the floating population of factory hands, & that only those Factories which had the most improved machinery in the place of manual labor could hope to succeed—the rest must go under. Here was a change! Five years before, labor was so abundant and so cheap that it was no object to save labor by machinery, but rather a charity not to do so. Five years before, Cotton was so very low that it was not worthwhile to be at the expense of perfect machinery and close management to prevent the wastage of raw material. But now labor and oil and Cotton had all gone up in price several hundred percent & were often not easy to control at any price. I began to regret bitterly that I had set my face against the improvements so far as to go on in the old way instead of keeping up with the times. In the Long Shoals Factory I had actually gone backwards, and adopted new machinery of the style ten years gone by. And I had been fool enough to make a virtue of my conservatism in so doing!

Fortunately for the Roswell Manufacturing Company, a son of Mr. Barrington King (James) was then at the North learning the business of Machinist. There he witnessed the rapid outcome of improvements that met the Tariff of '46. He witnessed the discussions of leading mechanics & adopted their new improvements, discarding what was spurious. The result was that the New Factory at Roswell was erected in a style to cope with the hardest times, and upon the success of that, the Old Factory was improved [on] the same model. Thereby securing the present high prosperity of that excellent institution, of which I am always proud.

For myself, I was not yet up to the times. A residence of six months at the North would set me right, but the plodding round of my old business and the growing necessity for hard work and close management blinded me quite.

Money was becoming very [plentiful] in Georgia and sought for investment. The system of Rail Roads could absorb no more capital, & the value of their stocks appreciated greatly. I had myself Georgia Rail Road stock which I had bought at 44 that had gone up to 110. The rate of Interest was reduced by law, and the question was often asked me if I could not invest more money for them in manufacturing. I ought to have said no. But my temperament is sanguine & hopeful, and finally I said yes; and I undertook, in an evil hour, to erect a new Cotton Spinning Factory in the town (City) of Greensboro. It was partly for the profit of the business, & partly to improve the value of property in the town, which was tending to decay.

Of course the Factory had to be propelled by steam power, but seeing Greensboro was a healthy place, I considered that the advantage of health among my hands more than compensated for the probable cost of steam compared with water power. Moreover, Greensboro was directly on the Rail Road, which was an advantage in the important matter of transportation. I thought I weighed the matter profoundly. I had a doubt about the sure supply of fuel, & stated that doubt to parties concerned, whereupon one of them came forward & set my mind at rest by entering into a written contract for a supply at satisfactory rates. A contract which he afterwards found means to evade & became my enemy accordingly, as men always do when they have done you wrong. . . . Another tendered the good offices of the Georgia Rail Road for the supply of wood, he being a Director in that Co. But the Georgia Rail Road, which began in good faith, had need of fuel itself &, coming to regard me as a rival in the wood-market, put up the price on me intolerably; and finally, under a new supt., they tore up the switch by which the car loads of wood were run in to the works. Those things baffled me afterwards. In the construction of the Factory buildings I was quite up to the times, & made the most of rather an indifferent and sidelong place. The bricks furnished me by another of the stock-holders were not well burned, but I had no remedy. I believe the building stands to this day, thanks to a strong cement which I attended to myself. . . . But it was not intended by a kind Providence that I should succeed in that undertaking. Again I was straitened in the purchase for machinery. At the moment I should have had the very best and most improved machinery. I was short of funds most unexpectedly, and had to be content with that which was very low-priced, although at the same time I was able to adopt some but not all of the current improvements.

# THE INDEX OF AMERICAN DESIGN

## 30 Playthings

The Index of American Design *was a New Deal program that provided work for unemployed commercial artists and documented the history of American design. The Index reflected the growing interest in American material culture that produced such reconstructions as Colonial Williamsburg and Old Sturbridge Village, as well as great museum collections of American folk art. From the drawing and watercolor renderings of such artifacts as clothing, furniture, tools, signs, folk art, and toys that make up the* Index, *artists and designers have found fresh inspiration and historians have learned much about the day-to-day lives of Americans.*

*Early America had no toy industry. Wealthier folk could provide their children with imported toys from Germany, but for most children, toys were either homemade or made by local artisans as a minor sideline to their main occupations. Toymakers principally used materials at hand such as wood, tin, pewter, clothes, rags, and cornhusks. Much, obviously, had to be left to children's imaginations.*

*Plate I is a marionette of wood and clothes representing Simon Legree, the cruel overseer from Harriet Beecher Stowe's* Uncle Tom's Cabin. *Plate II is a well-worn Quaker doll wearing the representative Quaker bonnet, with a papier-mâché head and padding rather than a formed body. Plate III is a mid-nineteenth century version of roller skates. The in-line wheels proved unsatisfactory until modern plastics made such skates practical more than a century later. The nineteenth-century rocking horse in Plate IV reflects a nineteenth-century economy of construction, but the elegant result will please most twentieth-century sensibilities.*

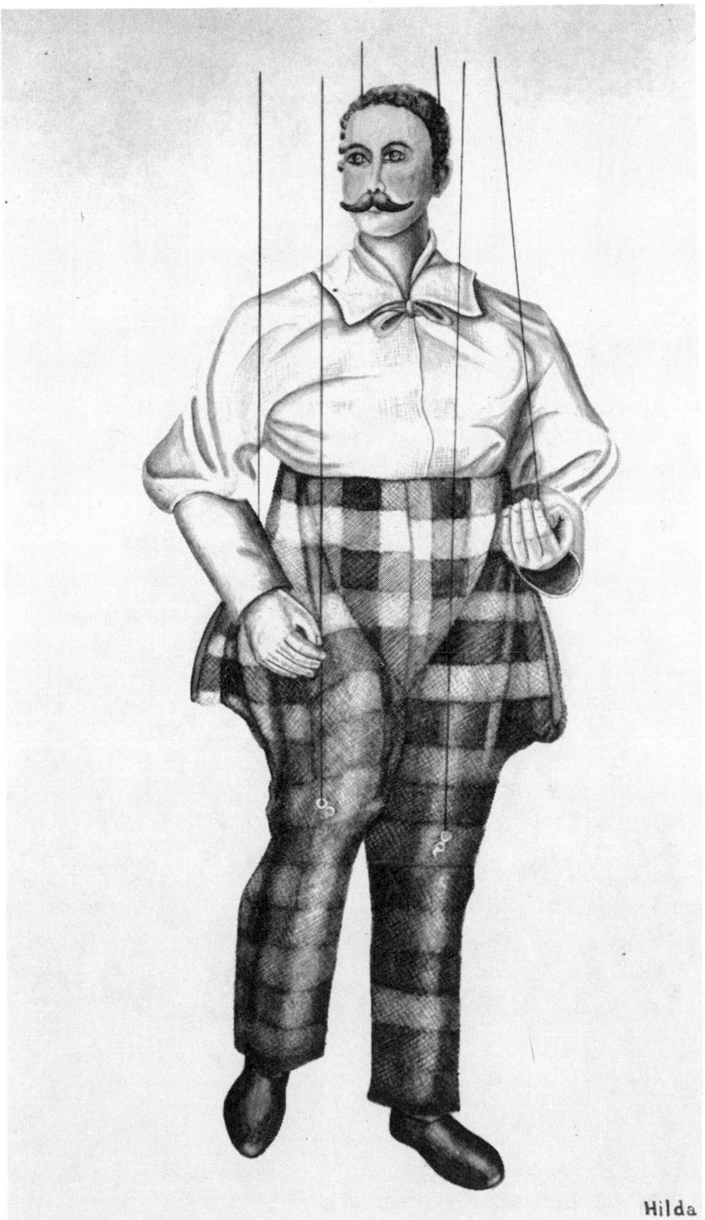


*Plate I*

Puppet of "Simon Legree" rendering by Elmer Weise, in *Index of American Design.* Copyright © 1994 Board of Trustees, National Gallery of Art, Washington.

*Plate II*

Quaker Costume Doll rendering by Charlotte Angus, in *Index of American Design*. Copyright © 1994 Board of Trustees, National Gallery of Art, Washington.

*Plate III*

Roller Skates rendering by Albert Rudin, in *Index of American Design*. Copyright © 1994 Board of Trustees, National Gallery of Art, Washington.

*Plate IV*

Wooden Rocking Horse rendering by Helen Gilman, in *Index of American Design*. Copyright © 1994 Board of Trustees, National Gallery of Art, Washington.

HARRIET JACOBS

# 31 A Perilous Passage in the Life of a Slave Girl

*Harriet Jacobs'* Incidents in the Life of a Slave Girl *is only now emerging as the classic narrative of a woman slave, a work to rank with the several autobiographies of Frederick Douglass. Published under a pseudonym in 1861, edited by a white abolitionist, and borrowing form and rhetoric from sentimental novels such as Harriet Beecher Stowe's* Uncle Tom's Cabin, *the authenticity of the work remained suspect for 120 years. Only in 1981, when Jean Fagan Yellin published documentary evidence for Jacobs' authorship (*American Literature *53 [Nov. 1981], 479–486), did recognition come that this is a major work of African-American literature, as well as an essential document for the history of antebellum slavery.*

*Jacobs (1813–1897), writing under the pseudonym of Linda Brent, added to the catalogue of slavery's evils an account of the sexual exploitation of a woman slave, deliberately discussing a forbidden subject. Yet her story is not that of a passive victim. To thwart the sexual advances of her master, she took as a lover a leading member of the white community. To prevent the permanent enslavement of her children, she hid for seven years in the attic of her grandmother's house, a tiny space only three feet high, while deceiving her master into thinking she had escaped to the North by smuggling out letters to be mailed from New York City and Boston. Finally she and then her children escaped from slave territory to discover the ambiguities of freedom in the so-called free states.*

## THE TRIALS OF GIRLHOOD

During the first years of my service in Dr. Flint's family, I was accustomed to share some indulgences with the children of my mistress. Though this seemed to me no more than right, I was grateful for it, and tried to merit the kindness by the faithful discharge of my duties. But I now entered on my fifteenth year—a sad epoch in the life of a slave girl. My master began to whisper foul words in my ear. Young as I was, I could not remain ignorant of their import. I tried to treat them with indifference or contempt. The master's age, my extreme youth, and the fear that his conduct would be reported to my grandmother, made me bear this treatment for many months. He was a crafty man, and resorted to many means to accomplish his purposes. Sometimes he had stormy, terrific ways, that made his victims tremble; sometimes he assumed a gentleness that he thought must surely subdue. Of the two, I preferred his stormy moods, although they left me trembling. He tried his utmost to corrupt the pure principles my grandmother had instilled. He peopled my young mind with unclean images, such as only a vile monster could think of. I turned from him with disgust and hatred. But he was my master. I was compelled to live under the same roof with him—where I saw a man forty years my senior daily violating the most sacred commandments of nature. He told me I was his property; that I must be subject to his will in all things. My soul revolted against the mean tyranny. But where could I turn for protection? No matter whether the slave girl be as black as ebony or as fair as her mistress. In either case, there is no shadow of law to protect her from insult, from violence, or even from death; all these are inflicted by fiends who bear the shape of men. The mistress, who ought to protect the helpless victim, has no other feelings towards her but those of jealousy and rage. The degradation, the wrongs, the vices, that grow out of slavery, are more than I can describe. They are greater than you would willingly believe. Surely, if you credited one half the truths that are told you concerning the helpless millions suffering in this cruel bondage, you at the north would not help to tighten the yoke. You surely would refuse to do for the master, on your own soil, the mean and cruel work which trained bloodhounds and the lowest class of whites do for him at the south.

Every where the years bring to all enough of sin and sorrow; but in slavery the very dawn of life is darkened by these shadows. Even the little child, who is accustomed to wait on her mistress and her children, will learn, before she is twelve years old, why it is that her mistress hates such and such a one among the slaves. Perhaps the child's own mother is among those hated ones. She listens to violent outbreaks of jealous passion, and cannot help understanding what is the cause. She will become prematurely knowing in evil things. Soon she will learn to tremble when she hears her master's footfall. She will be compelled to realize that she is no longer a child. If God has bestowed beauty upon her; it will prove her greatest curse. That which commands admiration in the white woman only hastens the degradation of the female slave. I know that some are too much brutalized by slavery to feel the humiliation of their position; but many slaves feel it most acutely, and shrink from the memory of it. I cannot tell how much I suffered in the presence of these wrongs, nor how I am still pained by the retrospect. My master met me at every turn, reminding me that I belonged to him, and swearing by heaven and earth that he would compel me to submit to him. If I went out for a breath of fresh air, after a day of unwearied toil, his footsteps dogged me. If I knelt by my mother's grave, his dark shadow fell on me even there. The light heart which nature had given me became heavy with sad forebodings. The other slaves in my master's house noticed the change. Many of them pitied me; but none dared to ask the cause. They had no need to inquire. They knew too well the guilty practices under that roof; and they were aware that to speak of them was an offence that never went unpunished.

I longed for some one to confide in. I would have given the world to have laid my head on my grandmother's faithful bosom, and told her all my troubles. But Dr. Flint swore he would kill me, if I was not as silent as the grave. Then, although my grandmother was all in all to me, I feared her as well as loved her. I had been accustomed to look up to her with a respect bordering upon awe. I was very young, and felt shamefaced about telling her such impure things, especially as I knew her to be very strict on such subjects. Moreover, she was a woman of a high spirit. She was usually very quiet in her demeanor; but if her indignation was once roused, it was not very easily quelled. I had been told that she once chased a white gentleman with a loaded pistol, because he insulted one of her daughters. I dreaded the consequences of a violent outbreak; and both pride and fear kept me silent. But though I did not confide in my grandmother, and even evaded her vigilant watchfulness and inquiry, her presence in the neighborhood was some protection to me. Though she had been a slave, Dr. Flint was afraid of her. He dreaded her scorching rebukes. Moreover, she was known and patronized by many people; and he did not wish to have his villany made public. It was lucky for me that I did not live on a distant plantation, but in a town not so large that the inhabitants were ignorant of each other's affairs. Bad as are the laws and customs in a slaveholding community, the doctor, as a professional man, deemed it prudent to keep up some outward show of decency. . . .

I once saw two beautiful children playing together. One was a fair white child; the other was her slave; and also her sister. When I saw them embracing each other, and heard their joyous laughter, I turned sadly away from the lovely sight. I foresaw the inevitable blight that would fall on the little slave's heart. I knew how soon her laughter would be changed to sighs. The fair child grew up to be a still fairer woman. From childhood to womanhood her pathway was blooming with flowers, and overarched by a sunny sky. Scarcely one day of her life had been clouded when the sun rose on her happy bridal morning.

How had those years dealt with her slave sister, the little playmate of her childhood? She, also, was very beautiful; but the flowers and sunshine of love were not for her. She drank the cup of sin, and shame, and misery, whereof her persecuted race are compelled to drink.

In view of these things, why are ye silent, ye free men and women of the north? Why do your tongues falter in maintenance of the right? Would that I had more ability! But my heart is so full, and my pen is so weak! There are noble men and women who plead for us, striving to help those who cannot help themselves. God bless them! God give them strength and courage to go on! God bless those, every where, who are laboring to advance the cause of humanity!

## *THE JEALOUS MISTRESS*

I would ten thousand times rather that my children should be the half-starved paupers of Ireland than to be the most pampered among the slaves of America. I would rather drudge out my life on a cotton plantation, till the grave opened to give me rest, than to live with an unprincipled master and a jealous mistress. The felon's home in a penitentiary is preferable. He may repent, and turn from the error of his ways, and so find peace; but it is not so with a favorite slave. She is not allowed to have any pride of character. It is deemed a crime in her to wish to be virtuous. . . .

I had entered my sixteenth year, and every day it became more apparent that my presence was intolerable to Mrs. Flint. Angry words frequently passed between her and her husband. He had never punished me himself, and he would not allow any body else to punish me. In that respect, she was never satisfied; but, in her angry moods, no terms were too vile for her to bestow upon me. Yet I, whom she detested so bitterly, had far more pity for her than he had, whose duty it was to make her life happy. I never wronged her, or wished to wrong her; and one word of kindness from her would have brought me to her feet.

After repeated quarrels between the doctor and his wife, he announced his intention to take his youngest daughter, then four years old, to sleep in his apartment. It was necessary that a servant should sleep in the same room, to be on hand if the child stirred. I was selected for that office, and informed for what purpose that arrangement had been made. By managing to keep within sight of people, as much as possible, during the daytime, I had hitherto succeeded in eluding my master, though a razor was often held to my throat to force me to change this line of policy. At night I slept by the side of my great aunt, where I felt safe. He was too prudent to come into her room. She was an old woman, and had been in the family many years. Moreover, as a married man, and a professional man, he deemed it necessary to save appearances in some degree. But he resolved to remove the obstacle in the way of his scheme; and he thought he had planned it so that he should evade suspicion. He was well aware how much I prized my refuge by the side of my old aunt, and he determined to dispossess me of it. The first night the doctor had the little child in his room alone. The next morning, I was ordered to take my station as nurse the following night. A kind Providence interposed in my favor. During the day Mrs. Flint heard of this new arrangement, and a storm followed. I rejoiced to hear it rage.

After a while my mistress sent for me to come to her room. Her first question was, "Did you know you were to sleep in the doctor's room?"

"Yes, ma'am."

"Who told you?"

"My master."

"Will you answer truly all the questions I ask?"

"Yes, ma'am."

"Tell me, then, as you hope to be forgiven, are you innocent of what I have accused you?"

"I am."

She handed me a Bible, and said, "Lay your hand on your heart, kiss this holy book, and swear before God that you tell me the truth."

I took the oath she required, and I did it with a clear conscience.

"You have taken God's holy word to testify your innocence," said she. "If you have deceived me, beware! Now take this stool, sit down, look me directly in the face, and tell me all that has passed between your master and you."

I did as she ordered. As I went on with my account her color changed frequently, she wept, and sometimes groaned. She spoke in tones so sad, that I was touched by her grief. The tears came to my eyes; but I was soon convinced that her emotions arose from anger and wounded pride. She felt that her marriage vows were desecrated, her dignity insulted; but she had no compassion for the poor victim of her husband's perfidy. She pitied herself as a martyr; but she was incapable of feeling for the condition of shame and misery in which her unfortunate, helpless slave was placed.

Yet perhaps she had some touch of feeling for me; for when the conference was ended, she spoke kindly, and promised to protect me. I should have been much comforted by this assurance if I could have had confidence in it; but my experience in slavery had filled me with distrust. She was not a very refined woman, and had not much control over her passions. I was an object of her jealousy, and, consequently, of her hatred; and I knew I could not expect kindness or confidence from her under the circumstances in which I was placed. I could not blame her. Slaverholders' wives feel as other women would under similar circumstances. The fire of her temper kindled from small sparks, and now the flame became so intense that the doctor was obliged to give up his intended arrangement.

I knew I had ignited the torch, and I expected to suffer for it afterwards; but I felt too thankful to my mistress for the timely aid she rendered me to care much about that. She now took me to sleep in a room adjoining her own. There I was an object of her especial care, though not of her especial comfort, for she spent many a sleepless night to watch over me. Sometimes I woke up, and found her bending over me. At other times she whispered in my ear, as though it was her husband who was speaking to me, and listened to hear what I would answer. If she startled me, on such occasions, she would glide stealthily away; and the next morning she would tell me I had been talking in my sleep, and ask who I was talking to. At last, I began to be fearful for my life. It had been often threatened; and you can imagine, better than I can describe, what an unpleasant sensation it must produce to wake up in the dead of night and find a jealous woman bending over you. Terrible as this experience was, I had fears that it would give place to one more terrible.

My mistress grew weary of her vigils; they did not prove satisfactory. She changed her tactics. She now tried the trick of accusing my master of crime, in my presence, and gave my name as the author of the accusation. To my utter astonishment, he replied, "I don't believe it; but if she did acknowledge it, you tortured her into exposing me." Tortured into exposing him! Truly, Satan had no difficulty in distinguishing the color of his soul! I understood his object in making this false representation. It was to show me that I gained nothing by seeking the protection of my mistress; that the power was still all in his own hands. I pitied Mrs. Flint. She was a second wife, many years the junior of her husband; and the hoary-headed miscreant was enough to try the patience of a wiser and better woman. She was completely foiled, and knew not how to proceed. She would gladly have had me flogged for my supposed false oath; but, as I have already stated, the doctor never allowed any one to whip me. The old sinner was politic. The application of the lash might have led to remarks that would have exposed him in the eyes of his children and grandchildren. How often did I rejoice that I lived in a town where all the inhabitants knew each other! If I had been on a remote plantation, or lost among the multitude of a crowded city, I should not be a living woman at this day.

The secrets of slavery are concealed like those of the Inquisition. My master was, to my knowledge, the father of eleven slaves. But did the mothers dare to tell who was the father of their children? Did the other slaves dare to allude to it, except in whispers among themselves? No, indeed! They knew too well the terrible consequences. . . .

Southern women often marry a man knowing that he is the father of many little slaves. They do not trouble themselves about it. They regard such children as property, as marketable as the pigs on the plantation; and it is seldom that they do not make them aware of this by passing them into the slave-trader's hands as soon as possible, and thus getting them out of their sight. I am glad to say there are some honorable exceptions.

I have myself known two southern wives who exhorted their husbands to free those slaves towards whom they stood in a "parental relation;" and their request was granted. These husbands blushed before the superior nobleness of their wives' natures. Though they had only counselled them to do that which it was their duty to do, it commanded their respect, and rendered their conduct more exemplary. Concealment was at an end, and confidence took the place of distrust.

Though this bad institution deadens the moral sense, even in white women, to a fearful extent, it is not altogether extinct. I have heard southern ladies say of Mr. Such a one, "He not only thinks it no disgrace to be the father of those little niggers, but he is not ashamed to call himself their master. I declare, such things ought not to be tolerated in any decent society!"

## *WHAT SLAVES ARE TAUGHT TO THINK OF THE NORTH*

Slaveholders pride themselves upon being honorable men; but if you were to hear the enormous lies they tell their slaves, you would have small respect for their veracity. I have spoken plain English. Pardon me. I cannot use a milder term. When they visit the north, and return home, they tell their slaves of the runaways they have seen, and describe them to be in the most deplorable condition. A slaveholder once told me that he had seen a runaway friend of mine in New York, and that she besought him to take her back to her master, for she was literally dying of starvation; that many days she had only one cold potato to eat, and at other times could get nothing at all. He said he refused to take her, because he knew her master would not thank him for bringing such a miserable wretch to his house. He ended by saying to me, "This is the punishment she brought on herself for running away from a kind master."

This whole story was false. I afterwards staid with that friend in New York, and found her in comfortable circumstances. She had never thought of such a thing as wishing to go back to slavery. Many of the slaves believe such stories, and think it is not worth while to exchange slavery for such a hard kind of freedom.

## *A PERILOUS PASSAGE IN THE SLAVE GIRL'S LIFE*

Dr. Flint contrived a new plan. He seemed to have an idea that my fear of my mistress was his greatest obstacle. In the blandest tones, he told me that he was going to build a small house for me, in a secluded place, four miles away from the town. I shuddered; but I was constrained to listen, while he talked of his intention to give me a home of my own, and to make a lady of me. Hitherto, I had escaped my dreaded fate, by being in the midst of people. My grandmother had already had high words with my master about me. She had told him pretty plainly what she thought of his character, and there was considerable gossip in the neighborhood about our affairs, to which the open-mouthed jealousy of Mrs. Flint contributed not a little. When my master said he was going to build a house for me, and that he could do it with little trouble and expense, I was in hopes something would happen to frustrate his scheme; but I soon heard that the house was actually begun. I vowed before my Maker that I would never enter it. I had rather toil on the plantation from dawn till dark; I had rather live and die in jail, than drag on, from day to day, through such a living death. I was determined that the master, whom I so hated and loathed, who had blighted the prospects of my youth, and made my life a desert, should not, after my long struggle with him, succeed at last in trampling his victim under his feet. I would do any thing, every thing, for the sake of defeating him. What *could* I do? I thought and thought, till I became desperate, and made a plunge into the abyss.

And now, reader, I come to a period in my unhappy life, which I would gladly forget if I could. The remembrance fills me with sorrow and shame. It pains me to tell you of it; but I have promised to tell you the truth, and I will do it honestly, let it cost me what it may. I will not try to screen myself behind the plea of compulsion from a master; for it was not so. Neither can I plead ignorance or thoughtlessness. For years, my master had done his utmost to pollute my mind with foul images, and to destroy the pure principles inculcated by my grandmother, and the good mistress of my childhood. The influences of slavery had had the same effect on me that they had on other young girls; they had made me prematurely knowing, concerning the evil ways of the world. I knew what I did, and I did it with deliberate calculation.

But, O, ye happy women, whose purity has been sheltered from childhood, who have been free to choose the objects of your affection, whose homes are protected by law, do not judge the poor desolate slave girl too severely! If slavery had been abolished, I, also, could have married the man of my choice; I could have had a home shielded by the laws; and I should have been spared the painful task of confessing what I am now about to relate; but all my prospects had been blighted by slavery. I wanted to keep myself pure; and, under the most adverse circumstances, I tried hard to preserve my self-respect; but I was struggling alone in the powerful grasp of the demon Slavery; and the monster proved too strong for me. I felt as if I was forsaken by God and man; as if all my efforts must be frustrated; and I became reckless in my despair.

I have told you that Dr. Flint's persecutions and his wife's jealousy had given rise to some gossip in the neighborhood. Among others, it chanced that a white unmarried gentleman had obtained some knowledge of the circumstances in which I was placed. He knew my grandmother, and often spoke to me in the street. He became interested for me, and asked questions about my master, which I answered in part. He expressed a great deal of sympathy, and a wish to aid me. He constantly sought opportunities to see me, and wrote to me frequently. I was a poor slave girl, only fifteen years old.

So much attention from a superior person was, of course, flattering; for human nature is the same in all. I also felt grateful for his sympathy, and encouraged by his kind words. It seemed to me a great thing to have such a friend. By degrees, a more tender feeling crept into my heart. He was an educated and eloquent gentleman; too eloquent, alas, for the poor slave girl who trusted in him. Of course I saw whither all this was tending. I knew the impassable gulf between us; but to be an object of interest to a man who is not married, and who is not her master, is agreeable to the pride and feelings of a slave, if her miserable situation has left her any pride or sentiment. It seems less degrading to give one's self, than to submit to compulsion. There is something akin to freedom in having a lover who has no control over you, except that which he gains by kindness and attachment. A master may treat you as rudely as he pleases, and you dare not speak; moreover, the wrong does not seem so great with an unmarried man, as with one who has a wife to be made unhappy. There may be sophistry in all this; but the condition of a slave confuses all principles of morality, and, in fact, renders the practice of them impossible.

When I found that my master had actually begun to build the lonely cottage, other feelings mixed with those I have described. Revenge, and calculations of interest, were added to flattered vanity and sincere gratitude for kindness. I knew nothing would enrage Dr. Flint so much as to know that I favored another; and it was something to triumph over my tyrant even in that small way. I thought he would revenge himself by selling me, and I was sure my friend, Mr. Sands, would buy me. He was a man of more generosity and feeling than my master, and I thought my freedom could be easily obtained from him. The crisis of my fate now came so near that I was desperate. I shuddered to think of being the mother of children that should be owned by my old tyrant. I knew that as soon as a new fancy took him, his victims were sold far off to get rid of them; especially if they had children. I had seen several women sold, with his babies at the breast. He never allowed his offspring by slaves to remain long in sight of himself and his wife. Of a man who was not my master I could ask to have my children well supported; and in this case, I felt confident I should obtain the boon. I also felt quite sure that they would be made free. With all these thoughts revolving in my mind, and seeing no other way of escaping the doom I so much dreaded, I made a headlong plunge. Pity me, and pardon me, O virtuous reader! You never knew what it is to be a slave; to be entirely unprotected by law or custom; to have the laws reduce you to the condition of a chattel, entirely subject to the will of another. You never exhausted your ingenuity in avoiding the snares, and eluding the power of a hated tyrant; you never shuddered at the sound of his footsteps, and trembled within hearing of his voice. I know I did wrong. No one can feel it more sensibly than I do. The painful and humiliating memory will haunt me to my dying day. Still, in looking back, calmly, on the events of my life, I feel that the slave woman ought not to be judged by the same standard of others.

The months passed on. I had many unhappy hours. I secretly mourned over the sorrow I was bringing on my grandmother, who had so tried to shield me from harm. I knew that I was the greatest comfort of her old age, and that it was a source of pride to her that I had not degraded myself, like most of the slaves. I wanted to confess to her that I was no longer worthy of her love; but I could not utter the dreaded words.

As for Dr. Flint, I had a feeling of satisfaction and triumph in the thought of telling *him*. From time to time he told me of his intended arrangements, and I was silent. At last, he came and told me the cottage was completed, and ordered me to go to it. I told him I would never enter it. He said, "I have heard enough of such talk as that. You shall go, if you are carried by force; and you shall remain there."

I replied, "I will never go there. In a few months I shall be a mother."

He stood and looked at me in dumb amazement, and left the house without a word. I thought I should be happy in my triumph over him. But now that the truth was out, and my relatives would hear of it, I felt wretched. Humble as were their circumstances, they had pride in my good character. Now, how could I look them in the face? My self-respect was gone! I had resolved that I would be virtuous, though I was a slave. I had said, "Let the storm beat! I will brave it till I die." And now, how humiliated I felt!

I went to my grandmother. My lips moved to make confession, but the words stuck in my throat. I sat down in the shade of a tree at her door and began to sew. I think she saw something unusual was the matter with me. The mother of slaves is very watchful. She knows there is no security for her children. After they have entered their teens she lives in daily expectation of trouble. This leads to many questions. If the girl is of a sensitive nature, timidity keeps her from answering truthfully, and this well-meant course has a tendency to drive her from maternal counsels. Presently, in came my mistress, like a mad woman, and accused me concerning her husband. My grandmother, whose suspicions had been previously awakened, believed what she said. She exclaimed, "O Linda! has it come to this? I had rather see you dead than to see you as you now are. You are a disgrace to your dead mother." She tore from my fingers my mother's wedding ring and her silver thimble. "Go away!" she exclaimed, "and never come to my house, again." Her reproaches fell so hot and heavy, that they left me no chance to answer. Bitter tears, such as the eyes never shed but once, were my only answer. I rose from my seat, but fell back again, sobbing. She did not speak to me; but the tears were running down her furrowed cheeks, and they scorched me like fire. She had always been so kind to me! *So* kind! How I longed to throw myself at her feet, and tell her all the truth! But she had ordered me to go, and never to come there again. After a few minutes, I mustered strength, and started to obey her. With what feelings did I now close that little gate, which I used to open with such an eager hand in my childhood! It closed upon me with a sound I never heard before.

Where could I go? I was afraid to return to my master's. I walked on recklessly, not caring where I went, or what would become of me. When I had gone four or five miles, fatigue compelled me to stop. I sat down on the stump of an old tree. The stars were shining through the boughs above me. How they mocked me, with their bright, calm light! The hours passed by, and as I sat there alone a chilliness and deadly sickness came over me. I sank on the ground. My mind was full of horrid thoughts. I prayed to die; but the prayer was not answered. At last, with great effort I roused myself, and walked some distance further, to the house of a woman who had been a friend of my mother. When I told her why I was there, she spoke soothingly to me; but I could not be comforted. I thought I could bear my shame if I could only be reconciled to my grandmother. I longed to open my heart to her. I thought if she could know the real state of the case, and all I had been bearing for years, she would perhaps judge me less harshly. My friend advised me to send for her. I did so; but days of agonizing suspense passed before she came. Had she utterly forsaken me? No. She came at last. I knelt before her, and told her the things that had poisoned my life; how long I had been persecuted; that I saw no way of escape; and in an hour of extremity I had become desperate. She listened in silence. I told her I would bear any thing and do any thing, if in time I had hopes of obtaining her forgiveness. I begged of her to pity me, for my dead mother's sake. And she did pity me. She did not say, "I forgive you;" but she looked at me lovingly, with her eyes full of tears. She laid her old hand gently on my head, and murmured, "Poor child! Poor child!"

*HARRIET TUBMAN*

# 32 | *A Biography by Her Contemporaries*

*This reading is based on a series of interviews with the escaped slave Harriet Tubman conducted by various people between 1859 and 1865 and published in 1865. Interviews of this sort were common during the Civil War, but here and elsewhere we usually do not know the precise sources. When the Civil War ended, Tubman continued to work for the betterment of her fellow African Americans. She went to North Carolina to assist in the education of freed slaves, although she herself was illiterate. She also founded an old-age home in Auburn, New York, where she died in 1913.*

One of the teachers lately commissioned by the New-England Freedmen's Aid Society is probably the most remarkable woman of this age. That is to say, she has performed more wonderful deeds by the native power of her own spirit against adverse circumstances than any other. She is well known to many by the various names which her eventful life has given her; Harriet Garrison, Gen. Tubman, &c.; but among the slaves she is universally known by her well-earned title of *Moses,*—Moses the deliverer. She is a rare instance, in the midst of high civilization and intellectual culture, of a being of great native powers, working powerfully, and to beneficent ends, entirely unaided by schools or books.

Her maiden name was Araminta Ross. She is the granddaughter of a native African, and has not a drop of white blood in her veins. She was born in 1820 or 1821, on the Eastern Shore of Maryland. Her parents were slaves, but married and faithful to each other, and the family affection is very strong. She claims that she was legally freed by a will of her first master, but his wishes were not carried into effect.

She seldom lived with her owner, but was usually "hired out" to different persons. She once "hired her time," and employed it in rudest farming labors, ploughing, carting, driving the oxen, &c., to so good advantage that she was able in one year to buy a pair of steers worth forty dollars.

When quite young she lived with a very pious mistress; but the slaveholder's religion did not prevent her from whipping the young girl for every slight or fancied fault. Araminta found that this was usually a morning exercise; so she prepared for it by putting on all the thick clothes she could procure to protect her skin. She made sufficient outcry, however, to convince her mistress that her blows had full effect; and in the afternoon she would take off her wrappings, and dress as well as she could. When invited into family prayers, she preferred to stay on the landing, and pray for herself; "and I prayed to God," she says "to make me strong and able to fight, and that's what I've allers prayed for ever since." It is in vain to try to persuade her that her prayer was a wrong one. She always maintains it to be sincere and right, and it has certainly been fully answered.

In her youth she received a severe blow on her head from a heavy weight thrown by her master at another slave, but which accidentally hit her. The blow produced a disease of the brain which was severe for a long time, and still makes her very lethargic. She cannot remain quiet fifteen minutes without appearing to fall asleep. It is not refreshing slumber; but a heavy, weary condition which exhausts her. She therefore loves great physical activity, and direct heat of the sun, which keeps her blood actively circulating. She was married about 1844 to a free colored man named John Tubman, but never had any children. Owing to changes in her owner's family, it was determined to sell her and some other slaves; but her health was so much injured, that a purchaser was not easily found. At length she became convinced that she would soon be carried away, and she decided to escape. Her brothers did not agree with her plans; and she walked off alone, following the guidance of the brooks, which she had observed to run North. The evening before she left, she wished very much to bid her companions farewell, but was afraid of being betrayed, if any one knew of her intentions; so she passed through the street singing,

> Good bye, I'm going to leave you,
> Good bye, I'll meet you in the kingdom,—

and similar snatches of Methodist songs. As she passed on singing, she saw her master, Dr. Thompson, standing at his gate, and her native humor breaking out, she sung yet louder, bowing down to him,—

> Good bye, I'm going for to leave you.

He stopped and looked after her as she passed on; and he afterwards said, that, as her voice came floating back in the evening air it seemed as if—

> A wave of trouble never rolled
> Across her peaceful breast.

Wise judges are we of each other!—She was only quitting home, husband, father, mother, friends, to go out alone, friendless and penniless into the world.

She remained two years in Philadelphia working hard and carefully hoarding her money. Then she hired a room, furnished it as well as she could, bought a nice suit of men's clothes, and went back to Maryland for her husband. But the faithless man had taken to himself another wife. Harriet did not dare venture into her presence, but sent word to her husband where she was. He declined joining her. At first her grief and anger were excessive. She said, "she did not care what massa did to her, she thought she would go right in and make all the trouble she could, she was determined to see her old man once more" but finally she thought "how foolish it was just for temper to make mischief" and that, "if he could do without her, she could without him," and so "he dropped out of her heart," and she determined to give her life to brave deeds. Thus all personal aims died out of her heart; and with her simple brave motto, "I can't die but once," she began the work which has made her Moses,—the deliverer of her people. Seven or eight times she has returned to the neighborhood of her former home, always at the risk of death in the most terrible forms, and each time has brought away a company of fugitive slaves, and led them safely to the free States, or to Canada. Every time she went, the dangers increased. In 1857 she brought away her old parents, and, as they were too feeble to walk, she was obliged to hire a wagon, which added greatly to the perils of the journey. In 1860 she went for the last time, and among her troop was an infant whom they were obliged to keep stupefied with laudanum* to prevent its outcries. This was at the period of great excitement, and Moses was not safe even in New-York State; but her anxious friends insisted upon her taking refuge in Canada. So various and interesting are the incidents of the journeys, that we know not how to select from them. She has shown in them all the characteristics of a great leader; courage, foresight, prudence, self-control, ingenuity, subtle perception, command over others' mind. Her nature is at once profoundly practical and highly imaginative. She is economical as Dr. [Benjamin] Franklin, and as firm in the conviction of supernatural help as Mahomet. A clergyman once said, that her stories convinced you of their truth by their simplicity as do the gospel narratives. She never went to the South to bring away fugitives without being provided with money; money for the most part earned by drudgery in the kitchen, until within the last few years, when friends have aided her. She had to leave her sister's two orphan children in slavery the last time, for the want of thirty dollars. Thirty pieces of silver; an embroidered handkerchief or a silk dress to one, or the piece of freedom to two orphan children to another! She would never allow more to join her than she could properly care for, though she often gave others directions by which they succeeded in escaping. She always came in the winter when the nights are long and dark, and people who have homes stay in them. She was never seen on the plantation herself; but appointed a rendezvous for her company

*A form of opium—Eds.

eight or ten miles distant, so that if they were discovered at the first start she was not compromised. She started on Saturday night; the slaves at that time being allowed to go away from home to visit their friends,—so that they would not be missed until Monday morning. Even then they were supposed to have loitered on the way, and it would often be late on Monday afternoon before the flight would be certainly known. If by any further delay the advertisement was not sent out before Tuesday morning, she felt secure of keeping ahead of it; but if it were, it required all her ingenuity to escape. She resorted to various devices, she had confidential friends all along the road. She would hire a man to follow the one who put up the notices, and take them down as soon as his back was turned. She crossed creeks on railroads bridges by night, she hid her company in the woods while she herself not being advertised went into the towns in search of information. If met on the road, her face was always to the south, and she was always a very respectable looking darkey, not at all a poor fugitive. She would get into the cars near her pursuers, and manage to hear their plans. By day they lay in the woods; then she pulled out her patchwork, and sewed together little bits, perhaps not more than [an] inch square, which were afterwards made into comforters for the fugitives in Canada.

The expedition was governed by the strictest rules. If any man gave out, he must be shot. "Would you really do that?" she was asked. "Yes," she replied, "if he was weak enough to give out, he'd be weak enough to betray us all, and all who had helped us; and do you think I'd let so many die just for one coward man." "Did you ever have to shoot any one?" was asked. "One time," she said, "a man gave out the second night; his feet were sore and swollen, he couldn't go any further; he'd rather go back and die, if he must." They tried all arguments in vain, bathed his feet, tried to strengthen him, but it was of no use, he would go back. Then she said, "I told the boys to get their guns ready, and shoot him. They'd have done it in a minute; but when he heard that, he jumped right up and went on as well as any body." She can tell the time by the stars, and find her way by natural signs as well as any hunter; and yet she scarcely knows of the existence of England or any other foreign country.

When going on these journeys she often lay alone in the forests all night. Her whole soul was filled with awe of the mysterious Unseen Presence, which thrilled her with such depths of emotion, that all other care and fear vanished. Then she seemed to speak with her Maker "as a man talketh with his friend"; her child-like petitions had direct answers, and beautiful visions lifted her up above all doubt and anxiety into serene trust and faith. No man can be a hero without this faith in some form; the sense that he walks not in his own strength, but leaning on an almighty arm. Call it fate, destiny, what you will, Moses of old, Moses of to-day, believed it to be Almighty God.

She loves to describe her visions, which are very real to her; but she must tell them word for word as they lie in her untutored mind, with endless repetitions and details; she cannot shorten or condense them, whatever be your haste. She has great dramatic power; the scene rises before you as she saw it, and her voice and language change with her different actors. Often these visions came to her in the midst of her work. She once said, "We'd been carting manure all day, and t'other girl and I were gwine home on the sides of the cart, and another boy was driving, when suddenly I heard such music as filled all the air" and, she saw a vision which she described in language which sounded like the old prophets in its grand flow; interrupted now and then by what t'other girl said, by Massa's coming and calling her to wake up, and her protests that she wasn't asleep.

One of her most characteristic prayers was when on board a steamboat with a party of fugitives. The clerk on the boat declined to give her tickets, and told her to wait. She thought he suspected her, and was at a loss how to save herself and her charge, if he did; so she went alone into the bow of the boat, and she says, "I drew in my breath, and I sent it out to the Lord. and I said, O Lord! you know who I am, and whar I am, and what I want; and that was all I could say; and again I drew in my breath and I sent it out to the Lord, but that was all I could say; and then again the third time, and just then I felt a touch on my shoulder, and looked round, and the clerk said, 'Here's your tickets.' "

Her efforts were not confined to the escape of slaves. She conducted them to Canada, watched over their welfare, collected clothing, organized them into societies, and was always occupied with plans for their benefit. She first came to Boston in the spring of 1859, to ask aid of the friends of her race to build a house for her aged father and mother. She brought recommendations from Berrit Smith, and at once won many friends who aided her to accomplish her purpose. Her parents are now settled in Auburn, and all that Harriet seems to desire in reward for her labors is the privilege of making their old age comfortable. She has a very affectionate nature, and forms the strongest personal attachments. She has great simplicity of character; she states her wants very freely, and believes you are ready to help her; but if you have nothing to give, or have given to another, she is content. She is not sensitive to indignities to her color in her own person; but knows and claims her rights. She will eat at your table if she sees you really desire it; but she goes as willingly to the kitchen. She is very abstemious in her diet, fruit being the only luxury she cares for. Her personal appearance is very peculiar. She is thoroughly negro, and very plain. She has needed disguise so often, that she seems to have command over her face, and can banish all expression from her features, and look so stupid that nobody would suspect her of knowing enough to be dangerous; but her eye flashes with intelligence and power when she is roused. She has the rich humor and the keen sense of beauty which belong to her race. She would like to dress handsomely. Once an old silk dress was given her among a bundle of clothes, and she was in great delight. "Glory!" she exclaimed; "didn't I say when I sold my silk gown to get money to go after my mother, that I'd have another some day?" She is never left in a room with pictures or statuary that she does not examine them and ask with interest about them.

I wish it were possible to give some of her racy stories; but no report would do them justice. She gives a most vivid description of the rescue of a slave in Troy. She fought and struggled so that her clothes were torn off her; but she was successful at last. Throughout all she shouted out her favorite motto, "Give me liberty or give me death," to which the popular heart never fails to respond. When she was triumphantly bearing the man off, a little boy called out, "Go it, old aunty! you're the best old aunty the fellow ever had." She is perfectly at home in such scenes; she loves action; I think she does not dislike fighting in a good cause; but she loves work too, and scorns none that offers.

She said once, just before the [Civil] war, when slavery was the one theme agitating the country,—"they say the negro has no rights a white man is bound to respect; but it seems to me they send men to Congress, and pay them eight dollars a day, for nothing else but to talk about the negro."

She says, "the blood of our race has called for justice in vain, and now our sons and brothers must be taken from our hearts and homes to bring the call for justice home to our hearts." She described a storm; "but the thunder's from the cannon's mouth, and the drops that fall are drops of blood."

She was deeply interested in John Brown; and it is said, that she was fully acquainted with his plans, and approved them. On the day when his companions were executed, she came to my room. Finding me occupied, she said, "I am not going to sit down, I only want you to give me an address" but her heart was too full, she must talk. "I've been studying and studying upon it," she said, "and its clar to me, it wasn't John Brown that died on that gallows. When I think how he gave up his life for our people, and how he never flinched, but was so brave to the end; its clar to me it wasn't mortal man, it was God in him. When I think of all the groans and tears and prayers I've heard on the plantations, and remember that God is a prayer-hearing God, I feel that his time is drawing near." Then you think, I said, that God's time is near. "God's time is always near," she said; "He gave me my strength, and he set the North star in the heavens; he meant I should be free." She went on in a strain of the most sublime eloquence I ever heard; but I cannot repeat it. Oh how sanguine and visionary it seemed then! but now four little years, and Maryland is free by her own act, and the bells are ringing out the declaration, that slavery is abolished throughout the land; and our Moses may walk, no longer wrapped in darkness, but erect and proud in her native State; and the name of him who was hung on the gallows is a rallying cry for victorious armies, and the stone which the builders rejected has become the head of the corner. What shall we fear whose eyes have seen this salvation?

When the war broke out Harriet was very anxious to go to South Carolina to assist the contrabands. The only condition she made was, that her old parents should be kept from want. It was wonderful to see with what shrewd economy she had planned all their household arrangements. She concluded that thirty dollars would keep them comfortable through the winter. She went to Port Royal, and was employed by Gen. Hunter, in scouting service, and accompanied Col. Montgomery in his expedition up the Combahee river. She was afterwards engaged by Gen. Saxton, to take a number of freed women under her charge, and teach them to do the soldiers' washing. She has also been making herb-medicine for the soldiers, which she gives away gratuitously, feeling it to be impossible to receive money from sick soldiers; and she has made cakes and pies for sale, in the intervals of other work.

She has had no regular support from Government; and she feels that she must have some certain income, which she wishes to apply to her parents' support. This society consider her labors too valuable to the freedmen to be turned elsewhere, and have therefore taken her into their service, paying her the small salary of ten dollars per month that she asks for. She is not adopted by any branch as she could not fulfill the condition of correspondence with them. She says, when the war is over she will learn to read and write, and then will write her own life. The trouble in her head prevents her from applying closely to a book. It is the strong desire of all her friends that she should tell her story in her own way at some future time. We think it affords a very cogent answer to the query, "Can the negro take care of himself?"

# 33 *Two Speeches*

*Born as Isabella, a slave, in New York State in 1795, Sojourner Truth became free in 1827 when the state completed its plan of gradual emancipation. She worked for some years as a domestic, then in 1841 experienced the call to testify to the sins against her people and her gender. Assuming the name Sojourner Truth, she became a well-known abolitionist speaker.*

*In the late 1840s she became closely identified with the woman's rights movement. She was particularly effective at answering male hecklers who were often part of the early rights meetings.*

*Many of the other abolitionists moved into the other reform movements that marked the period from the 1830s to the Civil War. Woman's rights, the peace effort, prohibition of alcoholic beverages, utopian communities, and a variety of dietary and health reforms were some of the movements that ripped through northern society in those years.*

*The first speech was given at a woman's convention in Akron, Ohio, in 1851; the second was delivered at a woman's rights convention in New York City in 1853.*

## *I*

Well, children, where there is so much racket there must be something out of kilter. I think that 'twixt the negroes of the South and the women at the North, all talking about rights, the white men will be in a fix pretty soon. But what's all this here talking about?

That man over there says that women need to be helped into carriages, and lifted over ditches, and to have the best place everywhere. Nobody ever helps me into carriages, or over mud-puddles, or gives me any best place! And ain't I a woman? Look at me! Look at my arm! I have ploughed and planted, and gathered into barns, and no man could head me! And ain't I a woman? I could work as much and eat as much as a man—when I could get it—and bear the lash as well! And ain't I a woman? I have borne thirteen children, and seen them most all sold off to slavery, and when I cried out with my mother's grief, none but Jesus heard me! And ain't I a woman?

Then they talk about this thing in the head; what's this they call it? [Intellect, someone whispers.] That's it, honey. What's that got to do with women's rights or negro's rights? If my cup won't hold but a pint, and yours holds a quart, wouldn't you be mean not to let me have my little half-measure full?

Then that little man in black there, he says women can't have as much rights as men, 'cause Christ wasn't a woman! Where did your Christ come from? Where did your Christ come from? From God and a woman! Man had nothing to do with Him.

If the first woman God ever made was strong enough to turn the world upside down all alone, these women together ought to be able to turn it back, and get it right side up again! And now they is asking to do it, the men better let them.

Obliged to you for hearing me, and now old Sojourner ain't got nothing more to say.

## *II*

Is it not good for me to come and draw forth a spirit, to see what kind of spirit people are of? I see that some of you have got the spirit of a goose, and some have got the spirit of a snake. I feel at home here. I come to you, citizens of New York, as I suppose you ought to be. I am a citizen of the State of New York; I was born in it, and I was a slave in the State of New York; and now I am a good citizen of this State. I was born here, and I can tell you I feel at home here. I've been lookin' round and watchin' things, and I know a little mite 'bout Woman's Rights, too. I come forth to speak 'bout Woman's Rights, and want to throw in my little mite, to keep the scales a-movin'. I know that it feels a kind o' hissin' and ticklin' like to see a colored woman to get up and tell you about things, and Woman's Rights. We have all been thrown down so low that nobody thought we'd ever get up again; but we have been long enough trodden now; we will come up again, and now I am here.

I was a-thinkin', when I see women contendin' for their rights, I was a-thinkin' what a difference there is now, and what there was in old times. I have only a few minutes to speak; but in the old times the kings of earth would[n't] hear a woman. There was a king in the Scriptures; and then it was the kings of the earth would kill a woman if she come into their presence; but Queen Esther come forth, for she was oppressed, and felt there was a great wrong, and she said I will die or I will bring my complaint before the king. Should the king of the United States be greater, or more crueler, or more harder? But the king, he raised up his sceptre and said: "Thy request shall be granted unto thee—to the half of my kingdom will I grant it to thee!" Then he said he would hang Haman on the gallows he had made up high. But that is not what women come forward to contend. The women want their rights as Esther. She only wanted to explain her rights. And he was so liberal that he said, "the half of my kingdom shall be granted to thee," and he did not wait for her to ask, he was so liberal with her.

Now, women do not ask half of a kingdom, but their rights, and they don't get 'em. When she comes to demand 'em, don't you hear how sons hiss their mothers like snakes, because they ask for their rights; and can they ask for anything less? The king ordered Haman to be hung on the gallows which he prepared to hang others; but I do not want any man to be killed, but I am sorry to see them so shortminded. But we'll have our rights; see if we don't; and you can't stop us from them; see if you can. You may hiss as much as you like, but it is comin'. Women don't get half as much rights as they ought to; we want more, and we will have it. Jesus says: "What I say to one, I say to all—watch!" I'm a-watchin'. God says: "Honor your father and your mother." Sons and daughters ought to behave themselves before their mothers, but they do not. I can see them a-laughin', and pointin' at their mothers up here on the stage. They hiss when an aged woman comes forth. If they'd been brought up proper they'd have known better than hissin' like snakes and geese. I'm 'round watchin' these things, and I wanted to come up and say these few things to you, and I'm glad of the hearin' you give me. I wanted to tell you a mite about Woman's Rights, and so I came out and said so. I am sittin' among you to watch; and every once and awhile I will come out and tell you what time of night it is.

THOMAS HENRY TIBBLES

# 34 With Old John Brown in Kansas

*Thomas Henry Tibbles was only sixteen in 1856, when he fought in "Bleeding Kansas" in the war between pro- and anti-slavery settlers. Caught by pro-slavery forces, he was ordered hanged, then escaped. Having captured the man who had sentenced him to death, he joined the staff of James H. Lane, who led the anti-slavery militia in Kansas. Then, in the incident described below, Tibbles briefly joined forces with John Brown, one of the most incendiary abolitionists in the United States. Brown planned to steal slaves to freedom; and shortly after the incident recounted here he hacked to death with broadswords five pro-slavery settlers near Pottawatomie Creek in retribution for a raid on an anti-slavery settlement.*

*Tibbles later served in the Civil War, was a freelance writer and newspaperman, a circuit preacher and a lecturer in the cause of the native American. He married a highly accomplished native-American woman in 1882. He became an important journalist and publisher of the Populist Party's national organ,* The Independent. *In 1904 he ran for Vice President of the United States on a ticket headed by Thomas E. Watson of Georgia in a forlorn and foredoomed People's Party campaign. Tibbles's career illustrates the remarkable links among reform movements over time in nineteenth-century America.*

[A] man came to tell me that Old John Brown wanted to see me. When I told Lane, he urged me to go and meet Brown, because he himself wanted to know "what that old lunatic intended to do next." It took me several hours to ride from Lawrence to the queer rendezvous Brown had appointed—the spot where he was encamped on the bank of a creek. The men in the group with him were queer too. Some of them were as high-minded and brave a lot of fanatics as ever fought for a cause, but I had then, as now, a suspicion that some were cutthroats and murderers who followed him for the prey and booty they could get in those disturbed times.

Brown had in his camp a fine-looking Negro, who said that he had run away from his master in Platte County, Missouri, because the man was going to sell him and his wife to a dealer who would take them south to Louisiana sugar plantations. The average Missouri Negro looked upon being sold south as one or two degrees worse than being sent straight to hell. This viewpoint was fostered by the masters, who always threatened, when things went wrong, to sell them down the river. John Brown had planned a raid into Platte County to rescue this Negro's wife and as many more slaves as possible.

He asked me, "Do you want a part in this holy crusade to free some of God's black children?"

"I do," I answered, "but I must report first to General Lane and get permission."

"That is proper and right," he agreed. Then he directed me, if Lane allowed me, to meet him at a certain place on a certain day.

When I reported to Lane, he laughed at me.

"Why, my boy," he argued, "if you go across the Missouri River stealing niggers, those Missourians will hang you sure! And this time they won't take the trouble to assemble a drumhead court-martial. They'll swing you up to the first tree they come to."

"They'd have to catch me first," I insisted.

"Catch you! The whole county over there would be after you, and every man in it is a Border Ruffian."

Though I pressed my request further, it was no use. Lane positively refused to let me go, but that evening he sent for me again.

He questioned me for a long time about Brown and his company, urging me to describe each man personally as nearly as I could. He inquired exactly what the old man had said to me, at what point he expected to cross the river, what types of arms they had, the condition of their horses, and many other matters of that nature. Then he asked abruptly:

"Do you still want to go?"

"I do," I answered.

"You may go; but you must file a request in writing with me so that I could prove, if there was any trouble, that I never ordered you to go. I would not order any man to go over into Platte County, much less a boy. I hope that someone of that crowd may get back, but I very much doubt if even one will escape. You go and see Brown, and after you get orders from him report to me before you make the trip."

When I reached Brown again, he told me that each man of his party would try to cross the river alone, keep hidden in the brush and the woods during the daytime, and meet at a designated place on a certain night at nine o'clock to receive further orders.

I reported again to Lane, who gave me a lot of written orders which I was to study until I knew them by heart. Then I was to burn them. Their substance was that I was to ride out of Lawrence after ten o'clock at night. After the first day I was to travel only by night. I was given the names of two Free State men who furnished Lane with information. I was also given a description of their houses and a rough map of the two little towns in which they lived on the west bank of the Missouri River. These men were of vast importance to the Free State cause, and I must do nothing that would bring suspicion on them in the slightest degree. I was to call upon them only after midnight, obtain what information and assistance I could, and get away without letting anyone else learn that I had been there. Before I had read that document half through, I saw the importance of burning it. I committed it to memory, and then put it into my first campfire.

That first night out I spent in an Indian camp, and traded for "jerked meat" some of the tobacco with which our New England friends, who had the sense to know that a man out of tobacco "wouldn't fight worth a cent," kept us well supplied. I got from the Indians enough meat, which could be eaten cooked or uncooked, wet or dry, to last me about ten days. All the next day Old Titus and I stayed in the camp and then stole away at nightfall.

I tried for two days to get to the house of one of those two Free State men. He lived in a tiny town of only two or three log houses and a shanty or two, but a guard was always posted there. Failing in my effort, I went to the other town, which was farther up the river. With its map indelibly printed on my brain, I easily found the house and the man.

He gave me a great deal of information which he advised me to carry straight back to Lane.

"Let Old John Brown do his 'nigger stealing' himself," he urged me. "It's vitally important for Lane to know some of these facts I'm telling you immediately."

The most important fact of all was that a lot of Border Ruffians were congregating at Westport and Independence in Missouri, preparing to make a raid into Kansas. When I refused to go back, he advised me to ride up along the river for some distance to where there was a flatboat ferry. I had not a cent of money—in fact had had none for a long time. The man gave me ten dollars—did Beecher sent it out there?—all in silver, as there would be no way for me to get change to pay small charges in that country.

Just before daylight [of August 27] I started on my way up the river; just before sundown that afternoon I appeared at the ferry and was carried across. On the Missouri side I "took to the brush" until it grew quite dark. During the night I made my way toward the appointed meeting place.

Once that night I was fired at by one of the "nigger patrols" which the slaveholders had organized to protect their property by riding around nightly in turn to see that none of their "niggers" ran away or were stolen. Finally I found a safe waiting spot in a mass of willows on low ground by the river, not more than two miles from the place where we were to meet. At dawn I left my horse, made my way to the nearest high ground, climbed a tree, and verified my location. I could plainly see on a hill the landmark house, which stood one mile east of our assembling point. Near me was a corncrib from which I carried away enough corn to give Old Titus three good feeds. As I went toward him, I all but stumbled over a "nigger" who very evidently had been out chicken stealing. He dropped his loot and ran for his life. I pretended I had not seen him.

This Platte County, into which John Brown had invited me, was thickly settled. Though most of the houses were built of logs, there were a few fine frame residences. Also, behind these residences, there were always "nigger quarters," ramshackle stables, and loom-houses where Negro women wove the jeans and linsey-woolsey which formed the outer clothing of the whole population. The planters' wealth was made up of fine horses, "likely niggers," and a rich soil which produced immense crops of corn and hemp. Though many of the owners of this countryside could neither read nor write, they were proud and rich. How long John Brown had been secretly lingering there near his chosen rendezvous, or how many men he had with him, I never knew.

Night settled down dark and moonless. Clouds hung low in the west. I had difficulty in making my way to the appointed place, but there I found Brown and the Negro whom I had seen in his camp. There were eight or ten dismounted men there also, who had left their horses across the Missouri. I learned from conversation I overheard that there were other men, farther down the river, who were mounted. These had crossed the river on a captured flatboat, and expected to recross by the same means before daylight. I noticed that Brown seemed to know the name of every slaveholder in that region, the number of his slaves, and the exact location of the road that led from his plantation to the river.

Brown directed our group to go to a certain cabin belonging to a certain house and get the slaves who were expecting us. We all were to take them to the river by a road he described. Then the rest of our group were to take these Negroes over the river in skiffs that would be found at a designated place, but I was to make my way back to the same ferry by which I had come and to cross by it as soon after daybreak as the man in charge turned up to navigate it.

Brown said there was a regular road in front of the house where we were to get the Negroes, but that, as it was guarded by the planters' patrol, our party was to enter the farm from the rear and approach the slave quarters through a cornfield. He bade me go alone a mile up the direct front road to watch for the patrol and keep our main party informed of any danger from that source. Just where a dim side road led off down to the river where the skiffs were waiting, he said, there was a certain sharp bend in the road. My orders were to tie my horse in a patch of pawpaw bushes nearby and take my station there in the turn itself, so that I could see in both directions.

When I objected to dismounting and separating myself from my horse, Brown told me with a metallic ring in his voice: "You will obey orders."

Doubtless if there had been more light, I should have seen a peculiar gleam in his eye. Anyone who had anything to do with Brown in Kansas learned that it was death, after one joined his band, to disobey any order he issued.

I went with his men as he had ordered. Because the night was so very dark, we had difficulty in finding the right place. I took my post in the bend, while the other men crept up through the cornfield. Just then the wind blew furiosly and the rain poured down. I could see nothing except when lightning flashed now and then. I stood in the road barely outside the bushes, impatiently waiting for our men and the Negroes to climb over the fence and follow with me that vague side road to the river. Without warning someone threw his arms around me from behind, pinioning my elbows to my sides. Instantly two more men leaped upon me, but before they could clap a hand over my mouth, I uttered the loudest yell that had ever come of me. It was the only warning I could give my associates.

My captors tied my hands and feet; they put a rope around my neck and dragged me along the ground by it for some distance. Then they lifted me to my feet, threw the rope end over the limb of a tree, and demanded:

"Tell us where the rest of this low-down gang of nigger stealers are, or up you go."

Without waiting for a reply they pulled away on the rope. When they let me down, I was "pretty tolerable mad." I gave them my opinion as to what sort of scoundrels they were. They cut that discourse short by swinging me up again. When next they let me down, they spent a few minutes in giving me their opinion of "nigger stealers." They wound up by declaring most solemnly that if I would tell them where the rest of the gang was, they would let me go and would hang the others.

I was not in condition to make a very good speech in reply. Still, I started—but before I had forced out a dozen words, they pulled away on the rope. One of them chuckled:

"We'll give him enough this time to make him reasonable."

Just at that moment pistols flashed. Two of the men who had been holding the rope dropped to the ground; the other ran away. My "gang," who had succeeded in creeping up through the cornfield and bringing away two Negro men and one woman, had then overheard the rather loud talk of the patrol at my "hanging bee." Thanks to the black night and the rain, they had stolen up to us unnoticed.

They soon had me on my feet and helped me to find Old Titus and mount him—for in fact there was little energy left in me. They said they would take the Negroes over the river, and they urged me to strike for the woods and reach my ferry by daybreak if possible. I noticed then that both my revolvers were gone, though I still had my Sharp's rifle, which I had left strapped to Titus's saddle. Two of my companions went back to the tree where the Platte County slaveholders had been giving me their "necktie reception," and soon brought me two revolvers, but only one of them was mine.

One of the Negroes pulled down the fence for me and told me to follow the corn rows to the other side of the field. If I tore down the fence there and went straight on, I would soon come to a road that led up the river. I rode away feeling rather uncomfortable.

Long before daylight it became obvious that the entire district was out on the warpath. I heard shots in several directions; I caught the baying of hounds; I saw signal fires both ahead of me and behind me. Twice I hid in the brush until bodies of armed men had passed. Certainly John Brown's "nigger stealing" raid into Platte County had started a tremendous uproar. By now, however, probably all the rest of Brown's men were safely back across the river, and here was I, at sixteen, left alone to fight the whole county.

Traveling through an unknown region in the night, with the population of an entire countryside, bloodhounds and all, on your trail and every man of the lot bent on swinging you up on a tree, as soon as caught, may make interesting reading when transferred to the printed page; it produces quite different sensations in the person chased, especially if his neck already is a bit sore from a recent hanging. I realized plainly before daylight that every approach to the river, as well as every road which ran north and south, was being guarded. Once I decided to strike out into the district to the east, but I had hardly made up my mind to that when I caught from that every direction such a racket of hounds and horns that I gave up the plan.

Just as day broke, I reached a dim lane that led toward the river. From sounds behind me I knew that not much over a mile away a large party was on my trail. After following that lane for a mile or so, I saw that a fence had been built across it, though there was not a human being in sight. I could hear the mob behind me drawing closer. In a moment I made my decision. I put my bridle reins in my teeth, took a revolver in each hand, and dashed toward the fence, trusting Old Titus to get over it somehow. I heard two shots fired at me from ambush, and I banged away right and left with my revolvers—and dug my spurs into Old Titus's sides. He went over the obstruction without touching a rail of it.

We forded quite a large stream and pressed on. Just as I was beginning to think that I had got well to the north of that whole raging section, with an open approach to my ferry, I saw ahead of me, to my disgust, a large group on horseback, gathered near a house which had just come into view. Hoping to escape notice, I leaped a fence into a cornfield—but they had seen me. I have never heard a more fiendish yell than they loosed then and there. I think that afterward, toned down several degrees, it became the famous "rebel yell," the battle cry of the Confederate troops. As that gang gave tongue to it, it fully convinced me that there was blood on the moon.

I plunged across the cornfield and finally reached the bottom lands of the river, which were covered in some places with grass as high as a man on horseback and in others with a dense growth of willows. My pursuers evidently had wholly lost my trail. At various times during the day I could see a patrol on the road that ran by the foot of the hills a mile or two away, but no one searched the bottom land where I was hiding. I stole out once during the day, crossed the road, and brought Old Titus an armful of corn from a field. The "jerked meat" I had bought from the Indians now did me good service.

Toward night I held a one-man council of war. It was clear that every road up or down the river was now patrolled both night and day. If I left the shelter of these willows and got back into the inhabited country, I must expect another night like the last. My only way of escape was to swim the Missouri River with its rapid current, its rushing, mud-colored water, and its treacherous quicksands. After much thought I decided to take the risk.

When evening closed down, I stripped. After tying all my clothing and accouterments to the top of my saddle, I led Old Titus down to the bank. I had expected to have a hard time to get him under way, but he went down the slope into the water without trouble and struck out for the far shore. I took hold of his tail and swam behind him; thus I not only relieved him of my weight, but was able to steer him wherever I wished. We landed in a wild and desolate spot.

I dressed and mounted. By riding all night I reached my Indian friends again at ten o'clock the next day. They all noticed my swollen neck and were very inquisitive about it. I concocted a story of how a lariat had got tangled around it. This satisfied them—and was not so very far from the truth, either.

*CLARA BARTON*

# 35 *Nursing on the Firing Line*

*Clara Barton (1821–1912) was the most famous woman in nineteenth-century America, indeed one of the most famous in the world. Although her humanitarian activities were seen as appropriate for women in Victorian times, Barton nevertheless broke many barriers, including the prohibition against respectable women going anywhere near active battle. Her initial fame derived from her nursing activities on the battlefields of the Civil War. Though the dominant image of Barton's work, presented in a stream of children's books, is one of ministering to the wounded, she in fact acted like a medical executive, raising funds, commandeering supplies, and organizing transportation and personnel, as well as personally serving the dying and wounded.*

*Barton created her image of "the angel of the battlefield" through carefully contrived letters, speeches, and gestures that appealed to the romantic sensibility of the age. In a long career that spanned the Civil War, the Franco-Prussian War, and the Spanish-American War, Barton lived as fully adventurous a life as any man. Her writings express a haunting ambivalence about war; recoiling with horror at its brutalities, she also found herself irresistibly drawn to it as an arena for sacrifice and the display of personal courage.*

## *AT CEDAR MOUNTAIN*

I was strong and thought I might go to the rescue of the men who fell. The first regiment of troops, the old 6th Mass. that fought its way through Baltimore, brought my playmates and neighbors, the partakers of my childhood; the brigades of New Jersey brought scores of my brave boys, the same solid phalanx; and the strongest legions from old Herkimer brought the associates of my seminary days. They formed and crowded around me. What could I do but go with them, or work for them and my country? The patriot blood of my father was warm in my veins. The country which he had fought for, I might at least work for, and I had offered my service to the government in the capacity of a double clerkship at twice $1400 a year, upon discharge of two disloyal clerks from its employ,—the salary never to be given to me, but to be turned back into the U.S. Treasury then poor to beggary, with no currency, no credit. But there was no law for this, and it could not be done and I would not draw salary from our government in such peril, so I resigned and went into direct service of the sick and wounded troops wherever found.

But I struggled long and hard with my sense of propriety—with the appalling fact that I was only a woman whispering in one ear, and thundering in the other the groans of suffering men dying like dogs—unfed and unsheltered, for the life of every institution which had protected and educated me!

I said that I struggled with my sense of propriety and I say it with humiliation and shame. I am ashamed that I thought of such a thing.

When our armies fought on Cedar Mountain, I broke the shackles and went to the field. . . .

Five days and nights with three hours sleep—a narrow escape from capture—and some days of getting the wounded into hospitals at Washington brought Saturday, August 30. And if you chance to feel, that the positions I occupied were rough and unseemly for a *woman*—I can only reply that they were rough and unseemly for *men*. But under all, lay the life of the nation. I had inherited the rich blessing of health and strength of constitution—such as are seldom given to woman—and I felt that some return was due from me and that I ought to be there.

/ / /

. . . Our coaches were not elegant or commodious; they had no windows, no seats, no platforms, no steps, a slide door on the side was the only entrance, and this higher than my head. For my manner of attaining my elevated position, I must beg of you to draw on your own imaginations and spare me the labor of reproducing the boxes, barrels, boards, and rails, which in those days, seemed to help me up and on in the world. We did not criticize the unsightly helpers and were only too thankful that the stiff springs did not quite jostle us out. This description need not be limited to this particular trip or train, but will suffice for all that I have known in Army life. This is the kind of conveyance by which your tons of generous gifts have reached the field with the precious freights. These trains through day and night, sunshine and rain, heat and cold, have thundered over heights, across plains, through ravines, and over hastily built army bridges 90 feet across the rocky stream beneath.

At 10 o'clock Sunday (August 31) our train drew up at Fairfax Station. The ground, for acres, was a thinly wooded slope—and among the trees on the leaves and grass, were laid the wounded who were pouring in by scores of wagon loads, as picked up on the field under the flag of truce. All day they came and the whole hillside was covered. Bales of hay were broken open and scattered over the ground like littering for cattle, and the sore, famishing men were laid upon it.

And when the night shut in, in the mist and darkness about us, we knew that standing apart from the world of anxious hearts, throbbing over the whole country, we were a little band of almost empty handed workers literally by ourselves in the wild woods of Virginia, with 3000 suffering men crowded upon the few acres within our reach.

After gathering up every available implement or convenience for our work, our domestic inventory stood 2 water buckets, 5 tin cups, 1 camp kettle, 1 stewpan, 2 lanterns, 4 bread knives, 3 plates, and a 2-quart tin dish, and 3000 guests to serve.

You will perceive by this, that I had not yet learned to equip myself, for I was no Pallas, ready armed, but grew into my work by hard thinking and sad experience. It may serve to relieve your apprehension for the future of my labors if I assure you that I was never caught so again.

You have read of adverse winds. To realize this in its full sense you have only to build a camp fire and attempt to cook something on it.

There is not a soldier within the sound of my voice, but will sustain me in the assertion that go whichsoever side of it you will, wind will blow the smoke and flame directly in your face. Notwithstanding these difficulties, within fifteen minutes from the time of our arrival we were preparing food, and dressing wounds. You wonder what, and how prepared, and how administered without dishes.

You generous thoughtful mothers and wives have not forgotten the tons of preserves and fruits with which you filled our hands. Huge boxes of these stood beside that railway track. Every can, jar, bucket, bowl, cup or tumbler, when emptied, that instant became a vehicle of mercy to convey some preparation of mingled bread and wine or soup or coffee to some helpless famishing sufferer who partook of it with the tears rolling down his bronzed cheeks and divided his blessings between the hands that fed him and his God. I never realized until that day how little a human being could be grateful for and that day's experience also taught me the utter worthlessness of that which could not be made to contribute directly to our necessities. The bit of bread which would rest on the surface of a gold eagle was worth more than the coin itself.

But the most fearful scene was reserved for the night. I have said that the ground was littered with dry hay and that we had only two lanterns, but there were plenty of candles. The wounded were laid so close that it was impossible to move about in the dark. The slightest misstep brought a torrent of groans from some poor mangled fellow in your path.

Consequently here were seen persons of all grades from the careful man of God who walked with a prayer upon his lips to the careless driver hunting for his lost whip,—each wandering about among this hay with an open flaming candle in his hands.

The slightest accident, the mere dropping of a light could have enveloped in flames this whole mass of helpless men.

How we watched and pleaded and cautioned as we worked and wept that night! How we put socks and slippers upon their cold, damp feet, wrapped your blankets and quilts about them, and when we had no longer these to give, how we covered them in the hay and left them to their rest!" . . .

The slight, naked chest of a fair-haired lad caught my eye, and dropping down beside him, I bent low to draw the remnant of his torn blouse about him, when with a quick cry he threw his left arm across my neck and, burying his face in the folds of my dress, wept like a child at his mother's knee. I took his head in my hands and held it until his great burst of grief passed away. "And do you know me?" he asked at length, "I am Charley Hamilton, who used to carry your satchel home from school!" My faithful pupil, poor Charley. That mangled right arm would never carry a satchel again.

About three o'clock in the morning I observed a surgeon with his little flickering candle in hand approaching me with cautious step far up in the wood. "Lady," he said as he drew near, "will you go with me? Out on the hills is a poor distressed lad, mortally wounded and dying. His piteous cries for his sister have touched all our hearts and none of us can relieve him but rather seem to distress him by our presence."

By this time I was following him back over the bloody track, with great beseeching eyes of anguish on every side looking up into our faces, saying so plainly, "Don't step on us."

"He can't last half an hour longer," said the surgeon as we toiled on. "He is already quite cold, shot through the abdomen, a terrible wound." By this time the cries became plainly audible to me.

"Mary, Mary, sister Mary, come,—O come, I am wounded, Mary! I am shot. I am dying—Oh come to me—I have called you so long and my strength is almost gone—Don't let me die here alone. O Mary, Mary, come!"

Of all the tones of entreaty to which I have listened, and certainly I have had some experience of sorrow, I think these sounding through that dismal night, the most heart-rending. As we drew near some twenty persons attracted by his cries had gathered around and stood with moistened eyes and helpless hands waiting the change which would relieve them all. And in the midst, stretched upon the ground, lay, scarcely full grown, a young man with a graceful head of hair, tangled and matted, thrown back from a forehead and a face of livid whiteness. His throat was bare. His hands, bloody, clasped his breast, his large, bewildered eyes turning anxiously in every direction. And ever from between his ashen lips pealed that piteous cry of "Mary! Mary! Come."

I approached him unobserved, and motioning the lights away, I knelt by him alone in the darkness. Shall I confess that I intended if possible to cheat him out of his terrible death agony? But my lips were truer than my heart, and would not speak the word "Brother," I had willed them to do. So I placed my hands upon his neck, kissed his cold forehead and laid my cheek against his.

The illusion was complete; the act had done the falsehood my lips refused to speak. I can never forget that cry of joy. "Oh Mary! Mary! You have come? I knew you would come if I called you and I have called you so long. I could not die without you, Mary. Don't cry, darling, I am not afraid to die now that you have come to me. Oh, bless you. Bless you, Mary." And he ran his cold, blood-wet hands about my neck, passed them over my face, and twined them in my hair, which by this time had freed itself from fastenings and was hanging damp and heavy upon my shoulders. He gathered the loose locks in his stiffened fingers and holding them to his lips continued to whisper through them "Bless you, bless you, Mary!" And I felt the hot tears of joy trickling from the eyes I had thought stony in death. This encouraged me, and wrapping his feet closely in blankets and giving him such stimulants as he could take I seated myself on the ground and lifted him on my lap, and drawing the shawl on my own shoulders also about his I bade him rest.

I listened till his blessings grew fainter and in ten minutes with them on his lips he fell asleep. So the gray morning found us. My precious charge had grown warm, and was comfortable.

Of course the morning light would reveal his mistake. But he had grown calm and was refreshed and able to endure it, and when finally he woke, he seemed puzzled for a moment but then he smiled and said:—"I knew before I opened my eyes that this couldn't be Mary. I know now that she couldn't get here but it is almost as good. You've made me so happy. Who is it?"

I said it was simply a lady, who hearing that he was wounded, had come to care for him. He wanted the name, and with childlike simplicity he spelled it letter by letter to know if he were right. "In my pocket," he said, "you will find mother's last letter, please get it and write your name upon it, for I want both names by me when I die."

"Will they take away the wounded?" he asked. "Yes," I replied, "the first train for Washington is nearly ready now." "I must go," he said quickly. "Are you able?" I asked. "I must go if I die on the way. I'll tell you why. I am poor mother's only son, and when she consented that I go to war, I promised her faithfully that if I were not killed outright, but wounded, I would try every means in my power to be taken home to her dead or alive. If I die on the train, they will not throw me off, and if I were buried in Washington, she can get me. But out here in the Virginia woods in the hands of the enemy, never. I *must* go!"

I sent for the surgeon in charge of the train and requested that my boy be taken.

"Oh impossible! Madam, he is mortally wounded and will never reach the hospital. We must take those who have a hope of life." "But you must take him." "I cannot."—"Can you, Doctor, guarantee the lives of all you have on that train?" "I wish I could," said he sadly. "They are the worst cases, nearly fifty per cent must die eventually of their wounds and hardships."

"Then give this lad a chance with them. He can only die and he has given good and sufficient reasons why he must go—and a woman's word for it, Doctor. You take him. Send your men for him." Whether yielding to argument or entreaty, I neither knew nor cared so long as he did yield nobly and kindly. And they gathered up the fragments of the poor, torn boy and laid him carefully on a blanket on the crowded train and with stimulants and food and a kind hearted attendant, pledged to take him alive or dead to Armory Square Hospital and tell them he was Hugh Johnson of New York, and to mark his grave.

Although three hours of my time had been devoted to one sufferer among thousands, it must not be inferred that our general work had been suspended or that my assistants had been equally inefficient. They had seen how I was engaged and nobly redoubled their exertions to make amends for my deficiencies.

Probably not a man was laid upon those cars who did not receive some personal attention at their hands, some little kindness, if it were only to help lift him more tenderly.

This finds us shortly after daylight Monday morning. Train after train of cars were rushing on for the wounded and hundreds of wagons were bringing them in from the field still held by the enemy, where some poor sufferers had lain three days with no visible means of sustenance. If immediately placed upon the trains and not detained, at least twenty-four hours must elapse before they could be in the hospital and properly nourished. They were already famishing, weak and sinking from loss of blood and they could ill afford a further fast of twenty-four hours. I felt confident that unless nourished at once, all the weaker portion must be past recovery before reaching the hospitals of Washington. If once taken from the wagons and laid with those already cared for, they would be overlooked and perish on the way. Something must be done to meet this fearful emergency. I sought the various officers on the grounds, explained the case to them and asked permission to feed all the men as they arrived before they should be taken from the wagons. It was well for the poor sufferers of that field that it was controlled by noble-hearted, generous officers, quick to feel and prompt to act.

They at once saw the propriety of my request and gave orders that all wagons would be stayed at a certain point and only moved on when every one had been seen and fed. This point secured, I commenced my day's work of climbing from the wheel to the brake of every wagon and speaking to and feeding with my own hands each soldier until he expressed himself satisfied.

Still there were bright spots along the darkened lines. Early in the morning the Provost Marshal came to ask me if I could use fifty men. He had that number, who for some slight breach of military discipline were under guard and useless, unless I could use them. I only regretted there were not five hundred. They came,—strong willing men,—and these, added to our original force and what we had gained incidentally, made our number something over eighty, and believe me, eighty men and three women, acting with well directed purpose will accomplish a good deal in a day. Our fifty prisoners dug graves and gathered and buried the dead, bore mangled men over the rough ground in their arms, loaded cars, built fires, made soup, and administered it. And I failed to discern that their services were less valuable than those of the other men. I had long suspected, and have been since convinced that a private soldier may be placed under guard, courtmartialed, and even be imprisoned without forfeiting his honor or manliness, that the real dishonor is often upon the gold lace rather than the army blue.

. . . The departure of this train cleared the grounds of wounded for the night, and as the line of fire from its plunging engines died out in the darkness, a strange sensation of weakness and weariness fell upon me, almost defying my utmost exertion to move one foot before the other.

A little Sibley tent had been hastily pitched for me in a slight hollow upon the hillside. Your imaginations will not fail to picture its condition. Rivulets of water had rushed through it during the last three hours. Still I attempted to reach it, as its white surface, in the darkness, was a protection from the wheels of wagons and trampling of beasts.

Perhaps I shall never forget the painful effort which the making of those few rods, and the gaining of the tent cost me. How many times I fell from sheer exhaustion, in the darkness and mud of that slippery hillside, I have no knowledge, but at last I grasped the welcome canvas, and a well established brook which washed in on the upper side at the opening that served as door, met me on my entrance. My entire floor was covered with water, not an inch of dry, solid ground.

One of my lady assistants had previously taken train for Washington and the other worn out by faithful labors, was crouched upon the top of some boxes in one corner fast asleep. No such convenience remained for me, and I had no strength to arrange one. I sought the highest side of my tent which I remembered was grass grown, and ascertaining that the water was not very deep, I sank down. It was no laughing matter then. But the recollection of my position has since afforded me amusement.

I remember myself sitting on the ground, upheld by my left arm, my head resting on my hand, impelled by an almost uncontrollable desire to lie completely down, and prevented by the certain conviction that if I did, water would flow into my ears.

How long I balanced between my desires and cautions, I have no positive knowledge, but it is very certain that the former carried the point by the position from which I was aroused at twelve o'clock by the rumbling of more wagons of wounded men. I slept two hours, and oh, what strength I had gained! I may never know two other hours of equal worth. I sprang to my feet dripping wet, covered with ridges of dead grass and leaves, wrung the water from my hair and skirts, and went forth again to my work.

## *AT FREDERICKSBURG*

No one has forgotten the heart sickness which spread over the entire country as the busy wires flashed the dire tidings of the terrible destitution and suffering of the wounded of the Wilderness whom I attended as they lay in Fredericksburg. But you may never have known how many hundredfold of these ills were augmented by the conduct of improper, heartless, unfaithful officers in the immediate command of the city and upon whose actions and indecisions depended entirely the care, food, shelter, comfort, and lives of that whole city of wounded men. One of the highest officers there has since been convicted a traitor. And another, a little dapper Captain quartered with the owners of one of the finest mansions in the town, boasted that he had changed his opinion since entering the city the day before,—that it was in fact a pretty hard thing for refined people like the people of Fredericksburg to be compelled to open their homes and admit "these dirty, lousy, common soldiers," and that he was not going to compel it.

This I heard him say and waited, until I saw him make his words good—till I saw, crowded into one old sunken hotel, lying helpless upon its bare, wet, bloody floors, 500 fainting men hold up their cold, bloodless, dingy hands, as I passed, and beg me in Heaven's name for a cracker to keep them from starving (and I had none); or to give them a cup that they might have something to drink water from, if they could get it (and I had no cup, and could get none), till I saw 200 six-mule army wagons in a line, ranged down the street to headquarters, and reaching so far out on the Wilderness road that I never found the end of it; every wagon crowded with wounded men, stopped, standing in the rain and mud, wrenched back and forth by the restless hungry animals all night from four o'clock in the afternoon till eight next morning and how much longer I know not.—The dark spot in the mud under many a wagon, told only too plainly where some poor fellow's life had dripped out in those dreadful hours.

I remembered one man who would set it right, if he knew it, who possessed the power and who would believe me if I told him, . . . I commanded immediately conveyance back to Belle Plain. With difficulty I obtained it, and four stout horses with a light army wagon took me ten miles at an unbroken gallop, through field and swamp, and stumps and mud to Belle Plain and a steam tug at once to Washington. Landing at dusk I sent for Henry Wilson, Chairman of the Military Committee of the Senate. A messenger brought him at eight, saddened and appalled like every other patriot in that fearful hour, at the weight of woe under which the nation staggered, groaned, and wept.

He listened to the story of suffering and faithlessness, and hurried from my presence, with lips compressed and face like ashes. At ten he stood in the War Department. They could not credit his report. He must have been deceived by some frightened villain. No official report of unusual suffering had reached them. Nothing had been called for by the military authorities commanding Fredericksburg.

Mr. Wilson assured them that the officers in trust there were not to be relied upon. They were faithless, overcome by the blandishments of the wily inhabitants. Still the department doubted. It was then that he proved that my confidence in his firmness was not misplaced, as facing his doubters he replies: "One of two things will have to be done—either you will send someone to-night with the power to investigate and correct the abuses of our wounded men at Fredericksburg—or the Senate will send some one to-morrow."

This threat recalled their scattered senses.

At two o'clock in the morning the Quartermaster-General and staff galloped to the 6th Street wharf under orders; at ten they were in Fredericksburg. At noon the wounded men were fed from the food of the city and the houses were opened to the "*dirty, lousy* soldiers" of the Union Army.

Both railroad and canal were opened. In three days I returned with carloads of supplies.

No more jolting in army wagons! And every man who left Fredericksburg by boat or by car owes it to the firm decision of one man that his grating bones were not dragged 10 miles across the country or left to bleach in the sands of that city.

GEORGE WARD NICHOLS

# 36 Marching with Sherman's Army

*George Ward Nichols'* The Story of the Great March *was one of the most popular accounts of Sherman's campaign through Georgia and the Carolinas. The book sold 60,000 copies within a year of its publication in 1865 and was reprinted in European newspapers. An aide-de-camp on the general's personal staff, Nichols shows Sherman in public with many groups: his field staff, his soldiers, and freed slaves. Nichols catches as well the eerie character of much of the march: the wait for enemies who do not materialize, the march at times through virtually empty country, the burning of the abandoned city of Atlanta.*

*Nichols (1831–1885), who had been active in the struggles in "Bleeding Kansas" in the 1850s, settled in Cincinnati after the war and became a leading figure in developing the city's museum, art school, and orchestra.*

## PREPARATIONS FOR THE SEAWARD MARCH—THE BURNING OF ATLANTA

General Sherman at once made preparations to abandon all the posts south of Dalton [Georgia]. From Gaylesville and Rome he issued his orders concerning the new movement. The sick and wounded, non-combatants, the machinery, extra baggage, tents, wagons, artillery, ammunition stores, every person and every thing not needed in the future campaigns, were sent back to Chattanooga. The army was stripped for fighting and marching.

/ / /

Let us for a moment look at General Sherman as he appeared at Gaylesville, seated upon a camp-stool in front of his tent, with a map of the United States spread upon his knees. . . . General Sherman's finger runs swiftly down the map until it reaches Atlanta; then, with unerring accuracy, it follows the general direction to be taken by the right and left wings, until a halt is made at Milledgeville. "From here," the general says, "we have several alternatives; I am sure we can go to Savannah, or open communication with the sea somewhere in that direction." After studying the map a while, tracing upon the tangled maze of streams and towns a line from Savannah north and east, at Columbia, South

Carolina, General Sherman looks up at General Howard with the remark, "Howard, I believe we can go there without any serious difficulty. If we can cross the Salkahatchie, we can capture Columbia. From Columbia"—passing his finger quickly over rivers, swamps, and cities to Goldsboro, North Carolina—"that point is a few days' march through a rich country. When we reach that important railroad junction—when I once plant this army at Goldsboro—Lee must leave Virginia, or he will be defeated beyond hope of recovery. We can make this march, for General Grant assures me that Lee can not get away from Richmond without his knowledge, nor without serious loss to his army."

To those who gazed upon the map, and measured the great distance to be traversed, from this quiet village away up in the mountains of Northern Alabama down to the sea, and thence hundreds of miles through a strange and impassable country away to the south again, and over wide rivers and treacherous bogs, the whole scheme, in the hands of any man but he who conceived it, seemed weird, fatal, impossible. But it was at that moment in process of operation. General Sherman at once communicated the first part of his plan to General Grant, subsequently receiving his hearty approval, with entire freedom to act as he should deem best. The army was at once set in motion; the numerous threads spreading over a wide field of operations were gathered up; out of confusion came exquisite order. Detachments guarding various dépôts were sent to their commands, outposts were withdrawn, the cavalry were concentrated in one division, under the lead of a gallant soldier. Compact, confident, and cheerful, this well-appointed host, guided by that master mind, moved grandly on to the fulfillment of its high mission. The field of operations now entered upon belonged, as has been said, to the genius of strategy. Those who have written of this campaign always date its commencement as from Atlanta. Inasmuch as we trod upon hitherto unconquered soil when we went out from Atlanta, this statement is true; but the march really began at Rome and Kingston, and it is from this point that we take up the diary of events which occurred within the experience and knowledge of the writer.

*November 13th.*—Yesterday the last train of cars whirled rapidly past the troops moving south, speeding over bridges and into the woods as if they feared they might be left helpless in the deserted land. At Cartersville the last communications with the North were severed with the telegraph wire. It bore the message to General Thomas, "All is well." And so we have cut adrift from our base of operations, from our line of communications, launching out into uncertainty at the best, on a journey whose projected end only the General in command knows. Its real fate and destination he does not know, since that rests with the goodness of God and the brave hearts and strong limbs of our soldiers. The history of war bears no similar example, except that of Cortés burning his ships. It is a bold, hazardous undertaking. There is no backward step possible here. Thirty days' rations and a new base: that time and those supplies will be exhausted in the most rapid march ere we can arrive at the nearest sea-coast; arrived there, what then? I never heard that manna grew on the sand-beaches or in the marshes, though we are sure that we can obtain forage on our way; and I have reason to know that General Sherman is in the highest degree sanguine and cheerful—sure even of success.

As for the soldiers, they do not stop to ask questions. Sherman says "Come," and that is the entire vocabulary to them. A most cheerful feature of the situation is the fact that the men are healthful and jolly as men can be; hoping for the best, willing to dare the worst.

Behind us we leave a track of smoke and flame. Half of Marietta was burned up—not by orders, however; for the command is that proper details shall be made to destroy all property which can ever be of use to the Rebel armies. Stragglers will get into these places, and dwelling-houses are leveled to the ground. In nearly all cases these are the deserted habitations formerly owned by Rebels who are now refugees.

Yesterday, as some of our men were marching toward the Chattahoochee River, they saw in the distance pillars of smoke rising along its banks—the bridges were in flames. Said one, hitching his musket on his shoulder in a free and easy way: "I say, Charley, I believe Sherman has set the river on fire." "Reckon not," replied the other, with the same indifference; "if he has, it's all right." And so they pass along; obeying orders, not knowing what is before them, but believing in their leader.

From Kingston to Atlanta the rails have been taken up on the road, fires built about them, and the iron twisted into all sorts of curves; thus they are left, never to be straightened again. The Rebel inhabitants are in agony of wonder at all this queer manœuvring. It appears as if we intended evacuating Atlanta; but our troops are taking the wrong direction for the hopes and purposes of these people.

Atlanta is entirely deserted by human beings, excepting a few soldiers here and there. The houses are vacant; there is no trade or traffic of any kind; the streets are empty. Beautiful roses bloom in the gardens of fine houses, but a terrible stillness and solitude cover all, depressing the hearts even of those who are glad to destroy it. In the peaceful homes at the North there can be no conception how these people have suffered for their crimes.

*Atlanta, Night of the 15th November.* A grand and awful spectacle is presented to the beholder in this beautiful city, now in flames. By order, the chief engineer has destroyed by powder and fire all the store-houses, dépôt buildings, and machine-shops. The heaven is one expanse of lurid fire; the air is filled with flying, burning cinders; buildings covering two hundred acres are in ruins or in flames; every instant there is the sharp detonation or the smothered booming sound of exploding shells and powder concealed in the buildings, and then the sparks and flame shoot away up into the black and red roof, scattering cinders far and wide.

These are the machine-shops where have been forged and cast the Rebel cannon, shot and shell that have carried death to many a brave defender of our nation's honor. These warehouses have been the receptacle of munitions of war, stored to be used for our destruction. The city, which, next to Richmond, has furnished more material for prosecuting the war than any other in the South, exists no more as a means for injury to be used by the enemies of the Union.

A brigade of Massachusetts soldiers are the only troops now left in the town: they will be the last to leave it. To-night I heard the really fine band of the Thirty-third Massachusetts playing "John Brown's soul goes marching on," by the light of the burning buildings. I have never heard that noble anthem when it was so grand, so solemn, so inspiring.

/ / /

News came from General Howard that the advance of the 17th Corps had arrived, at nine o'clock that morning, at a point thirteen miles from Cheraw, and had found the enemy intrenched in their front. It was said that Beauregard, Johnston, Hardee, and Hampton, with the garrisons of Charleston, Wilmington, and other points, were in Cheraw, and that a great battle was probable. The Rebels had certainly gathered an array of talent, in the way of generals, enough to appal this little army! The presence of all these men and any large force is doubtless an exaggeration, although there can be no question but the delays of the last few days have given the enemy an intimation of our plans, which they have improved by guarding the important outlet at Cheraw.

We were inclined to believe that the Rebels, not liking our society, would not interfere with our movements; indeed, that they would assist our passage through the country. The care with which they have laid in plentiful supplies of corn, fodder, hams, beef on the hoof, and other supplies, would have indicated this. Again, our infantry have hardly seen a Rebel soldier since we left Columbia until this morning. Our route from the Catawba crossed several creeks where there were valuable bridges uninjured, the destruction of any one of which would have delayed our column a day or more. Certainly we had every reason to suppose that the Rebels wished us a good riddance, and offered no objections to our speedy passage to the sea, or wherever we chose to go. Only one other hypothesis remained, and the presence of an enemy in our front to-night is a cogent argument in its favor. It is that the Rebel leaders did not divine the real movement until the last moment, and are now throwing obstacles in the way of our passage over the Pedee. We estimate that, without assistance from Virginia, they can not concentrate more than twenty-five thousand men in our front, and we will undertake to start that force in two or three days. Within that time we shall have brought up all our troops, and it will go hard with the Rebels, but we will have a pontoon floating quietly from either bank of the Pedee. Of course the hope of saving the bridge at Cheraw must be abandoned, and we must depend upon other resources.

Although for the last three days we have not seen the sun, and the rain has fallen now and then, the left wing has made some fine marches. The 14th Corps yesterday traveled over eighteen miles of the road which had already been used by the 20th Corps, and to-day the 20th Corps has marched twenty-one miles since daylight. Fortunately the route has led along the high ridges and through the pine barrens, where the soil is sandy, and better for the light fall of rain. Thus we were able to reach this place early in the afternoon, driving before us, at a good marching pace, Butler's, or rather Hampton's cavalry, who opposed the advance.

During the skirmishing, one of our men, a forager, was slightly wounded; but the most serious accident of the day occurred to a negro woman in a house where the Rebels had taken cover. When I saw this woman, who would not have been selected as the best type of South Carolina female beauty, the blood was streaming over her neck and bosom from a wound in the lobe of her ear, which the bullet had just clipped and passed by.

"What was it that struck you, aunty?" I asked.

"Lor bress me, massa, I dun know; I jus fell right down."

"Didn't you feel any thing, nor hear any sound?"

"Yes, now I 'member, I heerd a s-z-z-z-z-z, and den I jus knock down. I drap on de groun'. I'se so glad I not dead, for if I died den de Bad Man would git me, cos I dance lately a heap."

To-day is the first time within a week when I have seen a household where the women are neatly dressed and the children cleanly. The people who have inhabited the houses along the roads for fifty miles behind us are among the most degraded specimens of humanity I have ever seen. Many of the families I now refer to do not belong to the class known as the "poor whites" of the South, for these are large landowners, and holders of from ten to forty slaves.

The peasantry of France are uneducated, but they are usually cleanly in their habits. The serfs of Russia are ignorant, but they are semi-barbarous, and have, until lately, been slaves. A large proportion of the working classes in England are debased, but they work. But the people I have seen and talked to for several days past are not only disgustingly filthy in their houses and their persons, but are so provokingly lazy, or "shiftless," as Mrs. Stowe has it, that they appear more like corpses recalled to a momentary existence than live human beings, and I have felt like applying a galvanic battery to see if they could be made to move. Even the inroads of our foragers do not start them into life; they loll about like sloths, and barely find energy enough to utter a whining lamentation that they will starve.

During this campaign I have seen terrible instances of the horrors of slavery. I have seen men and women as white as the purest type of the Anglo-Saxon race in our army, who had been bought and sold like animals. I have looked upon the mutilated forms of black men who had suffered torture at the caprice of their cruel masters, and I have heard tales of woe too horrible for belief; but in all these cases I have never been so impressed with the degrading, demoralizing influence of this curse of slavery as in the presence of these South Carolinians. The higher classes represent the scum, and the lower the dregs of civilization. They are South Carolinians, not Americans.

The clean people whom I met this afternoon were a refreshing spectacle. Several of the young ladies—the men ran away at our approach—were attending school at this place, where a seminary has been situated for many years. One of these girls, in reply to my question why she had not gone to her home, forty miles down the river, answered:

"What is the use? Your people go every where; you overrun the state; and I am as well off here as at my father's house."

I acknowledged the wisdom of her action, for there is no doubting the fact that our presence is quite sensibly felt.

/ / /

I happened to be present this afternoon at one of those interviews which so often occur between General Sherman and the negroes. The conversation was piquant and interesting; not only characteristic of both parties, but the more significant because, on the part of the General, I believe it a fair expression of his feelings on the slavery question.

A party of ten or fifteen negroes had just found their way through the lines from Cheraw. Their owners had carried them from the vicinity of Columbia to the other side of the Pedee, with the mules and horses which they were running away from our army. The negroes had escaped, and were on their way back to find their families. A more ragged set of human beings could not have been found out of the slave states, or, perhaps, Italy. The negroes were of all ages, and had stopped in front of the General's tent, which was pitched a few feet back from the sidewalk of the main street.

Several officers of the army, among them General Slocum, were gathered round, interested in the scene. General Sherman said to them:

"Well, men, what can I do for you—where are you from?"

"We's jus come from Cheraw. Massa took us wid him to carry mules and horses away from youins."

"You thought we would get them; did you wish us to get the mules?"

"Oh yes, massa, dat's what I wanted. We knowed youins cumin, and I wanted you to hav dem mules; but no use; dey heard dat youins on de road, and nuthin would stop 'em. Why, as we cum along, de cavalry run away from de Yanks as if dey fright to deth. Dey jumped into de river, and some of dem lost dere hosses. Dey frightened at de berry name ob Sherman."

Some one at this point said: "That is General Sherman who is talking to you."

"God bress me! Is you Mr. Sherman?"

"Yes, I am Mr. Sherman."

"Dat's him, su' nuff," said one.

"Is dat de grre-aat Mr. Sherman dat we'se heard ob so long?" said another.

"Why, dey so frightened at your berry name dat dey run right away," shouted a third.

"It is not me that they are afraid of," said the General; "the name of another man would have the same effect with them if he had this army. It is these soldiers that they run away from."

"Oh no," they all exclaimed, "it's de name ob Sherman, su'; and we hab wanted to see you so long while you trabbel all roun' jis whar you like to go. Dey said dat dey wanted to git you a little furder on, and den dey whip all your soldiers; but, God bress me! you keep cumin' and a cumin', an' dey allers git out."

"Dey mighty 'fraid ob you, sar; dey say you kill de colored men too," said an old man, who had not heretofore taken part in the conversation.

With much earnestness, General Sherman replied:

"Old man, and all of you, understand me. I desire that bad men should fear me, and the enemies of the government which we are all fighting for. Now we are your friends; you are now free ('Tank you, Massa Sherman,' was ejaculated by the group). You can go where you please; you can come with us or go home to your children. Wherever you go you are no longer slaves. You ought to be able to take care of yourselves. ('We is; we will.') You must earn your freedom, then you will be entitled to it, sure; you have a right to be all that you can be, but you must be industrious, and earn the right to be men. If you go back to your families, and I tell you again you can go with us if you wish, you must do the best you can. When you get a chance, go to Beaufort or Charleston, where you will have a little farm to work for yourselves."

The poor negroes were filled with gratitude and hope by these kind words, which the General uttered in the kindest manner, and they went away with thanks and blessings on their lips.

# 37 | A Southern Woman's Wartime Journal

*Pauline DeCaradeuc Heyward's* Journal *offers a spirited account of a slaveholding family's experience of Sherman's march. Union soldiers, in Heyward's account, were determined to penalize South Carolina, the original seat of secession, for starting the Civil War. That the DeCaradeuc women managed to limit the damage done to their plantation and property indicates that even angry Union troops approaching the end of a terrible war continued to pay some homage to the code requiring gentlemen to respect feminine gentility.*

*The war cost the DeCaradeuc family the lives of two sons as well as most of their wealth. After the war Pauline married Geurard Heyward. When he failed as a planter, Pauline, Geurard, and their growing family moved to Savannah, Georgia, where they established a modest prosperity and continued to enlarge their family. Pauline maintained the role of a cultured, genteel southern wife and mother until her death in 1914.*

Feb. 14th, 1864

Carrie and I went over to Augusta yesterday, and really in spite of everything had a very amusing time. We bought several photographs of our most illustrious Gen's. I got Lee, Davis & Kirby Smith. John Cochran sent me word the other day that he had sent out to Richmond for Stonewall Jackson's for me, so that I'll have that too.

We visited Mr. Henry who is better, also Mrs. Foster, Mrs. Tubman & Mother's old friend, Mrs. Campbell. Then we tried to shop, but the only thing in the shape of a dress for myself that we saw, was a worsted stuff at $30.00 a yard.

I met Lieut. Col. Croft who stopped me & talked awhile on the street, he is most dreadfully, *agonizingly,* wounded in his right hand & looks very badly.

When we finished our business we sauntered round to the church yard & sat there 'till time to meet the train. When we reached the depot there was such a concourse of soldiers there that I begged an old lady who was going too, to let us remain with her. I was very uneasy as I never was in a crowd of men without a protector before, however, a young & handsome soldier came up & introduced himself, Major Beaufort of Va. and begged us to allow him to remain near us until the car was opened. When the doors were unlocked we got in & obtained good seats, some twenty- five ladies had to stand up & as many had to be left, & such crowds of soldiers!! An officer in front of us spread his blanket on the seat & begged us to keep it for him, but 'twas impossible & he couldn't even get in the car again. After a little while I heard a plaintive voice outside under the window, say: "Oh, Miss Pauline, ain't there any room in there for me?" I looked out & saw Col. Croft, of course, he couldn't get in our car; he asked me to look for his cousin in our car who was wounded & on crutches, but I couldn't even move, after talking a while he went into the conductor's car then I heard another voice say: "Miss Pauline, can't you get me a seat in front of you? I want to get in your car so much." What could I do? He was a very handsome Capt. I felt assured I knew him, his face & voice were perfectly familiar, but I could not remember his name, he conversed for awhile just like some old friend, seemed to know me well, but I don't yet remember who he is. Anyhow *he* too had to go off. Then our Va. Major came under the window to chat, & I gave him some cake I bought for the children, they would not allow soldiers to come in our car, without a lady; meanwhile a soldier on crutches stood near us looking sick & weak, he *stood* of course, & Carrie, noble as she always is rose & insisted on his taking her seat, but he would not hear of it, he then introduced himself, Captain Croft, the cousin, the Lieut. Col. asked me to look for, he remained with us the rest of the time & proved to be most agreeable.

After awhile we looked up & there was our kind Virginia Major standing by us, he pretended to the conductor that he had to see us out, & thus got into our car from which he did not again move, he is really quite charming & entertained us very nicely, two more Captains spoke to us & offered to assist us in any way, but our Va. friend didn't give them a chance, he saw us to the carriage at Johnston's & all but cried when we got off the car. I think somehow we will hear of him again, he was 'mazin kind & attentive to us, should like to return it.

/ / /

May 23, 1864

I have no heart to keep this Journal or tell of the dreadful, fatal battles in Va. Oh my God! my heart is too heavy, I am entirely miserable. Many whom I know are killed & wounded. Robert Taft and Col. Shooter are killed. Capt. Barnwell killed. George Lalane wounded. Wise's Brigade was subjected to a fearful firing from the enemy at Druery's Bluff. I suppose John Cochran is wounded, from the moment I saw him I felt that his life would be given to this devouring war; and I am assured that he is dead or wounded, for I *feel it.*

/ / /

Feb. 18th, 1865

The Yankees have come & gone. On the 10th Feb. they encamped at Johnstons. The whole of Kilpatrick's forces, they were turned on the country for forage, plunder, & provisions. The first we saw of them was about a dozen of them, dashing thro the gate shouting: "Here come the Yankees, look out now you d——d rebels." A moment after they were in the house, Mother & Grandmother met them at the door, but they didn't listen to a word they tried to say, but said, "Come give us your keys, where is your liquor? get your gold, get your silver, you old women, hurry yourselves, I say." I had a belt on under my dress, with my revolver, and a bag of bullets, caps & powder in my pocket, they rushed into the room, where all of us ladies were sitting, saying, "Give me your revolvers, d——d you, if we find them, you'd better look out, where are your pistols, we know you've got 'em." I felt it wouldn't do for them to find mine on me, infuriated as they were, so I took Tante's arm, hurried upstairs & threw the revolver between her sheets, hardly I had finished when the door burst open & the room was filled with them, they pulled the bed to pieces, of course.

We all went into the parlor, and by this time there were hundreds of them, in the house, upstairs, in the garret, in every chamber, under the house, in the yard, garden, &c., &c., some singing, shouting, whistling, and Oh, my God, *such cursing*. Both pianos were going at the same time, with axes they broke open every door, drawer, trunk that was locked, smashed a large French mirror, broke pieces of furniture, and flung every piece of clothing, that they didn't carry off, all over the floors, they got some of Fa.'s prettiest paintings and broke bottles of catsup over them, they carried off every piece of silver, every knife, jewel, & particle of possessions in the house & negro houses, every paper, letter, receipt, &c., they flung to the winds, all the roads are strewn with them. Mother and G. M. went among them like brave women, trying to save some few things in vain, at one time a horrid looking ruffian came into the parlor, seeing only women there, he entered shut both doors, & said in an undertone, "You cursed rebels, now empty your pockets." Ah, mon Dieu, mine had my bag of ammunition in it, I rose, & while he was grabbing Miss Hessie's pocket book, I dropped my bag in a corner & flung an old bonnet over it, in my pocket, he found my watch. "Ah," said he, "This is a pretty little watch, now where is the key, & does it go good?" & the villain put his hand on my shoulder, I rose & stood before him, with all possible dignity & he turned away. Then after taking Tante's watch and everybody's money, he walked up to Mother, grinding his teeth & looking her full in the face, said: "Now, you've just *got* to tell me where your gold & silver is buried, I know you've got it, and if you know what's good for yourself & all in this room, you'll tell me where it is." "I have no gold, my silver you have all taken with every other valuable in the house." "That's a d——d lie, now I'll burn your house this minute, if you don't tell me." "I have nothing more to tell, do you think I'd tell a lie?" " I don't know." Then he walked up & down the room cursing, swearing, threatening, & spitting on every side, then finding he could do nothing with us, took Solomon out, put a pistol to his head, saying he would blow his brains out, if he didn't tell. Solomon is as true to us as steel, so are they all, all faithful & friends to us.

About sundown, on the 10th they left off coming here. I then went to ascertain the fate of my revolver, there it was still rolled in the sheets, thrown on the floor with the chaos of clothing. I of course, sent it off. They took every blanket & pillow case & towel, the cases for bags to carry off what they took, & towels for handkerchiefs, they even made the servants get our chemises & tear them up into pocket handkerchiefs for them.

Well the next day, which was Saturday, they came just the same, hundreds of them, one of our villianous neighbors told them that our boys fired the first gun on Sumter, so they said this house was the root of the rebellion & burn it they would, but our good servants & Mother and G. Mother entreated in such a way that they desisted, then they said that they had to arrest and shoot every influential citizen in S.C., every mover of secession, & from the accumulation of wealth, the quantities of food, books & clothes in this house, the finest they had seen in these parts, that they knew Father was wealthy, literary, & influential, & they had heard enough of him, to make an example of him & catch him they would. We have no less than five large libraries of refugees, here, besides our own, & the accumulated clothing & valuables of four separate families, no wonder they found us so rich, & came here so often.

As to provisions, 'tis true, few was so bountifully supplied. We had 7 barrels of fine flour, 300 bushels of corn, 1 barrel & 1 box of nice sugar, &c., &c.

Out of that we have 15 bushels corn, 1 bag flour, 3 hams, they took all the wine & brandy. They had scouts out in every direction looking for Father. Thus passed Saturday, on Sunday morning they burned Uncle & Daughter's home *everything* & every building on their place, even the well, they are here with nothing but their clothes on, in the world, they searched uncle's person. After breakfast, 500 Yankees came here in a body & dispersed over the house & place, carrying off everything they could, they attempted to get into Aiken Saturday morning but were repulsed by Wheeler.

Well, on Saturday night, Father who was encamped in the woods, with the mules, horses & some provisions & one or two of the servants, sent us word that he could not evade the scouts longer & he was going to give himself up to K.ptr. [Gen. Kilpatrick] & demand protection, as a Frenchman, for himself & household, I went down in the swamp to see him & when half way between there & the house saw four Yankees entering the gate, my goodness didn't I run, it was a regular tug between them & me to see who could get to the house first, but I beat in safety, but I never ran so in my life.

Well, after Father went, we were filled with anxiety about him, knowing their threats about him, Oh, we were so frightened for him, when the door opened & a Yankee rushed in with a lit candle, he looked all 'round then ran into every room in the house to look for "that d——d rebel," he then went out saying he'd return during the night to fire the house,—pleasant intelligence—then he & two others asked the servants if there were any young ladies in the house, how old they were & where they slept, during all this I had on blue spectacles & my face muffled up, Carrie too.

When I heard of their questions to the servants I thought that burning the house was nothing; I was almost frantic, I sat up in a corner, without moving or closing my eyes once the whole night. My God! I suffered agony, I trembled *unceasingly* till morning; about eleven o'clock that night, two men went up the back stairs, we heard them walking over head, they went into the room over the parlour (we were in the parlour, of course, all together) and went to bed there, they stayed there all night.

Well, none of us undressed or went to bed for six nights. On Sunday, Mother & Grandmother determined to go out to the camp, to Kilpatrick & ask for protection & for Father's release, they went in the cart with a little blind mule, the only animal they left us, with pieces of yarn for bridle, as they carried off all the harness, &c., during their absence, quantities of Yankees came here, and walked in *every direction* sticking the ground with their swords, feeling for buried things. Wherever the ground was soft they dug, they found all Tante's silver, bonds & jewels, a quantity of provisions,—barrel of wine, one of china, a box of Confederate money & bonds, &c.

Fortunately, the bulk of our silver was sent off.

Mother returned from the camp, bringing Father and William whom they had captured.

Monday morning only a few Yankees came, about ten, I suppose, and then the entire force fell back, not wishing to engage our troops, the R.R., of course, cut & we knew nothing more of them.

Our own soldiers have been coming here constantly, these last two or three days. My goodness, how different they are to the Yankees, the commonest one is as gentle & respectful to us as can be.

Sherman was at Johnstons on Sunday. One dashing looking young officer entered the room where we were sitting on Saturday & Mother said, "Are you an officer, sir?" "I am Madam." "Then, sir, I entreate your protection for my helpless household." "I will, Madam, God knows I am disgusted with all this." He left the room, *we hoped,* to try to check the pillage, he walked into Miss Hessie's room, broke open her trunk and began stuffing his pockets.

They threw a good many shells at this house.

# 38 *African Americans' Reactions to Reconstruction*

*The Thirteenth, Fourteenth, and Fifteenth Amendments to the U.S. Constitution decreed an equality between the races that was not realized in fact. At first the federal government vigorously supported the Freedmen's Bureau and the efforts of Reconstruction governments in southern states to help the freed slaves, but within about a decade those efforts were abandoned as the northern public lost interest.*

*The social revolution brought about by emancipation caused severe problems for both African Americans and whites. Just as the slaves' experiences had varied widely, so the newly freed African Americans responded to their fresh situation in many different ways. Their needs were rarely understood by whites ill prepared to accept African Americans as equals or to support the long-term federal intervention that was required to make freedom an economic and social reality.*

*The interviews that follow were collected in the 1930s. Historians have found such accounts to be valuable sources for the history of slaves and Reconstruction.*

*FELIX HAYWOOD, from San Antonio, Texas. Born in Raleigh, North Carolina. Age at interview: 88.*

The end of the war, it come just like that—like you snap your fingers. . . . How did we know it! Hallelujah broke out—

> Abe Lincoln freed the nigger
>   With the gun and the trigger;
> And I ain't going to get whipped any more.
>   I got my ticket,
> Leaving the thicket,
>   And I'm a-heading for the Golden Shore!

Soldiers, all of a sudden, was everywhere—coming in bunches, crossing and walking and riding. Everyone was a-singing. We was all walking on golden clouds. Hallelujah!

Union forever,
  Hurrah, boys, hurrah!
Although I may be poor,
  I'll never be a slave—
Shouting the battle cry of freedom.

Everybody went wild. We felt like heroes, and nobody had made us that way but ourselves. We was free. Just like that, we was free. It didn't seem to make the whites mad, either. They went right on giving us food just the same. Nobody took our homes away, but right off colored folks started on the move. They seemed to want to get closer to freedom, so they'd know what it was—like it was a place or a city. Me and my father stuck, stuck close as a lean tick to a sick kitten. The Gudlows started us out on a ranch. My father, he'd round up cattle—unbranded cattle—for the whites. They was cattle that they belonged to, all right; they had gone to find water 'long the San Antonio River and the Guadalupe. Then the whites gave me and my father some cattle for our own. My father had his own brand—7 B)—and we had a herd to start out with of seventy.

We knowed freedom was on us, but we didn't know what was to come with it. We thought we was going to get rich like the white folks. We thought we was going to be richer than the white folks, 'cause we was stronger and knowed how to work, and the whites didn't, and they didn't have us to work for them any more. But it didn't turn out that way. We soon found out that freedom could make folks proud, but it didn't make 'em rich.

Did you ever stop to think that thinking don't do any good when you do it too late? Well, that's how it was with us. If every mother's son of a black had thrown 'way his hoe and took up a gun to fight for his own freedom along with the Yankees, the war'd been over before it began. But we didn't do it. We couldn't help stick to our masters. We couldn't no more shoot 'em than we could fly. My father and me used to talk 'bout it. We decided we was too soft and freedom wasn't going to be much to our good even if we had a education.

/ / /

*WARREN MCKINNEY, from Hazen, Arkansas. Born in South Carolina. Age at interview: 85.*

I was born in Edgefield County, South Carolina. I am eighty-five years old. I was born a slave of George Strauter. I remembers hearing them say, "Thank God, I's free as a jay bird." My ma was a slave in the field. I was eleven years old when freedom was declared. When I was little, Mr. Strauter whipped my ma. It hurt me bad as it did her. I hated him. She was crying. I chunked him with rocks. He run after me, but he didn't catch me. There was twenty-five or thirty hands that worked in the field. They raised wheat, corn, oats, barley, and cotton. All the children that couldn't work stayed at one house. Aunt Mat kept the babies and small children that couldn't go to the field. He had a gin and a shop. The shop was at the fork of the roads. When the war come on, my papa went to built forts. He quit Ma and took another woman. When the war close, Ma took her four children, bundled 'em up and went to Augusta. The government give out rations there. My ma washed and ironed. People died in piles. I don't know till yet what was the matter. They said it was the change of living. I seen five or six wooden, painted coffins piled up on wagons pass by our house. Loads passed every day like you see cotton pass here. Some said it was cholera and some took consumption. Lots of the colored people nearly starved. Not much to get to do and not much houseroom. Several families had to live in one house. Lots of the colored folks went up North and froze to death. They couldn't stand the cold. They wrote back about them dying. No, they never sent them back. I heard some sent for money to come back. I heard plenty 'bout the Ku Klux. They scared the folks to death. People left Augusta in droves. About a thousand would all meet and walk going to hunt work and new homes. Some of them died. I had a sister and brother lost that way. I had another sister come to Louisiana that way. She wrote back.

I don't think the colored folks looked for a share of land. They never got nothing 'cause the white folks didn't have nothing but barren hills left. About all the mules was wore out hauling provisions in the army. Some folks say they ought to done more for the colored folks when they left, but they say they was broke. Freeing all the slaves left 'em broke.

That reconstruction was a mighty hard pull. Me and Ma couldn't live. A man paid our ways to Carlisle, Arkansas, and we come. We started working for Mr. Emenson. He had a big store, teams, and land. We liked it fine, and I been here fifty-six years now. There was so much wild game, living was not so hard. If a fellow could get a little bread and a place to stay, he was all right. After I come to this state, I voted some. I have farmed and worked at odd jobs. I farmed mostly. Ma went back to her old master. He persuaded her to come back home. Me and her went back and run a farm four or five years before she died. Then I come back here.

/ / /

*LEE GUIDON, from South Carolina. Born in South Carolina. Age at interview: 89.*

Yes, ma'am, I sure was in the Civil War. I plowed all day, and me and my sister helped take care of the baby at night. It would cry, and me bumping it [in a straight chair, rocking.] Time I git it to the bed where its mama was, it wake up and start crying all over again. I be so sleepy.

It was a puny sort of baby. Its papa was off at war. His name was Jim Cowan, and his wife Miss Margaret Brown 'fore she married him. Miss Lucy Smith give me and my sister to them. Then she married Mr. Abe Moore. Jim Smith was Miss Lucy's boy. He lay out in the woods all time. He say no need in him gitting shot up and killed. He say let the slaves be free. We lived, seemed like, on 'bout the line of York and Union counties. He lay out in the woods over in York County. Mr. Jim say all the fighting 'bout was jealousy. They caught him several times, but every time he got away from 'em. After they come home Mr. Jim say they never win no war. They stole and starved out the South . . .

After freedom a heap of people say they was going to name theirselves over. They named theirselves big names, then went roaming round like wild, hunting cities. They changed up so it was hard to tell who or where anybody was. Heap of 'em died, and you didn't know when you hear about it if he was your folks hardly. Some of the names was Abraham, and some called theirselves Lincum. Any big name 'cepting their master's name. It was the fashion. I heard 'em talking 'bout it one evening, and my pa say, "Fine folks raise us and we gonna hold to our own names." That settled it with all of us. . . .

I reckon I do know 'bout the Ku Kluck. I knowed a man named Alfred Owens. He seemed all right, but he was a Republican. He said he was not afraid. He run a tanyard and kept a heap of guns in a big room. They all loaded. He married a Southern woman. Her husband either died or was killed. She had a son living with them. The Ku Kluck was called Upper League. They get this boy to unload all the guns. Then the white men went there. The white man give up and said, "I ain't got no gun to defend myself with. The guns all unloaded, and I ain't got no powder and shot." But the Ku Kluck shot in the houses and shot him up like lacework. He sold fine harness, saddles, bridles—all sorts of leather things. The Ku Kluck sure run them outen their country. They say they not going to have them round, and they sure run them out, back where they came from. . . .

For them what stayed on like they were, Reconstruction times 'bout like times before that 'cepting the Yankee stole out and tore up a scandalous heap. They tell the black folks to do something, and then come white folks you live with and say Ku Kluck whup you. They say leave, and white folks say better not listen to them old Yankees. They'll git you too far off to come back, and you freeze. They done give you all the use they got for you. How they do? All sorts of ways. Some stayed at their cabins glad to have one to live in and farmed on. Some running round begging, some hunting work for money, and nobody had no money 'cepting the Yankees, and they had no homes or land and mighty little work for you to do. No work to live on. Some going every day to the city. That winter I heard 'bout them starving and freezing by the wagon loads. I never heard nothing 'bout voting till freedom. I don't think I ever voted till I come to Mississippi. I votes Republican.

That's the party of my color, and I stick to them as long as they do right. I don't dabble in white folks' business, and that white folks' voting is their business. If I vote, I go do it and go on home.

I been plowing all my life, and in the hot days I cuts and saws wood. Then when I gets outa cotton-picking, I put each boy on a load of wood and we sell wood. The last years we got $3 a cord. Then we clear land till next spring. I don't find no time to be loafing. I never missed a year farming till I got the Bright's disease [one of several kinds of kidney ailments] and it hurt me to do hard work. Farming is the best life there is when you are able. . . .

When I owned most, I had six head mules and five head horses. I rented 140 acres of land. I bought this house and some other land about. The anthrax killed nearly all my horses and mules. I got one big fine mule yet. Its mate died. I lost my house. My son give me one room, and he paying the debt off now. It's hard for colored folks to keep anything. Somebody gets it from 'em if they don't mind.

The present times is hard. Timber is scarce. Game is about all gone. Prices higher. Old folks cannot work. Times is hard for younger folks too. They go to town too much and go to shows. They going to a tent show now. Circus coming, they say. They spending too much money for foolishness. It's a fast time. Folks too restless. Some of the colored folks work hard as folks ever did. They spends too much. Some folks is lazy. Always been that way.

I signed up to the government, but they ain't give me nothing 'cepting powdered milk and rice what wasn't fit to eat. It cracked up and had black something in it. A lady said she would give me some shirts that was her husband's. I went to get them, but she wasn't home. These heavy shirts give me heat. They won't give me the pension, and I don't know why. It would help me buy my salts and pills and the other medicines like Swamp Root. They won't give it to me.

/ / /

*TOBY JONES, from Madisonville, Texas. Born in South Carolina. Age at interview: 87.*

I worked for Massa 'bout four years after freedom, 'cause he forced me to, said he couldn't 'ford to let me go. His place was near ruint, the fences burnt, and the house would have been, but it was rock. There was a battle fought near his place, and I taken Missy to a hideout in the mountains to where her father was, 'cause there was bullets flying everywhere. When the war was over, Massa come home and says, "You son of a gun, you's supposed to be free, but you ain't, 'cause I ain't gwine give you freedom." So I goes on working for him till I gits the chance to steal a hoss from him. The woman I wanted to marry, Govie, she 'cides to come to Texas with me. Me and Govie, we rides the hoss 'most a hundred miles, then we turned him a-loose and give him a scare back to his house, and come on foot the rest the way to Texas.

All we had to eat was what we could beg, and sometimes we went three days without a bite to eat. Sometimes we'd pick a few berries. When we got cold we'd crawl in a brushpile and hug up close together to keep warm. Once in a while we'd come to a farmhouse, and the man let us sleep on cottonseed in his barn, but they was far and few between, 'cause they wasn't many houses in the country them days like now.

When we gits to Texas, we gits married, but all they was to our wedding am we just 'grees to live together as man and wife. I settled on some land, and we cut some trees and split them open and stood them on end with the tops together for our house. Then we deadened some trees, and the land was ready to farm. There was some wild cattle and hogs, and that's the way we got our start, caught some of them and tamed them.

I don't know as I 'spected nothing from freedom, but they turned us out like a bunch of stray dogs, no homes, no clothing, no nothing, not 'nough food to last us one meal. After we settles on that place, I never seed man or woman, 'cept Govie, for six years, 'cause it was a long ways to anywhere. All we had to farm with was sharp sticks. We'd stick holes and plant corn, and when it come up we'd punch up the dirt round it. We didn't plant cotton, 'cause we couldn't eat that. I made bows and arrows to kill wild game with, and we never went to a store for nothing. We made our clothes out of animal skins.

## *WHY ADAM KIRK WAS A DEMOCRAT*

*(House Report no. 262, 43 Cong., 2 Sess., p. 106. Statement of an Alabama Negro [1874].)*

A white man raised me. I was raised in the house of old man Billy Kirk. He raised me as a body servant. The class that he belongs to seems nearer to me than the northern white man, and actually, since the war, everything I have got is by their aid and their assistance. They have helped me raise up my family and have stood by me, and whenever I want a doctor, no matter what hour of the day or night, he is called in whether I have got a cent or not. And when I want any assistance I can get it from them. I think they have got better principles and better character than the republicans.

## SARAH JANE FOSTER

# 39 Teacher of the Freedmen

*Sarah Jane Foster's diary and letters are among the few autobiographical writings entirely capable of supplying the personal dimension to the great story of the hundreds of northerners who went south during and after the Civil War to educate former slaves. Foster, born in a country town in Maine in 1839, struggled as an educator and missionary in Martinsburg, West Virginia, to find the narrow ground where she might accept the slaves as equals, yet win acquiescence of her work by the white community. White rowdies and vandals attacked the school. Even her missionary brethren criticized her for turning for protection to the African-American men who accompanied her through the streets after school or religious services. There was probably no way for this rather naive and idealistic young woman to be fully accepted in Martinsburg, despite her apparent success in teaching and her moderate and conventional views on race, manners, and politics. Her matter-of-fact acceptance of the ex-slaves and her assumption that racial prejudices would rapidly melt away with the ending of slavery were enough to make her stay short and stormy. We will never know how she might have changed in the long run from her experiences in the South, for she died of yellow fever in 1868.*

Martinsburg, West Va., Feb. 11th, 1866

Dear Advocate [a Maine Newspaper]:—

/ / /

My day school . . . is growing larger. Its list is now seventy, while the night list approaches fifty. By the aid of the older scholars I have succeeded in cutting off about an hour and a half from my daily labors, but, even then, I spend not less than forty-two hours per week in the school-room, counting my Sabbath school and the meetings that I attend. Yet I am wonderfully sustained.—With all the changefulness of the climate and the humidity of the air, I find the place healthy, and never enjoyed better health anywhere. There has been no further disturbance, and I now walk home alone though the soldiers are yet in town, for I think it better to show no distrust. I understand that it was reported in the Baltimore American that our school was disturbed by returned rebel soldiers. I am not aware that such was in any instance the case, and think it but just to say I anticipate no trouble from them.

I spoke of good spelling in my last letter. Week before last a boy of sixteen, named Willoughby Fairfax, who chanced to recite alone, spelled seventy-five long words and only missed *two*. At the beginning of the year he was in words of four letters. He is one of my best pupils but not the best in spelling as good as he is. A girl of thirteen bears off the palm in that branch.

I now have several who are making creditable progress in cyphering, not to mention the boys who do easy sums on their slates, which I set to relieve the tedium of study. I have also several very good pupils in Geography, and actually hear some as good map lessons as I could expect to at home. Quite a number are learning fast to write. A great many are in Mental Arithmetic. I even have one small class in the night school who recite in the old but good Colburn's Arithmetic, which quite carries me back to my early school-days again. I have met with two copies each of Webster's and Town's spelling Books. Those most common are Comly's, which are not so good as either of the above. But, in spite of all the disadvantages, the scholars are bound to prove their capacity to learn. They are usually fond of school, and punctual in attendance, and, as a class, orderly on the street.

I daily become more and more interested in the school, and in all that concerns the welfare of the colored people here.

/ / /

Martinsburg, W. Va., Feb. 28th, 1866

Dear Advocate:—Again I snatch a few minutes to pen a short report of my school and its affairs. We are having now I judge about the fullest school that we shall have at all. The weather of late has been such as to allow the small children to come, and young men and women, who will soon be out at service for the summer, are now improving the time to come to school for a while. Even now the schools begin to change a little. The day school for a week or two has diminished a little, and the other has proportionately increased. One after another they come to me with the remark "Miss Jenny, I can't come to day-school anymore, I'm going to work, but I'll come at night," and they do so all that they can. The boy to whose spelling I alluded in my last will not be able to come any more than this week, for his father has bought a farm in the country and has work for him now: I regret to lose so good a scholar, but he will not fail to do well anywhere.

/ / /

The cognomen of "nigger teacher" seems to have died out, and I occasionally hear my own name as I pass in the street, or, more frequently some person is notified that "there goes the Freedmen's Bureau." I have not met with any annoyance on the street but once, and then a white man addressed an insolent remark to me as I was going into the school-room door. I don't mind such things at all. Report has married or engaged me several times to men connected with the school, and, Mrs. Vosburgh was actually asked by a neighbor the day I was there "if I was not part nigger." I hope they will believe it, for then surely they could not complain of my teaching the people of my own race. But Rev. Mr. Osborne preaches at our school room tonight, and I must prepare to go.

In haste, Sarah J. Foster

## *Diary, 1866*

Thursday, March 1

I have enjoyed today very much, for the air has been mild and spring-like. People are working their gardens. My school glides along smoothly too. Tonight Mary Brown came in to school to see me. Waited half an hour to talk with me afterward. We did not walk together on the street but she came after me and stopped at the shop window to call out Isaac. A lady(?) called out "Is that a 'nigger' or a white woman?" just as I passed her referring to Mary at the shop.

/ / /

Friday, March 2

A springlike overcast day. I fear it will rain tomorrow. My day and evening in school were as usual pleasant. Will Fairfax has done coming for now. He must work. I gave him a nice book. He seemed glad of it. I also gave him my last Advocate letter in which I had praised him.

Tonight two white men came in to school for about twenty minutes. They were civil, but will doubtless go off and be as hard as they can.

/ / /

Yesterday we made up a party for the Antietam battle-ground. We had a sky blue U.S. wagon, with a black oil-cloth cover that would roll up at the sides. That was filled and the rest of the party went on horse-back. The party included Mr. and Mrs. Brackett, Mr. Given, the Misses Dudley, Wright, Gibbs and Libby, Mrs. Smith and myself, besides a Mr. Ames formerly of Massachusetts—now trading here, and a Mrs. Clemmen and her daughter also from Massachusetts, a young colored man named Keyes, invited to go as a friend and to point out localities, and our sable driver. Mr. Ames and Mr. and Mrs. Brackett rode horse-back all the way, and Miss Clemmen nearly all, while Mr. Given and Mr.

Keyes alternated with each other. We made a merry party, and seemed to attract a great deal of attention. We first visited the Burnside bridge near which we lunched on the grass, drinking from a cold spring that has doubtless slaked the thirst of many a wounded and dying soldier. Then we moved over to the place where the Irish Brigade fought.—Dismounting we walked about among the trees which bore many scars of shot and shell—bits of shell yet remaining in some of them. Mr. Keyes got our party some water at a house not far beyond the battle field. They inquired where we were from. He told them from New England, and that we came to visit the battle ground. They seemed to think us a long way from home, and he did not correct the impression that we came on purpose to see Antietam. The lady of the house said that eight thousand dead bodies were interred on her farm, and previously Mr. Keyes had pointed out a large field, once filled with graves, now cultivated over. The lady spoke of it without seeming conscious of the horrible sacrilege of thus utilizing a nation's hallowed ground. We soon turned back from the plough polluted graveyard, and, coming to Bloody Lane, drove up it a little way, trying to fancy what it must have been when piled with reeking corpses, but the horror of the field beyond yet clung to us and no one alighted to search for relics. The place seemed too awful for tarrying.

/ / /

*Letter from Virginia*

Harper's Ferry, April 20th, 1866

Dear Advocate:—It is now two weeks since I opened school here. Miss Gibbs retains the school that she has had from the first, except that a few of the poorest scholars have been put in the other department. So she has a fine school, while mine are yet in the earliest stages of reading, or else unable to read at all. The coloured people here are scattered, and many of them in very destitute circumstances. They do not now come into school so well as they did last term. The older ones are gone out at service and smaller ones, who have long distances to come, fear to do so without protection; for the white boys will molest them when they find an opportunity. The boys of both races seem rather pugilistic about here. They have had several battles for the possession of this hill as a playground. The weapons were stones, and both parties were in earnest. My scholars at Martinsburg, though not destitute of spirit and courage, had the good sense to avoid collisions with the white boys, who often played marbles before the door. Jefferson County is much more aristocratic than Berkeley, and, as a consequence, the coloured people seem much more degraded as a class here than they are there. Here is a field for much mission labor. In Berkeley County there are more of the blacks who are competent to care for the interests of their race. But they are not dull here. Several children, who two weeks ago did not know the alphabet, are now reading in words of three letters. In the short time that we have taught out here, many, who did not know a letter, have learned to read in the Testament, and to spell well. The united testimony from all our schools is, that color is no barrier to progress.

I have four boys in my school who are so white that I should not suspect their lineage elsewhere. One has straight, light hair, and all are fine looking. Miss Gibbs has several little girls who are even whiter, or "brighter," as they call it here. One in particular, very appropriately named Lillie, has flaxen hair and grey blue eyes. One white boy comes to my school. His brother lives in the chambers here, and very wisely discards prejudice that he may have the benefit of a free school.

Last Sabbath our Sabbath school was reorganized here, some colored teachers being appointed; as Mr. Brackett wishes to get them prepared to continue the school after we go home in hot weather. Each of us takes a class. I do not know personally a member of mine, but hope to get acquainted soon.

/ / /

*Letter from Virginia*

Harper's Ferry, May 2d, 1866

Dear Advocate:—When I last wrote to you I thought it possible that I might be sent to Smithfield, but now my school has come up to a list of forty, with a prospect of nearly thirty daily in fair weather. As I have thirteen in the alphabet, and all are beginners in reading, I find enough to do. I have now got the school classified and systematized, and taught to come and go by strokes of the bell. The colored children fall into systematic regulations quite well, and seem to like them too. They annoy us most of all by whispering and laughing. The little ones will forget and whisper, and all laugh easily. They improve in that however. I sometimes use their laughter as a sort of spur to dull scholars, letting them laugh at their blunders, and it works well, for they are sensitive to ridicule. We have to use all ways and means to keep up their ambition and to encourage them to study. I tried, when I first began at Martinsburg, to avoid corporeal punishment. I found it impossible, but yet, by due severity when forced to punish, I did not have it to do very often. The fact is, the colored people are practical followers of Solomon. They show very great attachment to their children, making great efforts to reclaim them if they have been sold away, but they are very severe in governing them. They expect a teacher to be so too, and the children are of the same opinion. They really like a teacher better who compels them to perfect obedience. I followed the theory at once on acquaintance, and it worked well. I grew to like some of my pupils very much, and the attachment was mutual.

I spoke of the efforts of parents to recover children who had been sold away. One woman here has exerted herself to find her four children at great expense, though dependent on her own labor altogether. She has only been able to recover two, though she has made a journey to Richmond and back to try and obtain the others, who were sold away in that vicinity. Not only has she found those two, but she has bought clothing for them, and has never drawn a ration from the Bureau, though supporting her mother also. I know two young men who have gathered together their father and mother, a sister and two infant children, and four nephews and nieces from seven to fourteen years of age. By joint efforts the family dress neatly and live entirely unaided. Where are the white men who could voluntarily burden themselves with the children of deceased relatives, while young, single, and dependent on their daily labor? I think that parallel cases among us are rare, and yet we have been asked to believe that this race are only fit for chattels, and that they felt separation as little as the brutes. A deeper, darker falsehood was never palmed upon the public. It contradicts itself at every stage of our acquaintance with them. Stronger domestic affection I never saw than some of them exhibit.

/ / /

I have spoken of the variations of some familiar hymns. One occurs to me now, It is this:

"Jesus my all to heaven is gone,—
He's coming again by and by—
He whom I've fixed my hopes upon—
He's coming again by and by.
Christ's coming again, Christ's coming again,
He's coming again by and by,
He'll come this time, and He'll come no more,
He's coming again by and by."

And that is about the style of their peculiar hymns. They are nearly all chorus, but I like to hear them. They can all come in on the chorus after one or two repetitions, and, in a full meeting, the effect of their full melodious voices is thrilling and inspiring. As they sing they sway back and forth in time to the music, and some even step to it in a way that seems like dancing, only the whole body is in a quiver of excitement. At a meeting when a number are seeking the Savior, they will make a circle at the close around the "mourner's bench," where the seekers kneel meeting after meeting till they find peace. The circle then join hands, taking also the hands of their kneeling friends, and begin to sing, swaying as I have described, or lifting and dropping their hands in regular time. They will sing hymn after hymn with increasing earnestness, till the more excitable singers, and very likely some of the mourners, are shouting. The jumping, leaping and bodily contortions of a "shout" are beyond all description. They must be seen to be understood. For a long time I saw none of this at Martinsburg, and indeed the leading members there never practiced it, but they seem to think that converts can be brought out in no other way.

"They're going to sing over Isaac," said a colored woman to me, as I looked a little surprised to see them grouping around the bench at which one of my schoolboys was kneeling. I found that nearly all thought that the way to be "brought through." Some never yielded to it, and I am satisfied that none ever affected the emotion that convulsed those who were influenced by it. Even the white Methodists are very much the same about here; so it is not to be wondered at at all. On Saturday night we had here the most magnificent thunder shower that it was ever my lot to witness. The effect of the lightning, as the vivid chains lit up the darkness and played over the Heights, was sublime and awe-inspiring. It is quite chilly here now much of the time. We have needed a fire all day to-day. We have had some quite warm weather a day or two at a time, however, but we did not realize it much except when we descended to the village below the Hill. Here there is usually a breeze, and we can keep quite cool, I think, as long as we shall stay.

Some collisions are constantly occurring around here between the "chivalry" and the colored people. A sister of Mr. Keyes had an amusing triumph recently. A poor white neighbor struck her with no reasonable provocation, the fault being wholly her own. At first Mrs. Poles did not resent, but when the beating was recommenced, she retaliated in self-defense. The woman had her arrested, seeming not to know that a colored woman could have a right to defend herself, or that she was amenable to the law for having struck first. When the case was tried before a Justice in Bolivar, she gained a little valuable experience, and had the privilege of paying the costs. The justice, I learn, referred to the Civil Rights Bill, and also intimated that the Bureau had an influence upon his decision. Well it might here, for Major Welles is an excellent and efficient officer. Only this week a colored man was knocked down for remonstrating a little because some white men had broken open his stable, taking his horse to plow with, and refusing to give it back at his request. The Justice simply made them deliver up the horse, but he designs to bring a suit for assault, to see what will be done about it. An aggravated case of assault took place in Charlestown, the particulars of which I have not yet learned. I think that some test cases will have to be brought up to prove the extent and validity of the Civil Rights Bill. The Bureau officers will probably look out for that, and may thus benefit the Freedmen a great deal.

/ / /

# 40 | *A Sharecrop Contract*

*The ending of slavery and the impoverishment of the South in the aftermath of the Civil War seriously disrupted southern agriculture. Five years after the war's end, southern cotton production was still only about half of what it had been in the 1850s. The large plantations, no longer tended by gangs of slaves or hired freedmen, were broken up into smaller holdings, but the capital required for profitable agriculture meant that control of farming remained centralized in a limited elite of merchants and larger landholders.*

*Various mechanisms arose to finance southern agriculture. Tenants worked on leased land and small landowners gave liens on their crops to get financing. But the most common method of financing agriculture was sharecropping. Agreements like the Grimes family's sharecrop contract determined the economic life of thousands of poor rural families in the southern United States after the Civil War. Families, both African-American and white, lacking capital for agriculture were furnished the seed, implements, and a line of credit for food and other necessities to keep them through the growing season. Accounts were settled in the winter after crops were in. Under these conditions a small number of farmers managed to make money and eventually became landowners, but the larger part found themselves in ever deeper debt at the end of the year, with no choice but to contract again for the next year.*

To every one applying to rent land upon shares, the following conditions must be read, and *agreed to.*

To every 30 or 35 acres, I agree to furnish the team, plow, and farming implements, except cotton planters, and I *do not* agree to furnish a cart to every cropper. The croppers are to have half of the cotton, corn and fodder (and peas and pumpkins and potatoes if any are planted) if the following conditions are compiled with, but—if not—they are to have only two fifths ($\frac{2}{5}$). Croppers are to have no part or interest in the cotton seed raised from the crop planted and worked by them. No vine crops of any description, that is, no watermelons, muskmelons, . . . squashes or anything of that kind, except peas and pumpkins, and potatoes, are to be planted in the cotton or corn. All must work under my direction. All plantation work to be done by the croppers. My part of the crop to be *housed* by them, and the fodder and oats to be hauled and put in the house. All the cotton must be topped about 1st August.

If any cropper fails from any cause to save all the fodder from his crop, I am to have enough fodder to make it equal to one half of the whole if the whole amount of fodder had been saved.

For every mule or horse furnished by me there must be 1000 good sized rails . . . hauled, and the fence repaired as far as they will go, the fence to be torn down and put up from the bottom if I so direct. All croppers to haul rails and work on fence whenever I may order. Rails to be split when I may say. Each cropper to clean out every ditch in his crop, and where a ditch runs between two croppers, the cleaning out of that ditch is to be divided equally between them. Every ditch bank in the crop must be shrubbed down and cleaned off before the crop is planted and must be cut down every time the land is worked with his hoe and when the crop is "laid by," the ditch banks must be left clean of bushes, weeds, and seeds. The cleaning out of all ditches must be done by the first of October. The rails must be split and the fence repaired before corn is planted.

Each cropper must keep in good repair all bridges in his crop or over ditches that he has to clean out and when a bridge needs repairing that is outside of all their crops, then any one that I call on must repair it.

Fence jams to be done as ditch banks. If any cotton is planted on the land outside of the plantation fence, I am to have *three fourths* of all the cotton made in those patches, that is to say, no cotton must be planted by croppers in their home patches.

All croppers must clean out stables and fill them with straw, and haul straw in front of stables whenever I direct. All the cotton must be manured, and enough fertilizer must be brought to manure each crop highly, the croppers to pay for one half of all manure bought, the quantity to be purchased for each crop must be left to me.

No cropper to work off the plantation when there is any work to be done on the land he has rented, or when his work is needed by me or other croppers. Trees to be cut down on Orchard, House field & Evanson fences, leaving such as I may designate.

Road field to be planted from the *very edge of the ditch to the fence,* and all the land to be planted close up to the ditches and fences. *No stock of any kind* belonging to croppers to run in the plantation after crops are gathered.

If the fence should be blown down, or if trees should fall on the fence outside of the land planted by any of the croppers, any one or all that I may call upon must put it up and repair it. Every cropper must feed, or have fed, the team he works, Saturday nights, Sundays, and every morning before going to work, beginning to feed his team (morning, noon, and night *every day* in the week) on the day he rents and feeding it to and including the 31st day of December. If any cropper shall from any cause fail to repair his fence as far as 1000 rails will go, or shall fail to clean out any part of his ditches, or shall fail to leave his ditch banks, any part of them, well shrubbed and clean when his crop is laid by, or shall fail to clean out stables, fill them up and haul straw in front of them whenever he is told, he shall have only two-fifths ($\frac{2}{5}$) of the cotton, corn, fodder, peas and pumpkins made on the land he cultivates.

If any cropper shall fail to feed his team Saturday nights, all day Sunday and all the rest of the week, morning/ noon, and night, for every time he so fails he must pay me five cents.

No corn nor cotton stalks must be burned, but must be cut down, cut up and plowed in. Nothing must be burned off the land except when it is *impossible* to plow it in.

Every cropper must be responsible for all gear and farming implements placed in his hands, and if not returned must be paid for unless it is worn out by use.

Croppers must sow & plow in oats and haul them to the crib, but *must have no part of them.* Nothing to be sold from their crops, nor fodder nor corn to be carried out of the fields until my rent is all paid, and all amounts they owe me and for which I am responsible are paid in full.

I am to gin & pack all the cotton and charge every cropper an eighteenth of his part, the cropper to furnish his part of the bagging, ties, & twine.

The sale of every cropper's part of the cotton to be made by me when and where I choose to sell, and after deducting all they owe me and all sums that I may be responsible for on their accounts, to pay them their half of the net proceeds. Work of every description, particularly the work on fences and ditches, to be done to my satisfaction, and must be done over until I am satisfied that it is done as it should be.

No wood to burn, nor light wood, nor poles, nor timber for boards, nor wood for any purpose whatever must be gotten above the house occupied by Henry Beasley—nor must any trees be cut down nor any wood used for any purpose, except for firewood, without my permission.

# *Questions for Part IV*

1 How did Stanton's advocacy of women's rights grow out of her personal situation? How do her views of child-rearing relate to her belief in the need for women to have more power in society?

2 What do the letters from slaves tell you about their lives? Discuss some of the problems mentioned. How are they similar to or different from what you would expect to find in letters from poor but free people?

3 How does John Pendleton Kennedy's view, as expressed through Meriwether, of the capacity of Afro-Americans to direct their lives compare with what you read when black slaves and ex-slaves are writing about themselves? Why do you think Meriwether sees such limits to his slaves' abilities? What does this tell you about the institution of slavery?

4 What inspired Nat Turner to rebel? How would you describe his personality in general terms?

5 What does Douglass say about slave singing? How did he come to learn to read? What passage in Douglass' essay do you find most powerful?

6 How did Jacobs' sense of her own power make her life more livable?

7 What did Frederick Douglass, Harriet Jacobs, and Harriet Tubman have in common? Can you detect anything in their characters that would explain their "successes"?

8 How did being both black and a woman influence Sojourner Truth's view of women's rights?

9 What were the differing attitudes of General Lane and John Brown to the raid to free blacks in Missouri according to Tibbles' account?

10 What characteristics, exemplified by her actions, did Clara Barton reveal that made her so different from most Victorian ladies?

11 Discuss Sherman's march from the contrasting viewpoints of a participant, such as David Conyngham, and an observer, such as Dolly Lunt.

12 Based on the evidence you have read, what were some of the attitudes and expectations among freedmen after the Civil War?

13 Did Southern whites accept the consequences of the Civil War? Explain.

14 What kind of life did a sharecropping family lead? Give details.

# Acknowledgments

**Selection 1, page 3.** From *The Life of the Admiral Christopher Columbus by His Son Ferdinand* by Fernando Colon. Rutgers University Press. Translated and annotated by Benjamin Keen. Copyright ©1959 by Benjamin Keen. Reprinted by permission of Benjamin Keen.

**Selection 2, page 14.** From *Bartholomew de las Casas: His Life, His Apostolate, and His Writings* by Francis Augustus McNutt. G.P. Putnam's Sons, New York and London, 1909, pp. 314–321.

**Selection 3, page 19.** From *Legends, Traditions and Laws of the Iroquois, or Six Nations, and History of the Tuscarora Indians* by Elias Johnson (A Native Tuscarora Chief). Union Printing and Publishing Company, Lockport, New York, 1881, pp. 50–53.

**Selection 4, page 22.** From Richard Hakluyt, *The Principal Navigations.* London, George Bishop, 1589, Volume VIII, pp. 386, 390–398, 415–419. Spelling modernized.

**Selection 5, page 31.** From *The Jesuit Relations and Allied Documents: Travels and Explorations of the Jesuit Missionaries in New France, 1610–1791* by Reuben Gold Thwaites (editor). Cleveland, The Burrows Brothers Company, 1987. From Volume VI: pp. 157, 159, 161, 201, 203, 205, 225, 229, 231, 233, 243, 245, 247. From Volume VII: pp. 35, 37, 39, 41, 43.

**Selection 6, page 38.** Captain John Smith of Willoughby by Alford, Lincolnshire; President of Virginia and Admiral of New England. Works: 1608–1631. Edited by Edward Arber, The English Scholar's Library, No. 16. Birmingham, 1884, pp. 63–67.

**Selection 7, page 42.** Proceedings of the Massachusetts Historical Society, *Second Series,* Volume VIII: 1892–1894. Massachusetts Historical Society, Boston, 1894, pp. 471–473. Spelling modernized.

**Selection 8, page 45.** Samuel Willard, Minister at Groton, to Cotton Mather, 1672, in S.A. Green, *Groton in the Witchcraft Times.* Groton, Mass., 1883, pp. 17–20.

**Selection 9, page 61.** From *A Narrative of the Life of Mary Jemison: Deh-He-Wa-Mis.,* by James E. Seaver. Fourth edition. New York, Miller, Orton, and Mulligan, 1856, pp. 52, 53–63, 67–70, 72–74.

**Selection 10, page 68.** Gottlieb Mittelberger, *Journey to Pennsylvania in the Year 1750 and Return to Germany in the Year 1754.* Translated from the German by Carl Theo. Eben. Philadelphia, John Jos. McVey, 1898, pp. 19–29.

**Selection 11, page 73.** From *The Life of Olaudah Equiano, or Gustavus Vassa the African, Written by Himself,* by Olaudah Equiano. Isaac Knapp, 1837, pp. 41–52.

**Selection 12, page 79.** J. Hector St. John (Michael-Guillaume-Jean de Crèvecoeur), *Letters from an American Farmer; Describing Certain Provincial Situations, Manners and Customs Not Generally Known.* London, Thomas Davies, 1782, pp. 48–49, 51, 54–68, 71.

**Selection 13, page 87.** Captain Thomas Preston's Account of the Boston Massacre (13 March 1770), from British Public Record Office, C.O 5/759. Reprinted in Merrill Jensen (editor), *English Historical Documents,* Volume IX. London, 1964, pp. 750–53.

**Selection 14, page 91.** From *A Retrospect of the Boston Tea-Party, with a Memoir of George R.T. Hewes, a Survivor of the Little Band of Patriots who Drowned the Tea in the Boston Harbour in 1773, by a Citizen of New York,* by James Hawkes {supposed author}. New York, 1834, pp. 27–33, 36–41.

**Selection 15, page 97.** Illustration credits appear with illustrations in the selection.

**Selection 16, page 103.** From *The Crisis: Being a Series of Pamphlets in Sixteen Numbers,* by Thomas Paine. Reprinted in New York by D.M. Bennett, Liberal and Scientific Publishing House, 1877, pp. 3–11.

**Selection 17, page 110.** From *Ordinary Courage: The Revolutionary War Adventures of Joseph Plumb Martin,* by Joseph Plumb Martin and edited by James Kirby Martin, pp. 130–141. Copyright ©1993 by Brandywine Press. Reprinted by permission.

**Selection 18, page 122.** From *The Journals of Lewis and Clark* by Bernard DeVoto, pp. 202–206, 207–211, 213–214. Copyright ©1953 by Bernard DeVoto. © renewed 1981 by Avis DeVoto. Reprinted by permission of Houghton Mifflin Company. All rights reserved.

**Selection 19, page 131.** From *Autobiography of Peter Cartwright, The Backwoods Preacher,* by W.P. Strickland (editor). New York, Phillips and Hunt, 1856, pp. 34–38, 40–46, 48–53.

**Selection 20, page 140.** From *The Papers of Chief John Ross: Volume I, 1807–1839,* edited by Gary E. Moulton. Copyright ©1985 by the University of Oklahoma Press.

**Selection 21, page 148.** From "Letter of John Doyle to His Wife Fanny, January 25, 1818." *Journal of the American Irish Historical Society,* 12 (1913). Reprinted by permission of the *Journal of the American Irish Historical Society.*

**Selection 22, page 151.** From *The Pioneers, or the Sources of the Susquehanna,* Volume II, by James Fenimore Cooper. New York, Charles Wiley, 1823, pp. 41–50.

**Selection 23, page 157.** From *The Mexican Side of the Texas Revolution [1836]* compiled by Carlos E. Castaneda, pp. 109–118. Copyright ©1976 by Ayer Company Publishers, New Hampshire. Reprinted by permission.

**Selection 24, page 166.** From *Six Months in the Gold Mines* by Edward Gould Buffum, 1966, pp. 50–58, 60–65, 110–111. March of America Facsimile Series. Reprinted by permission of University Microfilms Inc., Ann Arbor, Michigan.

**Selection 25, page 174.** From *Loom and Spindle or Life among the Early Mill Girls,* by Harriet Hanson Robinson. New York, T.Y. Crowell, 1898, pp. 16–22, 37–43, 51–53. From a 1976 reprint by Press Pacifica.

**Selection 26, page 183.** From *Hearts of the West,* Volume 9, pp. 8–13, compiled by Kate B. Carter. Reprinted by permission of the International Society Daughters of Utah Pioneers.

**Selection 27, page 197.** From *Ten Nights in a Bar Room,* by Timothy Shay Arthur. Philadelphia, Henry Artemus, 1897, pp. 160–175.

**Selection 28, page 205.** From "Life under the Lash" by Charles Ball, Francis Henderson, Jacob Stroyer and Peter Randolph, *African-American Voices: The Life Cycle of Slavery,* edited by Steven Mintz, pp. 73–75, 78–79, 87–89, 111–113. Reprinted by permission of Brandywine Press.

**Selection 29, page 214.** From *The Autobiography of Henry Merrell: Industrial Missionary to the South,* edited by James L. Skinner III, pp. 134–135, 137, 140–142, 166–167, 198–201. Copyright ©1991 by James L. Skinner III. Reprinted by permission of the University of Georgia Press.

**Selection 30, page 220.** Illustration credits appear with illustrations in the selection.

**Selection 31, page 224.** From *Incidents in the Life of a Slave Girl,* by Harriet Jacobs. Boston, 1861, pp. 44–49, 51–55, 57–67, 82–89.

**Selection 32, page 235.** *Slave Testimony: Two Centuries of Letters, Speeches, Interviews, and Autobiographies,* ed. John W. Blassingame. Louisiana State University Press, 1977, pp. 457–465.

**Selection 33, page 242.** Sojourner Truth, *Two Speeches* (nothing cited).

**Selection 34, page 245.** From *Buckskin and Blanket Days, Memoirs of a Friend* by Thomas Henry Tibbles, pp. 46–55. Copyright ©1957 by Vivien K. Barris. Used by permission of Doubleday, a division of the Bantam Doubleday Dell Publishing Group, Inc.

**Selection 35, page 252.** From *Life of Clara Barton,* by Perry H. Epler. Macmillan, 1915, pp. 31–32, 35–43, 59, 96–98.

**Selection 36, page 261.** From *The Story of the Great March from the Diary of a Staff Officer,* by George Ward Nichols. New York, Harper & Brothers, 1865.

**Selection 37, page 268.** From *A Confederate Lady Comes of Age; The Journal of Pauline DeCaradeuc Heyward, 1863–1888,* edited by Mary D. Robertson, pp. 36–37, 65–69. Reprinted by permission of The University of South Carolina Press.

**Selection 38, page 273.** From *Lay My Burden Down: A Folk History of Slavery,* edited by B.A. Botkin (Chicago University Press, 1945), pp. 65–70, 223–224, 241–242, 246–247. Copyright ©1989 by Curtis Brown, Ltd. Reprinted by permission of Curtis Brown, Ltd.

**Selection 39, page 279.** From *Sarah Jane Foster, Teacher of the Freedmen: A Diary and Letters,* edited by Wayne E. Reilly (Charlottesville: Virginia, 1991), pp. 59–60, 66–68, 87–88, 95–96, 103–107. Reprinted by permission of the University Press of Virginia.

**Selection 40, page 286.** From the Grimes Family Papers (#3357), 1882. Held in the Southern Historical Collection, University of North Carolina, Chapel Hill.